D0511658

# AMATEUR THEATRE

Jennifer Curry has been interested in the theatre since her school days when she used to take part in amateur drama and write plays for her compeers. After gaining a teaching qualification she taught English and drama part-time and wrote part-time – frequently about the problems of teaching drama and the use of drama as a teaching agent.

She began writing plays in 1970 and had six performed in six years. Two of them were commissioned by schools in the area, two were written to be produced in Salisbury Playhouse during the Salisbury Festival of the Arts, one was written especially for the new Salisbury Playhouse, and the most recent, *Blonde on the Bonnet*, was performed by the New Hope Theatre Company at Richmond prior to its publication.

She has also been involved with St Edmund's Arts Centre, Salisbury where she is now Literature Officer, responsible for bringing visiting writers, poets, playwrights and novelists, to the city.

TEACH YOURSELF BOOKS

# AMATEUR THEATRE

## Jennifer Curry

*Illustrated by G. Hartfield Illustrators*

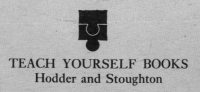

**TEACH YOURSELF BOOKS**
Hodder and Stoughton

# Contents

# Dedication

This book is dedicated, with affection and gratitude, to Roger Clissold and the company and staff of Salisbury Playhouse.

# Personal Acknowledgements

To Peter Alderton, John Curry, Jane Norman Walker, Jane Whittle and Salisbury Studio Theatre for their help, advice, and, most important, example.

# Foreword

Believing that the link between professional and amateur theatre is very strong and will continue to be, and knowing how beneficial the one can be to the other, I welcome and recommend this book which seems to me likely to be of benefit to both. It is generous in its intention to give assistance to the Actors' Benevolent Fund, and the contents I feel will be of invaluable help to all students in the theatre, both amateur and professional.

*Dame Peggy Ashcroft, DBE*

# I

# Choosing the Play

'The selection of a play will nearly always depend on two main factors:

(*a*) The extent to which the piece could be suitably cast from the available leading players and other acting members of the group;

(*b*) The general level of taste and sophistication of your audience. With regard to the latter it is no bad thing to present a play that is one intellectual notch above your assessment of this level and so stretch your audience – but not too much!

It is, of course, advisable to avoid presenting a play which has recently been seen on television, in the West End, or at your local professional theatre, thereby inviting unfair comparisons. This cannot always be checked but reasonable care should be taken.

If a classic is to be offered, choose Shakespeare only if your group is of the highest possible acting standard. For the rest – Sheridan, Wilde, Shaw, Ibsen, Chekhov – go for the best-known plays, for they are usually the ones with universal appeal: do *Hedda Gabler* but not *Brand*; *The Cherry Orchard* but not *Ivanov*; *The Importance of Being Earnest* but not *Salome*; *Pygmalion* rather than *Back to Methuselah* and so on.

The same applies to the modern classics. If you want to give them Pinter, condition them first with *The Caretaker* before tackling the lesser known, less universally entertaining ones. Samuel Beckett should be discreetly infiltrated into your list with *Waiting for Godot*, which is "effective theatre" for most people, if not wholly understood.

In the main, comedies of situation are safer than comedies of character. Most amateur groups would make a better job of a play like *Arsenic and Old Lace* than, say, Noel Coward's *Design For Living*. A thriller with a clever plot, from time to time, is better than one of mood.

Above all remember the size and adaptability of your stage; and the limitations of your lighting and sound. A good evening can be ruined by long stage waits, noisy scene changes, over-complicated and under-rehearsed lighting and sound effects; and an overcrowded stage.

Go for the text, the acting and the costumes. These are what count in the end.

Most amateur groups seem to contain an imbalance of male and female players. This state of affairs has led over the years to a glut of "All Female" plays for amateurs about Convents, Typing Pools, Japanese Camps for Women, Ladies' Colleges, Fishing Villages when the Herring Fleet is away at sea, and Welsh Villages when the men are away at the war. A dearth of men is limiting to your choice of plays and can only be rectified by intensive recruitment.

Finally, seek a public library with a strong drama section, containing the leading play publishers' catalogues, and that of The British Theatre Association (formerly The British Drama League), and be prepared to spend long and often fruitless hours to find the play that will fill your hall and stimulate interest and enjoyment on *both* sides of the footlights.'

**Alfred Shaughnessy**
*Writer and script editor*

'The play's the thing', as Shakespeare so rightly said, but it's an extremely difficult task to choose a totally satisfactory repertoire of plays for an amateur company – just as it is for a professional company though for different reasons. The professional theatre has to be particularly careful that the actors' wages will not outweigh its income and so it has to go for small-cast plays whenever possible, unless it is heavily subsidised. Any writer working in the professional theatre today knows that his chances of having a play accepted are much less hopeful if his cast list numbers more than six. The playwright working for the amateur theatre has no such restriction. Many companies require large-cast plays which will involve as many members of their society as possible. On the other hand, some are greatly over-weighted with women, or are composed entirely of women; some have very few young actors; some are made up entirely of teenagers. In fact, each society has its own specific needs – the only thing they have in common is that they don't have to pay their actors.

The most effective way of ensuring that there is always a good selection of plays available from which to make up a programme is:

(*a*) To appoint a play-reading committee, and

(*b*) To encourage *all* the members of the society to see, and read, and read about as many plays as possible, and to report to the committee about any which seem interesting.

Not all the plays which are put on in professional theatres are available to amateurs, but they are still worth considering because they will eventually be released for amateur production. It's just a question of being prepared to wait, and keeping an eye on *Amateur Stage* for details of new and forthcoming releases.

Ideally a *play-reading committee* should be composed of a group of people with several special assets. The first of these is the ability to 'lift a play from the page', to imaginatively envisage a performance when all that is available is the printed word. This skill can be developed through experience in reading and seeing plays, but only if there is a certain element of dramatic imagination to start with, so it is not a job for everyone.

The second required asset is the more practical one of having sufficient time and money to make it possible to experience a great deal of theatre. It is important to read a lot of plays, to watch televised drama, to go to the professional theatre, and to visit other amateur dramatic societies frequently.

The third asset is the ability to assess the practical problems involved in the staging of a particular play, and to work out whether the resources of the society – as regards its actors, stage management and technical strength, acting area and budget – make it a feasible proposition.

The fourth and final asset is a genuine enthusiasm for the job. A reluctant play-reading committee is worse than useless since it will do the job badly but its very existence will make sure that no one else will do the job at all.

Once the committee has been elected from members of the society who possess these assets, it should be given a brief to work by.

## Play-reading committee's working brief

The play must be right for the society. It should have a cast list which can be adequately supplied from the actors available, the production should not be beyond the skills or resources of the group as a whole, and the material should be sufficiently interesting and challenging to be thoroughly satisfying to all those concerned with its staging. It is essential to have a clear-eyed understanding of what the society is capable of, and it is as important not to under-rate its potential as it is not to over-rate it.

First, evaluate its acting skill. If it has some excellent middle-aged actresses, but none under the age of thirty, there is no point in trying to stage a play like *Mary Rose* or *The Day After The Fair*, both of which depend upon the youthful quality of one of the main characters. It is much more difficult to simulate youth than age, and it is unnecessary to undertake this thankless task since there are so many plays available for older actors and actresses; plays of the stature of David Storey's *Home*, for instance, or Marcelle Maurette's *Anastasia*. Similarly, if it is overweighted with women, choose a play to match. Never try to pass off a woman in a man's part unless the play demands it. That way disaster lies, and drama can easily topple into farce.

You will find that play publishers issue catalogues of plays divided into categories depending on the number and sex of the actors required, and this makes selection much easier. But beware of choosing a play only from its catalogue description or the advertising blurb. Looking for the right play is like house hunting – many that seem ideal from the description prove to be totally unsuitable on closer inspection.

A safer guide to available plays is the magazine *Amateur Stage* with its features on 'Play Selection' and 'New Play Reviews'. The British Theatre Association is also an invaluable aid with its comprehensive information and advisory service, extensive library, and quarterly theatre review, *Drama*. It is well worth the while of any amateur dramatic society to subscribe to both these excellent institutions if funds allow – if not, individual members might take it upon themselves.

Having assessed the acting strength of the company, the next step is to assess its technical strength.

1   Is the stage-management team efficient enough to put on a play which needs several sets and a number of scene changes?
2   Are the lighting technicians, and the lights themselves, capable of coping with a complicated lighting plot?
3   Are there sufficient competent craftsmen to build scenery and make a large number of props?
4   Is there an extensive wardrobe team with the time and talent to create elaborate costumes?

If not, avoid anything too demanding, and choose a play which can be staged very simply. Fortunately, the trend today is towards greater simplicity in play presentation. Partly because of the growth of fringe and alternative theatre both directors and writers are beginning to return to the philosophy of medieval theatre and feel that in many cases the words and the actors should be able to speak for themselves and create an imaginative environment rather than depend too strongly on a contrived set.

Then there is the question of the stage itself. If it is small avoid a large scale production with over thirty characters in it – it will be impossible to move them around with any degree of credibility or artistic flair.

Finally, it is very important to know what the company can afford to spend, and to choose a play which will not 'break the bank'. Obviously, period plays are expensive since, whether costumes are made or hired, they cost a lot of money. If period wigs are required they must be hired, and they are far from cheap.

Similarly any play set in a sophisticated indoor environment will require expensive props – even the cleverest craftsman will be hard-pressed to create a Chippendale chair from a couple of orange boxes. On the other hand, it might well be possible to borrow this kind of thing. The well-organised stage manager will have a prop book in which he will list any items which are available for loan in the area, with the name, address and telephone number of the cooperative owner (see also p. 129). Needless to say, anything of value should not only be treated with great care, but also insured. Accidents can happen even on the best-managed stage. It is also a courtesy to acknowledge the loan in the programme and to thank the owner with a couple of complimentary tickets.

Another significant expense is the performance fee. Each and every performance of a modern play has to be paid for, and the charge varies enormously. The writer's agent, or the publisher of the acting edition – named in the front of the playscript – will give you information about costs. Only if a play is out of copyright, that is, under normal circumstances, if the author has been dead for fifty years or more, can it be performed free of charge.

And then there is the cost of scripts, another detail which must be investigated.

1 Can scripts be obtained through your local library?
2 Should they be hired from the British Theatre Association?
3 Are they to be bought, and if so, will they be bought by the society or will the actors meet the cost themselves?
4 Is the play new and unpublished? In that case copies may well have to be made by the society, and unless one of the members has access to a copying machine this can again be a major financial outlay.

After consideration has been paid to the artistic, technical and financial demands of the play, some thought must be given to the nature of the play. I have seen good, lively societies grind to a halt because the committee has decided that they should stage a succession of music halls, pantomimes and revues when what the actors really wanted to do was Sartre, Pinter and Beckett. It must be equally galling for a group set upon recreating

*Salad Days* or *The Dancing Years* to find themselves struggling through *Mahagonny*.

Nevertheless, it is not good policy to allow what-the-actors-want to be the only yardstick for choosing a programme. What-the-audiences-want must be the second consideration on the brief of the play-reading committee. Amateur actors need an audience just as much as professional actors do, and it is self-indulgent to follow their own interests while holding those of the audience in contempt. Of course, there should be opportunities for them to explore their own particular enthusiasms occasionally – this is why play-readings and private performances should be built into the year's activities. But they should also discipline themselves to present a programme sufficiently attractive to bring in a large, paying audience. There are amateur dramatic societies which finance themselves so efficiently by jumble sales and coffee mornings that they are totally independent of box office takings, but this is an artificial and undesirable state of affairs. The successful society will, if necessary, create and then maintain its own audience, and their continuing partnership and shared dramatic experiences will enrich the lives of both.

It is quite wrong, and extremely patronising, to believe that audiences have lamentably bad taste in theatre, and will only go to see third-rate work, pot-boiler thrillers and unsubtle comedies. They do like to laugh, they do enjoy being excited or moved, but their emotions can be aroused just as effectively by well-wrought material as by a vulgar script.

For instance, the village where I live revels in pantomime and music hall, loves to participate noisily in melodrama, and joins in community singing with a will. Yet the plays which are best remembered and which caused most interest are *Mixed Doubles*, an entertainment created by writers of the calibre of Pinter, James Saunders and Alun Owen, and *In Camera*, the English version of *Huis Clos* by Jean-Paul Sartre.

It is important to get to know one's audience and their tastes, to coax them along to the theatre by clever advertising and subtle persuasion, and then, by high standards of performance and organisation, to build up their trust and confidence to such a pitch that they will become loyal and regular supporters.

But they will only remain loyal supporters if the standards remain high and the programme satisfyingly varied. In other words, by all means let the company have a go at *King Lear* if they are good enough and the prospect excites them, but follow it up with *Move Over Mrs Markham* or *Charley's Aunt*. A mixed diet of theatre is essential. Combine comedy, drama, revue, music hall, the new and the old, the 'highbrow' and the popular, and make sure that there is something for everyone. The only thing I would avoid, because it is phenomenally difficult, is farce. Treat discretion as the better part of valour and leave that to the experts.

Most audiences are attracted by something familiar – *Blithe Spirit* and *The Secretary Bird* will usually draw large houses – but it's a good idea to feed in one or two unfamiliar plays from time to time so that they have a chance to extend their experiences and broaden their theatrical horizons. David Mercer, Christopher Hampton, Woody Allen, John Arden, James Saunders, N. F. Simpson, David Storey, Colin Welland and Pam Gems are just a few of our rich supply of contemporary dramatists whose work, though available to amateurs, is not performed by them as often as it might be.

Once the society has consolidated a satisfactory relationship with its audience it might be a good idea to put out a suggestion box at the end of each performance and ask them to suggest plays they would like to see. It would be quite an easy matter to insert a slip of paper into the programme so that they could write down any ideas they might have. Some of the suggestions will almost certainly be impracticable but there might well be one or two worth following up. What is more, if the audience is invited to become involved in this way they are likely to take a more vital interest in the fortunes of the society.

When the play-reading committee has given due consideration to:
1 The requirements of the society, and
2 The requirements of the audience,
It should go on to contemplate:
3 The requirements of the area in which they live.

First of all, they should check on what other nearby amateur groups are doing. A few years ago three companies in my neighbourhood staged *Breath of Spring* within a few months of each other. This year they're at it again with *How The Other Half Loves*. It is not only bad box office policy, it also exposes them to the charge of being either careless, or unoriginal, or both.

Secondly, whether or not there is good repertory theatre easily accessible should figure largely in the committee's deliberations. There is little point in an amateur group putting on the same sort of programme, or even duplicating the same plays, as a nearby professional company. They will only invite invidious comparisons and split their potential audience. It is much more sensible for them to complement the repertoire of the local theatre by staging material which, for one reason or another, the professionals cannot undertake. Usually a theatre director will be happy to discuss his proposed programme with a competent amateur society, and make suggestions about possible plays for them, especially if he knows that members of the society will repay his cooperation by supporting his theatre.

The point has already been made that the professional theatre can rarely afford to put on large-cast plays, and this is one area in which amateurs can fill a sad gap. For instance, my local regional theatre can only manage to stage Shakespeare once in four or five years. Consequently a first-rate amateur company puts on a Shakespeare play every summer. It is always an open-air production, played against the romantic ruins of an ancient castle. It invariably draws large audiences and makes a lot of money. Standards of acting and presentation are always high, so both residents and holiday-makers in the city have come to realise that this is an experience not to be missed. Other large-cast plays which a small repertory company cannot afford nowadays need to be kept alive by amateurs. Peter Terson's *Zigger Zagger* is one, Thornton Wilder's *Our Town* another, as well as *The Royal Hunt of the Sun* by Peter Shaffer, and there are many more.

Similarly, financial pressures often prevent professional companies from putting on experimental or new drama unless they have a small studio theatre, and this is another field amateurs should explore. If there are professional writers in the area it is very possible that they are looking for an opportunity to get an initial staging of their plays so that they can see how they work, iron out any problems, and perhaps get their agent along to take a look. And in these circumstances they might even be prepared to waive a performance fee! If the society's publicity group is working effectively and the local paper, radio or television can be persuaded to take an interest and give the new play and its writer some coverage there should be no trouble in finding a good audience (see also Chapter 11, Publicity and Management). Alan Ayckbourn, talking at the Scarborough In-the-Round Festival in 1978, expressed his strongly-felt view that amateur societies should encourage new drama in its early stages and nurture their dramatists. Even though they have their own box office problems to solve, amateurs are generally in a stronger position to cooperate with up-and-coming dramatists, and this should be an important consideration in their programme planning.

Experimental drama often gets a showing in fringe theatres, but only a small proportion of it manages to transfer elsewhere. This is where the committee should be particularly alert. If a play creates interest on the fringe of the Edinburgh Festival, or another of the popular Arts Festivals, or has some success in one of London's alternative theatres, it might be worth contacting the author, finding out if he will allow amateurs to use his work, and offering play-goers in the area a chance to see a play that would be otherwise lost to them. The weekly paper, *The Stage*, carries reviews of much of the work of the Fringe, as well as plays being put on in major theatres and by provincial companies throughout the country, and is a very useful source of information.

If the company is large enough to have a pool of actors surplus to the requirements of the current play it is sensible to form them into an active play-reading group which will meet at least once a week to read sections of plays under consideration, or to go further and prepare staged or rehearsed readings. These will be done with the scripts, but should be given a certain amount of direction and rehearsal, and use a few props and costumes. In this way something of the total impact of the work will be created and the audience – made up of interested members of the society – will get a taste of the eventual flavour of the piece.

Rehearsed readings serve a double function. They try out possible plays to discover whether they deserve a place in the main programme, and they keep actors and directors interested and involved, providing them with useful experience and training while they are waiting their turn for a good part.

I believe it adds to the vitality of an amateur dramatic society if it occasionally writes, adapts or evolves its own dramatic material, and tailors it to fit the assets of the group and the specific interests of the audience.

If there are members of the society who are writers, or who are interested in writing, a *writers' group* could be formed, responsible for exploring themes or ideas. They could write either as a team, in partnerships, or as individuals, according to their own preference and temperament.

Pantomime is the prime example of an entertainment that can only benefit by being written especially for the company, and created to fit in with its special skills. The easiest way is to obtain a skeleton published script and to fill it out with additional material. A more satisfying way is to take a basic pantomime plot and to re-work it into a local version of the story. The best way is to take a local legend or historical event and to shape that into the traditional pantomime formula.

I have been involved in several home-made pantomimes of this kind. They were immensely popular, and caused much more interest than any re-hashed *Aladdin* or *Jack and the Beanstalk* ever achieved because the audience felt that they were written specially for them.

One of them was written for a village with a Manor House which was originally given by Queen Elizabeth I to the family of Sir Walter Raleigh. Legend has it that, when the gift was originally made, the house was in a state of crumbling disrepair, and was allowed to remain that way. Then, to Sir Walter's horror, the Queen suddenly took it into her head to visit him and examine her generous gift. Realising that time was short, and the Queen's disfavour to be avoided at all cost, he sailed a boat up the river, beached it nearby, dismantled it, and used the ship's timbers to refurbish his home, finishing his mammoth task just in time to receive his sovereign in the style she expected. This little story became the basic plot of the pantomime, with Queen Elizabeth as a termagant, red-headed Dame, and the Raleigh ladies as the Ugly Sisters – or rather, Ugly Mother and Daughter.

## A RUFF FOR BESS – DOWNTON AMATEUR DRAMATIC SOCIETY

(The authors wish to declare that any resemblance to historical accuracy is purely accidental.)

### ACT I SCENE I

SIR WALTER, MUMSY, SIS, MESSENGER, JAKE, CHORUS

*Legend has it that Queen Elizabeth decided to come to visit the Manor House before they'd finished modernising it, so the play opens with* SIR WALTER, *his* MOTHER *and* SISTER, *with* JAKE *in attendance, examining the progress of the builders, a few of whom are standing around, looking quaint, and indulging in a variety of picturesque Tudor crafts.*

SIR WALTER [*rather languid and precious*]: I say, chaps, not bad. Not bad at all. Coming along splendidly. What do you think, Mumsy dear?

MUMSY: Charming, quite charming. [*Crosses to look out of the window, stage right*] Just look at that view.

SIS: [*stage left, chatting up a workman, and functioning on an entirely different wavelength than her mother's*]: Oh! You are clever. And so strong. Ooh! and what lovely muscles you have! Mumsy, just look at this one.

MUMSY [*imagining* SIS *is referring to the view from window, stage left*]: No darling. I prefer this one.

SIS: Oh! you can't be serious. This one is absolutely beautiful.

MUMSY: But look at this – the shape, the breadth, the colour ...

SIS: But look at *this* – the strength, the rippling muscles ...

MUMSY [*astonished, swinging around to look at* SIS]: Rippling

muscles! Darling, do put the man *down*. You don't know where
he's been. I can't take you anywhere. Walter, we must find her a
husband. Surely one of your nice young friends ...

SIR WALTER: But Mumsy, look at her!

[*They both stare miserably at* SIS, *in darkening despair.* SIS,
*too dim to understand what is going on, beams back at them,
hideously*]

MUMSY: I see what you mean.

SIR WALTER: Tell you what. First we'll get the new house sorted out,
then we'll have a go at the ancient monument over there.

[*Enter* MESSENGER, *very elaborately dressed, very breathless,
bearing a scroll*]

MESSENGER: Sir Walter Raleigh. A letter.

SIR WALTER: A letter? Good heavens. And I haven't sent out my
change of address cards yet. Who is it from?

MESSENGER: The Queen.

MUMSY AND SIS: The Queen? [*Very excited*]

CHORUS: The Queen! [*Very impressed*]

SIR WALTER: The Queen. [*Very depressed*] What does she want
this time? Not another trip to America, I hope. I'm still trying to
give up smoking! Besides, she knows how sea-sick I get. I just
ruined my plum-coloured doublet last time. It's these terrible
sailing ships that cause the trouble. If only they'd get a move on
and invent the engine.

MUMSY: Walter, dear. What does she say?

SIR WALTER: What? Oh yes, the letter. [*Reads*] Dear Wal, Just
longing to see your country nook. Sounds divine. Popping down
for the weekend to give it a dekko. Toodle-oo. Bess.

[*The* CHORUS, MUMSY *and* SIS *dissolve into an instant tizz.* SIR
WALTER *looks horrified, but resigned*]

I might have known. You never can keep her away from Downton.
It always was her favourite place. But Bess, for the weekend.
And just look at the place!

CHORUS [*rushing around the stage examining its bare unfinished state,
and exchanging frantic glances*]: The Queen! What are we going
to do? Where will she sleep? What will she say?

[*Then they burst into song, to the tune of 'This Old House' –
Rosemary Clooney's hit*]

SONG NO. 1 [*individual lines to be sung by individual singers*]:

This new house is not yet finished,
This new house is just half done.
There's no tiling on the roof yet,
There's no shelter from the sun.
When it rains the water pours in,
When it snows we all get wet,

When the wind blows, how we shiver!
And we have no mod cons. yet.

*etc.*

Now this house is all made ready,
Now this house has all been done,
There's a chimney from the fireplace,
And some logs for us to burn.
There's a table for our victuals,
And an armchair by the hearth.
We've got pictures, and some curtains ...
But we haven't got a 'bearth'.

WORKMAN 1: A bath?
WORKMAN 2: Yes, a bath.
WORKMAN 1: But who wants a bath?
WORKMAN 2: [*sniffing ostentatiously*]: Pooh! You do.

We've got all we need for comfort,
Quite the best you've ever seen.
There's no doubt at all about it,
It's a house fit for a Queen.

CHEERLEADER: What are we going to do, sir?
SIR WALTER: Do? Get on with it, of course. Don't hang around there.
Come on. Get moving.
> [*The* CHORUS *and* SIR WALTER *and* JAKE *carry on all the props and dress the stage, while the piano plays 'This Old House' softly in the background. No words are spoken, but there is some comic horseplay before the work is complete. Loo and bath are carried across stage and dumped in the wings*]
So it is. Fit for a queen. Splendid. But what are we going to *do* with the woman all weekend? It's bound to rain. I know, I'll ask old Phil to come over from Wilton and help us out.
SIS: Sir Philip Sydney? Oh, yes *please*. I *like* him. He's got gorgeous muscles.
MUMSY [*eyeing* SIS *speculatively*]: Sir Philip? Yes. He could be just the one. Yes, do send for him, dear. He'll be most – er – useful.
SIR WALTER: Jake, my boy. Just gallop along to Wilton House and ask Sir Philip to pop over for a day or two. Tell him the Queen's coming. No, that's no good. Tell him my mother and sister would like to see him. No, that's even worse. I know, tell him the Queen's coming, and bringing her very prettiest maids-in-waiting. That'll fetch him ... Then he can look after old Bess, and I'll wait on the maids! Come on, folks. Time's short. She'll be here before you can hoist your petard.

*[All exeunt]*

Other good local material that can be used comes from contemporary events, the issues that closely affect the lives of the community, and about which they care deeply. The closing of a large factory, for instance, the building of an industrial complex in a small town, the discovery of oil, the creation of a motorway, the demolition of an old, but much-loved area of a city – all these events intimately involve those concerned. They tend to be confused about the rights and wrongs of the situation, apprehensive about the outcome, and anxious to have the matter thoroughly aired. A competent writing group could take advantage of this sort of dispute and turn it into good documentary drama which would be genuinely relevant to the lives of its audience, and help them to understand the *pros* and *cons*. To give it total authenticity the script could include some of the actual comments, reports, letters and speeches which will have appeared in the local press and television coverage while the matter has been under discussion.

It's worth noting that though this is serious theatre, it is not necessarily unfunny. In fact, the most effective drama is often that which deals with important issues in a funny way. Alan Plater's play, *Close The Coalhouse Door*, is an excellent example of this. He set out to create, for the Newcastle Playhouse, a documentary musical to praise the miners of north east England, to show that they had been unfairly used throughout the history of the industry, and continued to be abused despite nationalisation. He wrapped his 'message' in a framework of vibrant dialogue, songs, dance, projected slides and music hall humour, and created an entertainment that was at the same time hilariously funny, immensely moving, and yet made an important statement about a vital issue. Some of the quality of the writing can be experienced in this excerpt, though anyone interested in contemporary documentary drama should read the whole play.

While few amateur dramatic societies are likely to match up to the combined talents of Alan Plater and his song-writer, Alex Glasgow, nevertheless there is no reason why some members should not combine to produce the same sort of material, based on the shared community experience of their area. The most important ingredients are thorough research, and sympathy with, and understanding of, the subject matter.

### CLOSE THE COALHOUSE DOOR – ACT III

WILL: What about rationalisation? [*Pause*]

JACKIE: Rationalisation?

WILL: Aye.

JACKIE: Nobody's talking about rationalisation ...

WILL: I'm talking about it.

THOMAS: The subject on the agenda is nationalisation.

WILL: Bust the agenda, I'm talking about rationalisation.

MARY: I don't know what anybody's talking about.

RUTH: Me neither.

THOMAS: It's nowt to do with women.

FRANK: What about rationalisation?

WILL: And you a scholar ...

FRANK: I'm sorry, I don't see the connection ...

WILL: The connection is that this village, and this pit, got rationalisation. [*Pause*]

JACKIE: Aye.

GEORDIE: That's right.

THOMAS: I know.

VICAR: How do you mean? The pit got rationalisation?

WILL: I mean, the NCB says we've got to rationalise the industry
... we've got to rationalise Brockenback pit ... [*Pause*] I mean,
they closed the bugger.

> [*Music link, a lighting change and the Labour Exchange door is
> pushed on again.* THOMAS, WILL, JACKIE *and* GEORDIE *form a
> queue*]
> [*Slide: 1961*]

THOMAS: 1961. Harold Macmillan.

JACKIE: Selwyn Lloyd.

WILL: Huckleberry Hound.

GEORDIE: Yogi Bear.

THOMAS: Harold Macmillan. [*Pause*] We're here again, lads.

WILL: This is what they mean by rationalisation.

JACKIE: Marginal adjustments in the national economy.

GEORDIE: Safeguarding the strength of sterling.

JACKIE: Our world role.

WILL: Wor* seat at the conference table.

THOMAS: Well, it still feels like the dole to me.

JACKIE: Only one thing to do.

WILL: Whitehall it'll have to be.

> [*Marching music building up quietly*]

* 'Wor' – Geordie dialect: 'our'.

GEORDIE: We'll have to stir the conscience of the nation.

[*The old banners are brought out*]

THOMAS: Are you ready, lads?

[*The music building up*]

By the left . . . quick march . . .

[*Just as they are about to set off, the* EXPERT *comes on from the opposite side. He is dressed as a high Cabinet man, and carries a brief case*]

EXPERT: Don't you go to all that trouble, chaps, we'll come to you.

[*And he crosses to them. They are stunned*]

THOMAS: Ye what?

EXPERT: I am coming to you.

THOMAS: Wey, that's a turn-up.

EXPERT: Well, you see, I'm on a fact-finding mission.

JACKIE: What sort of facts do you expect to find?

EXPERT: One can't really say that, till one has, as it were, found them.

[*He roots around the stage looking for facts*]

The point is, gentlemen . . . chaps . . . lads . . . we are very worried about the results of nationalisation and, er . . . rationalisation, in this area . . .

THOMAS: So are we!

JACKIE: What are ye ganna dae about it?

EXPERT: We have perfected a new policy . . . regionalisation! [*Fanfare*]

THOMAS: Regionalisation?

WILL: Getaway.

JACKIE: That sounds grand.

GEORDIE: But what is it?

EXPERT: It simply means that from now on, we in Whitehall are determined to take a fresh look at you splendid chaps, lads in Durham and Northumberland and . . . Yorkshire's quite near as well, isn't it?

JACKIE: You mean we'll get a bigger slice of the national cake.

EXPERT: Yes . . . and very nicely put, if I may say so.

JACKIE: Ta.

THOMAS: But you're all Tories, aren't you?

EXPERT: Well lads, we're all Tories now, unless we're Socialists . . .

WILL: That's true enough.

EXPERT: My friends . . .

THOMAS: Watch him . . .

EXPERT: My friends . . . we're all brothers in the same family . . .

THOMAS: Prove it!

EXPERT: I can prove it, friends . . . because I have brought with me on my fact-finding mission our new secret weapon. Our new symbol of liberty, equality and fraternity.

[*As the music starts he brings out of his brief case a cloth cap, two sizes too large ... and sings ...*]

[*Slides: Hailsham, Home, Macmillan, George Brown in caps*]

[*He makes the song a triumphal procession ending with a big flourishing exit. The men are left feeling quite pleased until they realise they are still standing at the Labour Exchange door*]

THOMAS: Well, it's all very well but I divven feel any different.

[*The* VICAR *walks across to them*]

VICAR: I hear they're closing the pit.

THOMAS: That's right.

VICAR: Perhaps I could say a few suitable words ...

GEORDIE: We've already said a few suitable words ...

WILL: And it's staying closed.

VICAR: Well, haven't they made any arrangements?

THOMAS: Oh, aye, they're looking after us ... me and Will here, we're ganna look after the pumps ...

JACKIE: And me and Geordie, we're ganna be redeployed to Datton Colliery ... temporarily ...

VICAR: Temporarily?

JACKIE: Till they build the perfume factory.

VICAR: They're going to build a perfume factory here?

GEORDIE: To take up the slack of unemployment ...

JACKIE: They're not actually building it yet ... They're doing a feasibility study ... to see whether it's the right place for a perfume factory.

THOMAS: There's got to be an adequate water supply before you can build a perfume factory.

WILL: And proper sewage disposal.

GEORDIE: And the right kind of prevailing winds.

JACKIE: You can't just bash a perfume factory down anywhere.

GEORDIE: Diversification.

WILL: What?

GEORDIE: Diversification ... that's what they call it when they close a pit and build a perfume factory ...

WILL: Look, for God's sake, Geordie man, we've had nationalisation and rationalisation ... and then regionalisation ... and now diversification ... I divven think I can take any more ...

GEORDIE: All we lack's constipation.

JACKIE: I've got news for you.

GEORDIE: Oh, I'm sorry ... keep taking the tablets ...

**by Alan Plater**

(*Copyright 1969 Alan Plater, lyrics Alex Glasgow, published 1969 by Methuen*)

Another form of theatre which a group might be able to create is revue. There is no need to write all the material, for published sketches and monologues can be obtained without difficulty, either from libraries or publishers, and used as a basis, but it is good to add to these extra material which has been written by and for the society. It's also quite easy to substitute new and relevant words to familiar tunes – once the rhythm is worked out you'll find that words should fall into place without too much trouble. If there are good dancers in the society use their skills too to add visual variety and glamour. The whole thing can then be tied together by a link-man with his own line in patter and humour. This sort of combination of song, dance, comedy and visual and verbal wit usually provides a popular evening's entertainment. If you prefer to keep it short and sharp, and limit it to about an hour, the rest of the evening might be devoted to a disco and buffet supper or something similar. One word of warning – to work well, revue must be slickly directed with impeccable stage management and split-second timing. Pace is of the essence.

Finally, if your writing group feels unable to create any original material it can still evolve a good theatrical event by choosing a theme and using available literature to work into an anthology.

The anthology might take as its subject matter a theme of particular interest – perhaps 'Country Life' for a village society; 'The City' for an urban group; 'The Faces of Woman' for a Townswomen's Guild or Women's Institute; 'Growing Up' for a youth club – or it could be created around a topic of general interest – 'Parents and Children' usually works well, as does 'In Love', and 'Magics and Marvels'. All that is required is wide reading so that a comprehensive range of unfamiliar as well as popular material – poems, prose excerpts, letters, jokes, riddles, limericks, nursery rhymes, as well as sections of newspaper and magazine articles and possibly music, too – can be discovered and then woven together to make a well-shaped and balanced whole.

The other way of choosing a theme is to select a personality who is being celebrated because of some significant anniversary, and build the anthology around his/her life and work. In 1978, the fiftieth anniversary of Hardy's death, several societies mounted good anthologies based on Hardy and his Wessex. They were able to draw on his novels, poems and short stories, on Frank Harvey's dramatisation, *The Day After The Fair*, on letters, on the large body of critical work that has grown up around his literary output, and on peripheral material which brings together the novels and the Wessex that he immortalised. In many cases the anthology was unified by slides of the incomparable countryside he portrayed so well.

The *Writers' and Artists' Yearbook* can be consulted in any public library and contains a Journalists' Calendar which lists imminent anniversaries. Alternatively, study the *Encyclopaedia of Dates and Events* (L. C. Pascoe, Teach Yourself Books, 1979) which is crammed with valuable information.

Before embarking on this sort of activity, I would recommend any writing group to study John Barton's excellent anthology, *The Hollow Crown*, based upon the kings and queens of England. It is a splendid example of the genre and one that has proved itself an artistic and commercial success for amateurs and professionals alike.

Staging an anthology is not difficult since no sets are required, and props and costumes are minimal. The main problem is the avoidance of visual monotony, so it is desirable to design good lighting, and to equip the stage with a selection of rostra which will provide a variety of levels from which the actors can work. If possible, the projection of slides will also create extra interest.

### Exercise 1 – Choosing a programme

Imagine that you are on the play-reading committee of a village dramatic society which has seventeen members (twelve women and five men). They have to share all the work – lighting, stage management, props, etc. as well as the acting. None of the women is younger than twenty-five, two are in their sixties. One of the men is seventeen, two are in their early thirties, one is forty, the other in his mid-fifties.

There is a repertory theatre six miles away, and another fifteen miles away, but neither is able to put on very modern or unusual work.

The society has about fifty pounds in its bank account and is able to earn more money quite effectively by holding jumble sales and similar functions. For their productions they have the use of a well-equipped village hall which has a reasonably-sized stage, with curtains, and basic stage lighting.

Work out a varied programme for two years of activities which will include three public productions each year, plus one or two private events for friends and members only. Remember that your double aim should be to satisfy and occupy all the members of the society and to please your audience so much that it not only remains loyal, but also grows.

# A Job for Everyone

' "A Job for Everyone" ' – it sounds like an election slogan for the Old Testament Prophets' Party! But, of course, your aim is pleasure, not profit. Both? – very good.

The exciting thing about a company of people agreeing to create a production for the pleasure of an audience and the increase of skills by themselves is that everybody can try new avenues of exploration.

Did you hear someone suddenly bursting into song? Get them to sing in the play – add a song if there isn't one.

Does that shy stage manager play the guitar? He could record the play-in music – perhaps write it as well.

That lady who can't act without giggling but always has bright ideas – perhaps she could direct instead?

Why not create a show written by the company, or by local people, and performed by the company with everyone having a go at directing sketches, songs or poems?

There is always a job for everyone, but it isn't always the one you expect! Be brave, ask people to rise to occasions – they always do.'

**Denise Coffey**
*Actress, writer and director*

Most of the people who join amateur dramatic societies are, naturally enough, would-be actors. Many profess to have little interest or competence in the more practical skills of stagecraft. These two combined factors often make it very difficult for amateur groups to choose varied and interesting plays, and to stage them effectively.

Obviously, the situation has to be manipulated to the advantage of the company. This can be done in several ways. First of all, those members who aren't given acting parts in the current production must be encouraged and, if necessary, trained, to do some of the other jobs that are of equal importance, but less glamorous, in the staging of a play. These range from directing to publicity, and take in such responsibilities as painting scenery, acquiring props, rigging lights, applying make-up, making tea, organising front-of-house requirements, making and maintaining costumes, and prompting, to name but a few.

Besides these, the business of reading and assessing plays, writing special material, arranging staged rehearsals, as well as visiting professional theatres and other amateur groups, should go on all year round, whether or not there is a production in the pipe-line.

There will also be the organisational work of the group – making sure that the subscriptions come in and the budget is balanced, putting out a newsletter, recruiting and enrolling new members, arranging regular meetings for the committee and any sub-committees that exist, and generally keeping the society in healthy working order. It all takes time and manpower, and it's important that the work should be fairly distributed instead of resting too heavily on the shoulders of a harassed handful.

I feel very strongly that full membership of an amateur dramatic society should only be granted to those who are prepared to do some other job than acting, when called upon, and that this should be clearly stated on the membership application form they sign when they join. In the professional theatre many of our most distinguished actors began their careers sweeping the stage as assistant stage managers, and were happy to do any job connected with the theatre just to get a foot in the door of the profession they loved. Yet, all too often, amateurs who don't get parts in a play simply opt out until the next auditions are held. Quite apart from the fact that this creates fearful difficulties for the director, who will probably be left with a skeleton stage staff, it is also very bad for the actors themselves who can learn a great deal about their craft from becoming involved in non-acting tasks. So, whenever auditioning for a part, actors should be asked to state what other tasks they will be prepared to undertake in the event of their not being cast in the play (see the audition form on p. 91).

All the experienced members of the company should look upon it as part of the job to pass on their own acquired skills to inexperienced members, and each major production should employ a combination of old hands and new in every department. Once they have had a certain amount of training in this way, people should be ready to practise what they have learnt in a more responsible capacity, preferably, to start with, in a private performance of a one-act play which will give them the practice they need to become perfect without putting too heavy demands upon them.

A second way of making sure that the society has sufficient manpower to cope with the requirements of the current programme is to look beyond the membership for specialised work. For instance, groups studying dress design at the local college, senior school, or in adult education classes might be prepared to design and/or make the costumes as part of their practical work if it can be tied in with an existing syllabus or project. Similarly, student carpenters and joiners might be persuaded to make scenery and props, and art students to design and paint them. The latter could be invited to design posters and programmes too. Teachers very often jump at the chance of presenting their pupils with a practical project rather than one which is of merely academic interest. And, the results can often be quite dazzling.

For a recent production of *Joseph and his Amazing Technicolor Dreamcoat*, my local theatre ran a competition throughout local schools in the city to see which child could design the best dreamcoat. The winning drawing was transformed into a superb and highly dramatic costume by the theatre's wardrobe mistress. This was also a very clever publicity exercise, of course, and there's no reason at all why amateurs should not adopt similar tactics to get some of their work done for them and to extend their potential audiences. The only snag is that this sort of exercise needs to be planned well ahead so that it can be organised properly. It can only be really useful to those who make up their programme on at least an annual, if not biennial, basis.

Apart from the schools and colleges, societies and clubs which might be prepared to give group help, there are often individuals with particular interests who can be of great value to a dramatic society, even though they may not be particularly interested in drama. For instance, I have come across a dedicated sound recordist and an excellent photographer, both of whom were delighted to lend their skills, and their equipment, to a particular production on an 'expenses only' basis. For them, it was an opportunity to indulge in a favourite hobby and meet an unusual challenge without being out of pocket. For the amateur dramatic society it meant, in one case, sound effects of professional standard which enabled them to put on a technically demanding play, in the other, superb publicity photographs which went into a central shop window, as well as into the programme, and sold dozens of seats through the interest they aroused. And it was also useful publicity for the photographer.

In a village or close-knit community the society will usually know of people like these who can be approached with a request to give specific help. In a more urban or scattered environment it might be worth advertising for them in a local paper.

The third way of getting the best results from a dramatic society with limited membership is – to extend the membership.

This is not as difficult as it might seem if the society has something attractive to offer. Not many newcomers are going to be drawn to a dramatic group which presents a programme of dreary plays indifferently staged. However, if it puts on exciting work in an exciting way, maintaining high standards of acting, direction and technical expertise, and if it combines this achievement with effective publicity, it should attract a constant stream of new members.

It's not a good idea for a society which wants to grow to stage all its plays in the same place, whether that place is its own little theatre, village hall, school assembly hall, or whatever. Actors must occasionally be prepared to go out and find new audiences and new members, and not expect them to make the first move. Mobility, flexibility and versatility are the key words.

It might be possible to put on an open-air lunchtime show in the courtyard of a pub, or in a central space in a pedestrian precinct – but always check with the authorities first. Some schools, colleges, factories and hospitals will welcome a good amateur group which wants to do a show specially for them if it can be fitted into their timetable. At Easter or Christmas the society might like to put on a religious play in a local church or chapel, maybe tying it in with the service as an alternative to the sermon. An ancient tradition this, which dates back to medieval times, and one which can only enhance both the life of the church and the experience of the dramatic society.

Another old tradition which is well worth reviving is that of the Mummers' Play. In my village Mummers still visit the pubs in the week before Christmas with their strange tale of the death and resurrection of St George, and in this way their acting is seen and enjoyed by many people who would never consider going anywhere near a theatre, either amateur or professional.

When taking drama to the people the society should seize the opportunity to publicise its activities as effectively as possible. Striking posters and photographs should be displayed, and handbills distributed describing the activities of the club, outlining its future programme, and asking for new members. If the local paper, radio or television can be persuaded to take an interest in the event and give a certain amount of coverage, so much the better.

It is vital to get across the important message that the society does not only need actors. It also needs technicians, artists, musicians, needlewomen, carpenters, joiners, writers, people with secretarial skills and people prepared to make coffee, sell programmes, distribute posters, organise the car park or just be general supporters. Very often there are those who would like to join but are shy about offering their services since they feel they have no acting talent. They should always be encouraged to become members because there really is a job for everyone in the work of the theatre – acting is only one of the many.

A lot of dramatic societies also offer *associate membership* to those who merely want to show a close and continuing interest. For a reduced subscription they are kept well-informed about the club's activities, and future programme, are invited to participate in social events, and are offered an early choice of tickets for each production at a slightly reduced price. In return, they form the nucleus of a loyal, regular and enthusiastic audience, and are often prepared to help in other ways, by displaying posters perhaps, by lending props and costumes, and by sharing some of the front-of-house jobs.

Another way of attracting new members is to make sure that the work of the dramatic society is done within a framework of enjoyable social activities – outings, competitions, folk concerts, discos, talks, demonstrations and discussions, for example – and this will be an added incentive. It's important to remember that most people join societies because they are, as the name indicates, essentially social.

You may also expand your membership and your audience by giving free tickets to fully paid-up members for the less popular plays. This can be a real perk for theatre enthusiasts, and one they'll find difficult to resist if the society has a good reputation for imaginative play selection and high performance standards.

To recruit young members it's necessary to put on plays which are specially suited to their interests and abilities, and have probably been written with them in mind. There are some good ones from which to choose – Peter Terson's *The Apprentices* and *Zigger Zagger* written originally for the National Youth Theatre, and Don Taylor's *Long March to Jerusalem*, based on the Children's Crusade, and involving a large supporting cast of children as well as twenty-four major parts for young people and fifteen for adults – a marvellous experience for all concerned. Or, as an alternative to pantomime, written specially for the Young Vic and intended principally for eight- to twelve-year-olds, there's Denise Coffey's fun-play, *The Incredible Vanishing !!!!*

Better still, have a show written for them by a writer living in the area who will probably evolve special material to suit their interests and abilities. This is often the stuff from which good theatre is created, and it also gives rise to good publicity.

Too many amateur dramatic societies have a staid, middle-aged image. It's well worth making a positive effort to develop a lively and flourishing young membership. It can always be channelled into a separate Young Drama Group if it works better that way, but at least there's always a pool of trained youthful talent from which to draw when the need arises, and the mutual advantages can be immensely rewarding.

Finally, if it proves impossible to build up the membership to suit the plays, it's essential to choose the plays to suit the membership. If you have a marvellous stage-lighting team use them to the full and choose a play like John Mortimer's *A Voyage Round My Father* which depends upon lighting to set its various scenes. If you have a trained choreographer in the company, exploit his skills in pantomime and revue. If there is a lot of musical talent available, either choose musical entertainments, or build the play of your choice into a framework of music. In other words, learn to play to your strengths and avoid your weaknesses, while making absolutely sure that everyone is happily and usefully employed.

# 3

# The Craft of Acting

'I've always found it difficult to talk about acting. It's such an ephemeral craft but I believe its basic requirements are stamina, energy, observance, discipline, economy and a sense of humour – not necessarily in that order.

The work of the actor is to convey the intention of the author, through the director and himself, to the audience. On paper that looks simple enough, but the process of getting there can be strangely elusive. As Ralph Richardson once said, "Acting is a great mystery. One day it's there and the next day nowhere to be seen."

The more you learn about it the more difficult it becomes, and there's never an end to the learning.'

**Judi Dench**
*Actress*

The first step towards good acting lies in a thorough understanding of the character to be played, as it is revealed in the play.

Clues to interpretation are to be found in many areas of the script. First of all, in the words that the character actually says. The actor and director should work very closely together to arrive at a careful interpretation of each line of dialogue, bearing in mind that many sentences are capable of various interpretations, depending on mood, tone and situation.

I had my first lesson in interpretation from a seven-year-old about to play the lead in his school play. He was taking his responsibilities very seriously. 'It's my first speech that is the difficult one,' he said. 'Jane

says to me, "What are you doing, Peter?" and I have to say, "Thinking".'
I couldn't, at first, see where the difficulty lay. 'But you see,' he explained,
'I could say "Think*ing*" in a slow, thoughtful way. Or I could be
annoyed at being interrupted and say "*Think*ing" in a cross way. Or I
could be matter-of-fact and just say "Thinking" in an ordinary way. Or
I could be pretending I had a secret and say "Thinking" in a sing-song,
teasing way. Or I. . . .'

He was right. He had a problem of interpretation, and that problem
could only be resolved by a complete study of the play, an analysis of
Peter's character, and an understanding of his relationship with Jane and
the situation in which he found himself when she asked her question. And
he'd learnt his first important lesson as an actor — to act his part well
he must first of all understand it.

Character is revealed not only in the lines the person says himself. It
is also revealed by the lines addressed to him by other characters, by
remarks made about him, by what he does or omits to do in the context
of the play's action, and by his reaction to other people.

It is also essential to realise that characters in plays, just like people
in real life, often use words to disguise what they are thinking, feeling
and doing, rather than to illuminate it, so it is just as necessary to read
between and beneath the lines — to study the *sub-text* as it is called — as
to consider exactly what is being said.

Here, for instance, in fine comic vein, is Jack Worthing trying desperately to conceal the identity of Cecily from his friend Algernon, in
*The Importance of Being Earnest*. Any actor tackling the part must make
it quite clear that 'aunt' Cecily is a rather unconvincing figment of Jack's
imagination, and that he is struggling to make his story credible.

> [*Enter* LANE]
> LANE: Mr Ernest Worthing.
> > [*Enter* JACK. LANE *goes out*]
>
> ALGERNON: How are you, my dear Ernest? What brings you up to
> town?
> JACK: Oh, pleasure, pleasure! What else should bring one anywhere?
> Eating as usual, I see, Algy!
> ALGERNON [*stiffly*]: I believe it is customary in good society to take
> some slight refreshment at five o'clock. Where have you been
> since last Thursday?
> JACK [*smiling down on the sofa*]: In the country.
> ALGERNON: What on earth do you do there?

JACK [*pulling off his gloves*]: When one is in town one amuses oneself. When one is in the country one amuses other people. It is excessively boring.

ALGERNON: And who are the people you amuse?

JACK [*airily*]: Oh, neighbours, neighbours.

ALGERNON: Got nice neighbours in your part of Shropshire?

JACK: Perfectly horrid! Never speak to one of them.

ALGERNON: How immensely you must amuse them! [*Goes over and takes sandwich*] By the way, Shropshire is your county, is it not?

JACK: Eh? Shropshire? Yes, of course. Hallo! Why all these cups? Why cucumber sandwiches? Why such reckless extravagance in one so young? Who is coming to tea?

ALGERNON: Oh! merely Aunt Augusta and Gwendolen.

JACK: How perfectly delightful!

ALGERNON: Yes, that is all very well; but I am afraid Aunt Augusta won't quite approve of your being here.

JACK: May I ask why?

ALGERNON: My dear fellow, the way you flirt with Gwendolen is perfectly disgraceful. It is almost as bad as the way Gwendolen flirts with you.

JACK: I am in love with Gwendolen. I have come up to town expressly to propose to her.

ALGERNON: I thought you had come up for pleasure? ... I call that business.

JACK: How utterly unromantic you are!

ALGERNON: I really don't see anything romantic in proposing. It is very romantic to be in love. But there is nothing romantic about a definite proposal. Why, one may be accepted. One usually is, I believe. Then the excitement is all over. The very essence of romance is uncertainty. If I ever get married, I'll certainly try to forget the fact.

JACK: I have no doubt about that, dear Algy. The Divorce Court was specially invented for people whose memories are so curiously constituted.

ALGERNON: Oh! there is no use speculating on that subject. Divorces are made in Heaven...

[JACK *puts out his hand to take a sandwich.* ALGERNON *at once interferes.*]

Please don't touch the cucumber sandwiches. They are ordered specially for Aunt Augusta. [*Takes one and eats it*]

JACK: Well, you have been eating them all the time.

ALGERNON: That is quite a different matter. She is my aunt. [*Takes plate from below*] Have some bread and butter. The bread and butter is for Gwendolen. Gwendolen is devoted to bread and butter.

JACK [*advancing to table and helping himself*]: And very good bread and butter it is too.

ALGERNON: Well, my dear fellow, you need not eat as if you were going to eat it all. You behave as if you were married to her already. You are not married to her already, and I don't think you ever will be.

JACK: Why on earth do you say that?

ALGERNON: Well, in the first place girls never marry the men they flirt with. Girls don't think it right.

JACK: Oh, that is nonsense.

ALGERNON: It isn't. It is a great truth. It accounts for the extraordinary number of bachelors that one sees all over the place. In the second place, I don't give my consent.

JACK: Your consent!

ALGERNON: My dear fellow, Gwendolen is my first cousin. And before I allow you to marry her, you will have to clear up the whole question of Cecily. [*Rings bell*]

JACK: Cecily! What on earth do you mean? What do you mean, Algy, by Cecily! I don't know any one of the name of Cecily.
[*Enter* LANE]

ALGERNON: Bring me that cigarette case Mr Worthing left in the smoking-room the last time he dined here.

LANE: Yes, sir.

[LANE *goes out*]

JACK: Do you mean to say you have had my cigarette case all this time? I wish to goodness you had let me know. I have been writing frantic letters to Scotland Yard about it. I was very nearly offering a large reward.

ALGERNON: Well, I wish you would offer one. I happen to be more than usually hard up.

JACK: There is no good offering a large reward now that the thing is found.

[*Enter* LANE *with the cigarette case on a salver.* ALGERNON *takes it at once.* LANE *goes out*]

ALGERNON: I think that is rather mean of you, Ernest, I must say. [*Opens case and examines it*] However, it makes no matter, for, now that I look at the inscription inside, I find that the thing isn't yours after all.

JACK: Of course it's mine. [*Moving to him*] You have seen me with it a hundred times, and you have no right whatsoever to read what is written inside. It is a very ungentlemanly thing to read a private cigarette case.

ALGERNON: Oh! it is absurd to have a hard and fast rule about what one should read and what one shouldn't. More than half of modern culture depends on what one shouldn't read.

JACK: I am quite aware of the fact, and I don't propose to discuss modern culture. It isn't the sort of thing one should talk of in private. I simply want my cigarette case back.

ALGERNON: Yes; but this isn't your cigarette case. This cigarette case is a present from some one of the name of Cecily, and you said you didn't know any one of that name.

JACK: Well, if you want to know, Cecily happens to be my aunt.

ALGERNON: Your aunt!

JACK: Yes. Charming old lady she is, too. Lives at Tunbridge Wells. Just give it back to me, Algy.

ALGERNON [*retreating to back of sofa*]: But why does she call herself little Cecily if she is your aunt and lives at Tunbridge Wells? [*Reading*] 'From little Cecily with her fondest love.'

JACK [*moving to sofa and kneeling upon it*]: My dear fellow, what on earth is there in that? Some aunts are tall, some aunts are not tall. That is a matter that surely an aunt may be allowed to decide for herself. You seem to think that every aunt should be exactly like your aunt! That is absurd! For Heaven's sake give me back my cigarette case. [*Follows* ALGERNON *round the room*]

ALGERNON: Yes. But why does your aunt call you her uncle? 'From little Cecily, with her fondest love to her dear Uncle Jack.' There is no objection, I admit, to an aunt being a small aunt, but why an aunt, no matter what her size may be, should call her own nephew her uncle, I can't make out. Besides, your name isn't Jack at all; it is Ernest.

JACK: It isn't Ernest; it's Jack.

ALGERNON: You have always told me it was Ernest. I have introduced you to every one as Ernest. You answer to the name of Ernest. You look as if your name was Ernest. You are the most earnest-looking person I ever saw in my life. It is perfectly absurd your saying that your name isn't Ernest. It's on your cards. Here is one of them. [*Taking it from case*] 'Mr Ernest Worthing, B. 4, The Albany.' I'll keep this as a proof that your name is Ernest if ever you attempt to deny it to me, or to Gwendolen, or to any one else. [*Puts the card in his pocket*]

JACK: Well, my name is Ernest in town and Jack in the country, and the cigarette case was given to me in the country.

ALGERNON: Yes, but that does not account for the fact that your small Aunt Cecily, who lives at Tunbridge Wells, calls you her dear uncle. Come, old boy you had much better have the thing out at once.

JACK: My dear Algy, you talk exactly as if you were a dentist. It is very vulgar to talk like a dentist when one isn't a dentist. It produces a false impression.

(*From 'The Importance of Being Earnest' by Oscar Wilde*)

Or, in a very different mood, you might like to consider another concealing conversation, again between two central male characters. By the end of Act 2 of Samuel Beckett's *Waiting for Godot* Estragon and Vladimir know very well that Godot will never come, and that they will never go, yet they refuse to acknowledge the fact, even to themselves. In this case the actors must make apparent to the audience the rift between the men's words and their expectations if the conclusion of the play is to have its desired effect.

ESTRAGON: Didi.
VLADIMIR: Yes.
ESTRAGON: I can't go on like this.
VLADIMIR: That's what you think.
ESTRAGON: If we parted? That might be better for us.
VLADIMIR: We'll hang ourselves tomorrow. [*Pause*] Unless Godot comes.
ESTRAGON: And if he comes?
VLADIMIR: We'll be saved.
  [VLADIMIR *takes off his hat* (LUCKY'S), *peers inside it, feels about inside it, shakes it, knocks on the crown, puts it on again*]
ESTRAGON: Well? Shall we go?
VLADIMIR: Pull on your trousers.
ESTRAGON: What?
VLADIMIR: Pull on your trousers.
ESTRAGON: You want me to pull off my trousers?
VLADIMIR: Pull ON your trousers.
ESTRAGON [*Realising his trousers are down*]: True. [*He pulls up his trousers*]
VLADIMIR: Well? Shall we go?
ESTRAGON: Yes, let's go.
  [*They do not move*]

CURTAIN

(*Copyright 1955 and 1956 Samuel Beckett, published by Faber and Faber*)

It becomes clear then that before an actor begins to create a role he should have studied every aspect of his part, so far as it reveals itself in both text and sub-text, until he has totally absorbed the character, and understood how it fits into the total pattern of the play.

There is sometimes another rich source of information that should be considered most assiduously, and that is the playwright's introduction and stage directions. The characters in the play, even if they are based on real people, are, as they stand, imaginative creations of the writer, and he will often try to breathe extra life into them by telling actor and director what sort of people they are, how they dress, move, react, what they look like, and so on.

In his note on the historical accuracy of *The Crucible* Arthur Miller wrote, 'As for the characters of the persons, little is known about most of them excepting what may be surmised from a few letters, the trial record, certain broadsides written at the time, and references to their conduct in sources of varying reliability. They may therefore be taken as creations of my own, drawn to the best of my ability.' And that ability combined dialogue and stage direction to create pure drama, as in this short section from John Proctor's last meeting with his wife, Elizabeth.

*Alone.* PROCTOR *walks to her, halts. It is as though they stood in a spinning world. It is beyond sorrow, above it. He reaches out his hand as though towards an embodiment not quite real, and as he touches her, a strange soft sound, half laughter, half amazement, comes from his throat. He pats her hand. She covers his hand with hers. And then, weak, he sits. Then she sits, facing him.*

PROCTOR: The child?
ELIZABETH: It grows.
PROCTOR: There is no word of the boys?
ELIZABETH: They're well. Rebecca's Samuel keeps them.
PROCTOR: You have not seen them?
ELIZABETH: I have not. [*She catches a weakening in herself and downs it*]
PROCTOR: You are a – marvel, Elizabeth.
ELIZABETH: You – have been tortured?
PROCTOR: Aye.
    [*Pause. She will not let herself be drowned in the sea that threatens her*]
  They come for my life now.
ELIZABETH: I know it.

In my opinion the writer's directions should always be studied carefully if the aim of the director is to recreate his vision as truthfully as possible. If the stage directions are not the writer's, but simply a spin-off from an earlier production of the play, later incorporated into an acting edition, they need not be taken so seriously but are probably worth noting, even if they may be discarded eventually.

Unfortunately, it is not always easy to discover the source of script directions, but it is worth making an effort. The author's agent, whose name will be found at the beginning of a copyright play, or alternatively, his publisher may be able and willing to help. As a general rule, the older a play is, the less likely it is to have the writer's original staging included – how Shakespeare intended his characters to move and speak is rarely specified. On the other hand, many contemporary playwrights – Tom Stoppard, Trevor Griffiths and Tennessee Williams, for example – take great pains to direct the directors of their work, even while apologising about it. E. A. Whitehead cleverly gives a nutshell analysis of the two characters of his play, *Alpha Beta* in one short paragraph of his production note.

> 'It is also important to suggest the areas of ambiguity in the two characters: in the woman, between "Norma Elliot", the vulnerable and passionate human being, and "Mrs Elliot", the implacable wife, completely committed to the standards brain-washed into her; and in the man, between the "social catalyst" (as he sees himself) and the pub orator and permanent adolescent forever justifying his own sexual capriciousness (as she certainly sees him).'

Given such help by the playwright, actors should have at least a good starting point from which to master the following scene which concludes the play.

> We've been separated for three years. The law – the *law* – allows us to divorce by mutual consent after two years. [*Then nervously*] We could do that now. [*Silence*] But it also allows unilateral divorce after *five* years. So that I can divorce you, without your consent, in two years from now. [*Pause*] Which I *will*. [*Pause*] Why the hell not face up to it now, start again, get a job … [*Then pleading*] You know I'll look after you and the kids … [*Now forceful*] So why not be adult about the situation and …
>
> MRS ELLIOT [*snaps*]: What about her?
> MR ELLIOT: Who?
> MRS ELLIOT: YOUR SLUT!
>    [*Pause.* MR ELLIOT *looks grim but ignores her*]
>    How long is that going to last?
> MR ELLIOT: It's a permanent relationship.

MRS ELLIOT: Huh! The only permanent relationships you have are with the past!

MR ELLIOT: She's my last and only love.

MRS ELLIOT: Huh . .

MR ELLIOT: You think I'm beyond redemption?

MRS ELLIOT: Beyond repair.

[*Pause. Then with some exasperation*]

MR ELLIOT: Look ... what are *you* suggesting we do? Are you suggesting we play the social game? So I live here ... on a loose rein ... and I'm allowed out every Friday night for some wild revel in the woods, after which I return – exhausted and seed-freed – to the old barred cell? Balls! I'm through with all that. [*Pause.* MR ELLIOT *walks to the window. Very restless. His tone is urgent now, sincere*] Look ... there's no need for ... despair! O.K. you *may* wonder about the neighbours ... but it's a nine-day wonder with them and they're probably consumed with envy in any case. [*Pause*] They don't matter. [*Pause*] And the children ... I have a better relationship with them than I ever had. I used to curse their existence but now I ... I'm proud of them, I'm happy with them ... I love them, for Christ's sake!

MRS ELLIOT [*harsh*]: Because they're older ...

MR ELLIOT [*snaps*]: Not just because they're *older* ... because ...

[*Pause*]

MRS ELLIOT: What?

MR ELLIOT [*determined*]: I'm happier with them because I'm happier without them.

MRS ELLIOT: Hmmm.

[*Pause.* MR ELLIOT *turns to face her. She moves to the chair facing the window*]

MR ELLIOT: I wish it was simpler.... You're an attractive woman ... a good, selfless mother ... and a jealous, vindictive wife. I wish you were just a one-hundred-per-cent bitch. It'd be a hell of a lot easier!

MRS ELLIOT [*sarcastic*]: I'm sorry ...

MR ELLIOT [*very serious*]: Can I tell you something you won't believe?

[*Silence*]

I have no wish to hurt you.

[*She looks at him sourly*]

I don't want to damage you! I know your quality ... and I don't want to humiliate you, to cheat you, to exploit you ... to emotionally destroy you. That's why I left you!

[*Silence*]

MRS ELLIOT [*withering*]: Thanks.

MR ELLIOT [*dispirited*]: Ahhh.

MRS ELLIOT [*cynical*]: Still the old saviour? [*Laughs*] Listen, the truth is, you do exactly what you want to do and you don't give a bugger who you destroy in the process. So ... so carry on, do what you want to do, but just don't ask for my blessing.

MR ELLIOT: And what about you? Aren't you trying to force me to do what *you* want me to do?

MRS ELLIOT: Only the things you undertook – vowed – to do!

MR ELLIOT: Oh – not again!

MRS ELLIOT: So you did.

MR ELLIOT: So I did ... subject to satisfaction.

MRS ELLIOT: You can't have marriage on free approval.

MR ELLIOT [*heated*]: And when a marriage breaks down – there's no law that would tolerate this sort of emotional blackmail! [*Points to the glasses*] This ... there's no law, moral or otherwise, that entitles you to threaten that you will kill yourself and murder the children ... just so that you can 'have your way' with your errant husband.

MRS ELLIOT: My knight-errant husband.

MR ELLIOT [*raging*]: It's just blackmail!

MRS ELLIOT [*deadly pleasant*]: You know ... you've given me an idea. If you really want to help ...

   [*Pause.* MR ELLIOT *looks at her*]

It would be easier ... and tidier ... and we know how you care about tidiness ... if *you* took the deadly draught, wouldn't it? Not here, of course ... not in this room ... [*Light laugh*] You wouldn't want any corpses littering the lounge and frightening the children, would you? But somewhere ... I know! In your penthouse! What about that? In your penthouse! Suicide seems more appropriate to a penthouse anyway, doesn't it? [*Very brightly*] And I tell you what ... maybe *she* would take a sip too ... from the same glass! Yes ... maybe you could *share the same glass* of nembutal, with different straws, of course ... and sink simultaneously down together ... like you always wanted! Then the children and I ... would live happily ever after. How about that?

   [*Silence.* MR ELLIOT *gives several slow handclaps*]

The playwright who is most famous for his explicit acting directions is G. B. Shaw. The following scene from *You Never Can Tell* amply demonstrates the detail with which he orchestrated his characters' tones of voice, facial expressions and smallest movements to achieve theatrical perfection.

PHILIP: The fact is, Mr Valentine, we are the children of the celebrated Mrs Lanfrey Clandon, an authoress of great repute – in Madeira. No household is complete without her works. We came to England to get away from them. They are called the Twentieth Century Treatises.

DOLLY: Twentieth Century Cooking.

PHILIP: Twentieth Century Creeds.

DOLLY: Twentieth Century Clothing.

PHILIP: Twentieth Century Conduct.

DOLLY: Twentieth Century Children.

PHILIP: Twentieth Century Parents.

DOLLY: Cloth limp, half a dollar.

PHILIP: Or mounted on linen for hard family use, two dollars. No family should be without them. Read them, Mr Valentine: they'll improve your mind.

DOLLY: But not till we've gone, please.

PHILIP: Quite so: we prefer people with unimproved minds. Our own minds have successfully resisted all our mother's efforts to improve them.

VALENTINE [*dubiously*]: Hm!

DOLLY [*echoing him inquiringly*]: Hm? Phil: he prefers people whose minds are improved.

PHILIP: In that case we shall have to introduce him to the other member of the family: the Woman of the Twentieth Century: our sister Gloria!

DOLLY [*dithyrambically*]: Nature's masterpiece!

PHILIP: Learning's daughter!

DOLLY: Madeira's pride!

PHILIP: Beauty's paragon!

DOLLY [*suddenly descending to prose*]: Bosh! No complexion.

VALENTINE [*desperately*]: May I have a word?

PHILIP [*politely*]: Excuse us. Go ahead.

DOLLY [*very nicely*]: So sorry.

VALENTINE [*attempting to take them paternally*]: I really must give a hint to you young people . . .

DOLLY [*breaking out again*]: Oh come! I like that. How old are you?

PHILIP: Over thirty.

DOLLY: He's not.

PHILIP [*confidently*]: He is.

DOLLY [*emphatically*]: Twenty-seven.

PHILIP [*imperturbably*]: Thirty-three.

DOLLY: Stuff.

PHILIP [*to Valentine*]: I appeal to you, Mr Valentine.

VALENTINE [*remonstrating*]: Well, really – [*Resigning himself*] Thirty-one.

PHILIP [*to Dolly*]: You were wrong.

DOLLY: So were you.

PHILIP [*suddenly conscientious*]: We're forgetting out manners, Dolly.

DOLLY [*remorseful*]: Yes, so we are.

PHILIP [*apologetic*]: We interrupted you, Mr Valentine.

DOLLY: You were going to improve our minds, I think.

VALENTINE: The fact is, your . . .

PHILIP [*anticipating him*]: Our manners?

DOLLY: Our appearance?

VALENTINE [*ad misericordiam*]: Oh do let me speak.

DOLLY: The old story. We talk too much.

PHILIP: We do. Shut up, both. [*He seats himself on the arm of the operating chair*]

DOLLY: Mum! [*She sits down in the writing-table chair, and closes her lips with the tips of her fingers*]

VALENTINE: Thank you. [*He brings the stool from the bench in the corner; places it between them; and sits down with a judicial air. They attend to him with extreme gravity. He addresses himself first to Dolly*] Now may I ask, to begin with, have you ever been in an English seaside resort before?

[*She shakes her head slowly and solemnly. He turns to Phil, who shakes his head quickly and expressively*]

I thought so. Well, Mr Clandon, our acquaintance has been short; but it has been voluble; and I have gathered enough to convince me that you are neither of you capable of conceiving what life in an English seaside resort is. Believe me, it's not a question of manners and appearance. In those respects we enjoy a freedom unknown in Madeira.

[*Dolly shakes her head vehemently.*]

Oh yes, I assure you. Lord de Cresci's sister bicycles in knicker-bockers; and the rector's wife advocates dress reform and wears hygienic boots.

[*Dolly furtively looks at her own shoe: Valentine catches her in the act, and deftly adds*]

No, that's not the sort of boot I mean.

[*Doll's shoe vanishes*]

We don't bother much about dress and manners in England, because, as a nation, we don't dress well and we've no manners. But – and now will you excuse my frankness?

[*They nod*]

Thank you. Well, in a seaside resort there's one thing you must have before anybody can afford to be seen going about with you; and that's a father, alive or dead. Am I to infer that you have omitted that indispensable part of your social equipment?

[*They confirm him by melancholy nods*]

Then I'm sorry to say that if you are going to stay here for any length of time, it will be impossible for me to accept your kind invitation to lunch. [*He rises with an air of finality, and replaces the stool by the bench*]

PHILIP [*rising with grave politeness*]: Come, Dolly. [*He gives her his arm*]

DOLLY: Good morning.

   [*They go together to the door with perfect dignity*]

VALENTINE [*overwhelmed with remorse*]: Oh stop! stop!

   [*They halt and turn, arm in arm*]

You make me feel a perfect beast.

DOLLY: That's your conscience: not us.

VALENTINE [*energetically, throwing off all pretence of a professional manner*]: My conscience! My conscience has been my ruin. Listen to me. Twice before I have set up as a respectable medical practitioner in various parts of England. On both occasions I acted conscientiously, and told my patients the brute truth instead of what they wanted to be told. Result, ruin. Now I've set up as a dentist, a five shilling dentist; and I've done with conscience for ever. This is my last chance. I spent my last sovereign on moving in; and I haven't paid a shilling of rent yet. I'm eating and drinking on credit; my landlord is as rich as a Jew and as hard as nails; and I've made five shillings in six weeks. If I swerve by a hair's breadth from the straight line of the most rigid respectability, I'm done for. Under such circumstances is it fair to ask me to lunch with you when you don't know your own father?

DOLLY: After all, our grandfather is a canon of Lincoln Cathedral.

VALENTINE [*like a castaway mariner who sees a sail on the horizon*]: What! Have you a grandfather?

DOLLY: Only one.

VALENTINE: My dear good friends, why on earth didn't you tell me that before? A canon of Lincoln! That makes it all right, of course. Just excuse me while I change my coat. [*He reaches the door in a bound and vanishes*]

(*From 'You Never Can Tell' copyright details from The Society of Authors*)

At this stage, armed with text, sub-text, and author's production directions if available, the actor should be able to understand and re-create his character's thoughts, feelings and ideas, whether they are stated or merely implied. He should also have come to some conclusions about the character's past and future. No real person exists only in the present – he is a combination of what has already happened and what he hopes or fears will happen, as well as what is currently happening. The following exercise, linked with the play being rehearsed, will test whether the actor has managed to make this imaginative leap.

## Exercise 1 – Character realisation

The director should ask each actor to think himself into the part he is about to play, and then to answer questions put to him by the rest of the cast as if he were the dramatic character. The questions should be carefully considered, ranging through and beyond the play's limits of time and place, but always remaining totally relevant to characterisation. Some of the answers will be in the text, others will depend upon the actor's hypothetical analysis of his character. This sounds difficult, but we all analyse character often and automatically, without even realising what we are doing. Every time we arrange a party or outing for our friends, choose a gift for a relative, plan a holiday involving other people, or even simply chat, we are, in fact, making assumptions, based upon information, observation and speculation, about those we are connected with.

Here, as an example to base your work on, is a list of questions that could be put to the lead actress in the comedy, *Move Over Mrs Markham*, by Ray Cooney and John Chapman.

> MRS MARKHAM: What sort of family background do you come from? What sort of school did you go to? Were you clever? Were you a prefect? Did you have any boyfriends before you met Philip? How old were you when you got married? Where did you go for your honeymoon? Do you consider yourself happily married? Do you consider your husband a successful man? Are you interested in his publishing business? What is your idea of luxury? Why did you choose Alistair as your Interior Designer? Have you any children? If not, do you plan to have any?

If the actor is a little diffident of being cross-questioned in this way – though from my experience I'm sure that most will join in with great gusto – it is quite easy to direct the questions to a pair, rather than an individual. In this instance Mr Markham could be involved too, answering queries about his professional, personal and social life.

Having captured the essence of his character in his head, the actor's next step is to communicate it to the audience. To do this he must create an illusion of reality by means of the manipulation of his voice and the movements of his body. In other words, his mastery of the role must be physical as well as imaginative.

# The voice

The first demand an audience makes of an actor is that it should be able to hear him. This does not mean, of course, that an actor should 'elocute' in a totally artificial voice, merely that he should learn to project his voice so that it can be heard from every seat, even when he is apparently speaking in a whisper. Basically, it's a matter of finding the correct pitch, and this only comes with experience which eventually becomes almost instinctive. You will notice that if you are trying to talk to friends at a noisy party you automatically adjust your voice so that it can be heard above the babble by your immediate group without overwhelming the entire room. The same technique is required on stage. However, since the acoustics of every hall or theatre are different, the required degree of voice projection can only be determined in the first place by stationing members of the company in and around the hall at the beginning of the rehearsal period and having them report on audibility.

The second necessity an actor should always have in his mind is the avoidance of tonal monotony. The voice is an instrument capable of great variety. It has a large range of notes, and all have their part to play in producing a performance which is always interesting, never boring. The monotone is to be avoided at all costs, except on those rare occasions when it is dictated by character.

The third thing that an amateur actor should bear in mind is that he should never allow himself to be rushed through his part by nervousness, or the fear that if he doesn't grab at his words quickly he might forget them. He must try to develop the confidence to relax, sit back on his lines, make a pause where the script will benefit from it – either to emphasise a word or phrase, or to denote thought or reflection – and to slow down the dialogue occasionally for dramatic effect. Often the biggest difference between the amateur and the professional actor is simply that the latter dares to take his time.

Once an actor has achieved the correct pitch to make himself heard, a satisfactory tonal range, and sufficient confidence to pace his lines effectively, he can get down to the important task of acquiring the right voice to make his character live. To gain complete mastery over the quality of the sounds he produces he must first of all be relaxed. A certain nervousness can improve an actor's performance, adding tension and energy, but too much can play havoc with his voice.

Here are two exercises for relaxation and breathing which the actor will find a useful pre-rehearsal and pre-performance routine.

## Exercise 2 – Relaxation

Lie on your back in a comfortable position. Concentrate on the joints of your toes. First tense them as tightly as possible, and then relax them as completely as possible. Next do the same with your ankle joints, your knee joints, and so on up the whole length of your body, finishing with the neck and shoulders. By the time you have completed this exercise you should have achieved total relaxation.

## Exercise 3 – Breath control

Breathe in deeply and, remaining totally relaxed, hold your breath as long as possible without becoming uncomfortable. Breathe out deeply, and hold your breath for as long as you can. Repeat these two actions, one after the other, for about five minutes.

If you practise this exercise daily the chances are that you will find that you can hold your breath for an increasing length of time, and can organise your breathing to see you through the most taxing demands of your part. Some of Shakespeare's long speeches, for example, need very disciplined breath control. Try to borrow some gramophone records or tapes of Shakespearean readings from your nearest record library. Listen carefully to the way the actor uses his voice and breath to deliver the longer speeches, and see if you can match his expertise. Try coping with this famous passage from *Othello* before you have begun regular breathing exercises, and try it again after a few weeks of practice. You should find that you have gained much greater control over both phrasing and pitch.

> OTHELLO: Her father loved me; oft invited me;
> Still questioned me the story of my life
> From year to year, the battle, sieges, fortune
> That I have passed.
> I ran it through, even from my boyish days
> To th' very moment that he bade me tell it.
> Wherein I spoke of most disastrous chances,
> Of moving accidents by flood and field,
> Of hairbreadth scapes i' th'imminent deadly breach,
> Of being taken by the insolent foe
> And sold to slavery, of my redemption thence
> And portance in my travel's history,
> Wherein of anters vast and deserts idle,
> Rough quarries, rocks, and hills whose heads touch heaven,
> It was my hint to speak. Such was my process.

And of the Cannibals that each other eat,
The Anthropophagi, and men whose heads
Grew beneath their shoulders. These things to hear
Would Desdemona seriously incline;
But still the house affairs would draw her thence;
Which ever as she could with haste dispatch,
She'd come again, and with a greedy ear
Devour up my discourse. Which I observing,
Took once a pliant hour, and found good means
To draw from her a prayer of earnest heart
That I would all my pilgrimage dilate,
Whereof by parcels she had something heard,
But not intentively. I did consent,
And often did beguile her of her tears
When I did speak of some distressful stroke
That my youth suffered. My story being done,
She gave me for my pains a world of kisses.
She swore in faith 'twas strange, 'twas passing strange;
'Twas pitiful, 'twas wondrous pitiful.
She wished she had not heard it; yet she wished
That heaven had made her such a man. She thanked me,
And bade me, if I had a friend that loved her,
I should but teach him how to tell my story,
And that would woo her. Upon this hint I spake.
She loved me for the dangers I had passed,
And I loved her that she did pity them.
This only is the witchcraft I have used.

This same speech is a useful one through which to study pace, timing and variety of tone, to build in light and shade, and to experiment with change of emphasis and inflection. As the variables are altered you will notice that the nature of the words becomes subtly different and throws a different light on Othello's character. Consequently, the way an actor interprets Othello will decide the way in which he paces the lines, the inflection he adopts, and the words he stresses. At the same time, of course, he must always remember that the speech is in blank verse, with five stresses to a line, and the underlying rhythms should not be destroyed.

A case can be made out for each of two conflicting views of Othello's mood when he delivers this speech. First of all, he could be consumed with fury and resentment that he, a distinguished soldier, should be charged with pagan witchcraft by a man who had formerly been a friendly and generous host. The claim that his black skin would, in the normal course of events, have made him hideous in the eyes of the woman he loved and had just married, could rouse him to an intense hatred of Brabantio, the father-in-law who was seeking to ruin his reputation and his marriage by these cruel and unfounded charges.

Interpreted in this way the speech should be coloured by a passion which would affect pace, pitch, emphasis and inflection. It should probably be delivered quite fast, in a voice heightened by emotion. The first lines:

> Her father loved me; oft invited me;
> Still questioned me the story of my life ...

should be emphatic, especially the three verbs, and spoken with a falling inflection which tends to sound dogmatic and preclude disagreement, as opposed to a rising inflection which sounds tentative or querying.

Othello should constantly stress the fact that his story-telling had been dictated by Brabantio, not by his own inclination, and that merely as an act of courtesy to his host he almost casually 'ran it through' because '*he bade* me tell it'. Similarly, when describing Desdemona's response to his tales, he should emphasise that *she* was the one who was the persuader, he was merely the one who 'did consent'. In conclusion, the penultimate line should be raised to a defiant shout of self-defence, again on a descending inflection. 'This *only* is the witchcraft I have used.'

This is merely the bare bones of one possible approach to the speech. Another actor might approach it quite differently. He could draw from the text sufficient evidence to suggest that Othello would *not* necessarily react to Brabantio's charges with fury. Othello is a mature man. His services to the state of Venice are known and valued, his family is distinguished, his wife loves him deeply. Consequently, he is secure and self-assured, and not easily roused to wrath. His lines could therefore be interpreted as the rather amused, but incredulous, response of a sophisticated mind to a totally unfounded and stupidly prejudiced accusation. They should therefore be delivered in a voice pitched lower, at a more leisured, thoughtful pace, with more pauses, different emphases, and less tendency towards positive inflection. For instance, he could pause before the first 'loved' as if he were searching for the right word to describe the earlier state of their relationship and concluding, after thought, that it was one of real affection. When describing the growth of love between himself and Desdemona he would balance her emotions with his own.

> *She* loved *me* for the dangers I had passed,
> And *I* loved *her* that she did pity them.

Having proved that his wife's love is based on something very different from black magic, he can then go on to mock Brabantio's suspicions by emphasising the word 'witchcraft' with devastating irony. 'This only is the – *witchcraft* I have used.'

It will have become obvious through this brief study of one of Othello's speeches that the meaning or tone of a sentence can be quite changed by the positioning of emphases.

## Exercise 4 – Emphasis

Here is an apparently straightforward sentence. 'She thought her garden was the prettiest in the village.' Try placing an emphasis on each word in turn to find out how many different shades of meaning you can elicit from it. For instance, '*She* thought her garden . . .', 'She *thought* her garden . . .', etc. It seems to me that only the second 'the' refuses to be emphasised, and that there are, in fact, nine possible interpretations of this group of ten words.

To study more carefully the effect of pace and pause on mood and meaning there is a lot we can learn from Harold Pinter, who is a master at communicating with his audience not so much by what is said but more by how it is said. *The Birthday Party*, for example, is pervaded by threat, violence, cold menace, pathos, mystery and humour which together, in Pinter's hands, add up to brilliant theatre. Yet the basic plot of the two strangers who visit a seedy boarding-house, interrogate a lonely, unsuccessful pier-pianist, organise a birthday party for him, and eventually take him away a gibbering wreck of a man is so full of unanswered questions and evasions that no one knows exactly what has happened or why. Despite this, it works superbly, calling up a response from both actors and audience that is imaginative rather than cerebral. (It's interesting to note that Beckett works in much the same way and does not welcome any attempt at intellectual analysis.)

Here are the two strangers, Goldberg and McCann, addressing themselves to Stanley, the pianist, just before they drive him off to some unspecified fate. The section begins slowly, almost gently, with the pauses giving a superficial feeling of calm before the urgent pace and staccato rhythms of the following lines, and the horrific images called up in them, catapult the victim into final disaster.

[MCCANN *goes to the door, left, and goes out. He ushers in* STANLEY, *who is dressed in a dark well-cut suit and white collar. He holds his broken glasses in his hand. He is clean-shaven.*

MCCANN *follows and closes the door.* GOLDBERG *meets* STANLEY, *seats him in a chair*]

GOLDBERG: How are you, Stan? [*Pause*] Are you feeling any better? [*Pause*] What's the matter with your glasses? [GOLDBERG *bends to look*] They're broken. A pity.

[STANLEY *stares blankly at the floor*]

MCCANN [*at the table*]: He looks better, doesn't he?

GOLDBERG: Much better.

MCCANN: A new man.

GOLDBERG: You know what we'll do?

MCCANN: What?

GOLDBERG: We'll buy him another pair.

[*They begin to woo him, gently and with relish. During the following sequence* STANLEY *shows no reaction. He remains, with no movement, where he sits*]

MCCANN: Out of our own pockets.

GOLDBERG: It goes without saying. Between you and me, Stan, it's about time you had a new pair of glasses.

MCCANN: You can't see straight.

GOLDBERG: It's true. You've been cockeyed for years.

MCCANN: Now you're even more cockeyed.

GOLDBERG: He's right. You've gone from bad to worse.

MCCANN: Worse than worse.

GOLDBERG: You need a long convalescence.

MCCANN: A change of air.

GOLDBERG: Somewhere over the rainbow.

MCCANN: Where angels fear to tread.

GOLDBERG: Exactly.

MCCANN: You're in a rut.

GOLDBERG: You look anaemic.

MCCANN: Rheumatic.

GOLDBERG: Myopic.

MCCANN: Epileptic.

GOLDBERG: You're on the verge.

MCCANN: You're a dead duck.

GOLDBERG: But we can save you.

MCCANN: From a worse fate.

GOLDBERG: True.

MCCANN: Undeniable.

GOLDBERG: From now on, we'll be the hub of your wheel.

MCCANN: We'll renew your season ticket.

GOLDBERG: We'll take tuppence off your morning tea.

MCCANN: We'll give you a discount on all inflammable goods.

GOLDBERG: We'll watch over you.

MCCANN: Advise you.

GOLDBERG: Give you proper care and treatment.

MCCANN: Let you use the club bar.

GOLDBERG: Keep a table reserved.

MCCANN: Help you acknowledge the fast days.

GOLDBERG: Bake you cakes.

MCCANN: Help you kneel on kneeling days.

GOLDBERG: Give you a free pass.

MCCANN: Take you for constitutionals.

GOLDBERG: Give you hot tips.

MCCANN: We'll provide the skipping rope.

GOLDBERG: The vest and pants.

MCCANN: The ointment.

GOLDBERG: The hot poultice.

MCCANN: The fingerstall.

GOLDBERG: The abdomen belt.

MCCANN: The ear plugs.

GOLDBERG: The baby powder.

MCCANN: The back scratcher.

GOLDBERG: The spare tyre.

MCCANN: The stomach pump.

GOLDBERG: The oxygen tent.

MCCANN: The prayer wheel.

GOLDBERG: The plaster of Paris.

MCCANN: The crash helmet.

GOLDBERG: The crutches.

MCCANN: A day and night service.

GOLDBERG: All on the house.

MCCANN: That's it.

GOLDBERG: We'll make a man of you.

MCCANN: And a woman.

GOLDBERG: You'll be re-orientated.

MCCANN: You'll be rich.

GOLDBERG: You'll be adjusted.

MCCANN: You'll be our pride and joy.

GOLDBERG: You'll be a mensch.

MCCANN: You'll be a success.

GOLDBERG: You'll be integrated.

MCCANN: You'll give orders.

GOLDBERG: You'll make decisions.

MCCANN: You'll be a magnate.

GOLDBERG: A statesman.

MCCANN: You'll own yachts.

GOLDBERG: Animals.

MCCANN: Animals.

[GOLDBERG *looks at* MCCANN]

GOLDBERG: I said animals. [*He turns back to* STANLEY] You'll be able to make or break, Stan. By my life.

[*Silence.* STANLEY *is still*]

Well? What do you say?

[STANLEY'S *head lifts very slowly and turns in* GOLDBERG'S *direction*]

What do you think? Eh, boy?

[STANLEY *begins to clench and unclench his eyes*]

MCCANN: What's your opinion, sir? Of this prospect, sir?

GOLDBERG: Prospect. Sure. Sure it's a prospect.

[STANLEY'S *hands clutching his glasses begin to tremble*]

What's your opinion of such a prospect? Eh, Stanley?

[STANLEY *concentrates, his mouth opens, he attempts to speak, fails and emits sounds from his throat*]

STANLEY: Uh-gug ... uh-gug ... eeehhh-gag ... [*On the breath*] Caahh ... caahh....

[*They watch him. He draws a long breath which shudders down his body. He concentrates*]

GOLDBERG: Well, Stanny boy, what do you say, eh?

[*They watch. He concentrates. His head lowers, his chin draws into his chest, he crouches*]

STANLEY: Uh-gughh ... uh-gughhh....

MCCANN: What's your opinion, sir?

STANLEY: Caahhh ... caaahh....

MCCANN: Mr Webber! What's your opinion?

GOLDBERG: What do you say, Stan? What do you think of the prospect?

MCCANN: What's your opinion of the prospect?

[STANLEY'S *body shudders, relaxes, his head drops, he becomes still again, stooped*]

(*Copyright, Harold Pinter 1959, published Methuen*)

After the crisis the pace slows again by means of changed rhythms and pauses until it becomes melancholy, languid – almost dream-like.

For your next exercise try to put the most effective pauses into these lines from which the author's instructions have been omitted. If you wish to mark a pause within or at the end of a sentence, use three dots. If you wish to place a pause between lines of dialogue, simply write the word 'pause'.

## Exercise 5 – Pauses

MEG [*coming downstage*]: The car's gone.

PETEY: Yes.

MEG: Have they gone?
PETEY: Yes.
MEG: Won't they be in for lunch?
PETEY: No.
MEG: Oh, what a shame. [*She puts her bag on the table*] It's hot out.
  [*She hangs her coat on a hook*] What are you doing?
PETEY: Reading.
MEG: Is it good?
PETEY: All right.
  [*She sits by the table*]
MEG: Where's Stan? Is Stan down yet, Petey?
PETEY: No, he's
MEG: Is he still in bed?
PETEY: Yes, he's still asleep.
MEG: Still? He'll be late for his breakfast.
PETEY: Let him sleep.
MEG: Wasn't it a lovely party last night?
PETEY: I wasn't there.
MEG: Weren't you?
PETEY: I came in afterwards.
MEG: Oh. It was a lovely party. I haven't laughed so much for years.
  We had dancing and singing. And games. You should have been
  there.
PETEY: It was good, eh?
MEG: I was the belle of the ball.
PETEY: Were you?
MEG: Oh yes. They all said I was.
PETEY: I bet you were, too.
MEG: Oh, it's true. I was. I know I was.

Now compare your version of the passage with the printed one.

MEG [*coming downstage*]: The car's gone.
PETEY: Yes.
MEG: Have they gone?
PETEY: Yes.
MEG: Won't they be in for lunch?
PETEY: No.
MEG: Oh, what a shame. [*She puts her bag on the table*] It's hot out.
  [*She hangs her coat on a hook*] What are you doing?
PETEY: Reading.
MEG: Is it good?
PETEY: All right.
  [*She sits by the table*]
MEG: Where's Stan?
  [*Pause*]

Is Stan down yet, Petey?

PETEY: No ... he's. ...

MEG: Is he still in bed?

PETEY: Yes, he's ... still asleep.

MEG: Still? He'll be late for his breakfast.

PETEY: Let him ... sleep.

[*Pause*]

MEG: Wasn't it a lovely party last night?

PETEY: I wasn't there.

MEG: Weren't you?

PETEY: I came in afterwards.

MEG: Oh.

[*Pause*]

It was a lovely party. I haven't laughed so much for years. We had dancing and singing. And games. You should have been there.

PETEY: It was good, eh?

[*Pause*]

MEG: I was the belle of the ball.

PETEY: Were you?

MEG: Oh yes. They all said I was.

PETEY: I bet you were, too.

MEG: Oh, it's true. I was.

[*Pause*]

I know I was.

## CURTAIN

The conscientious actor will rapidly discover that once he thoroughly understands the character he is to play he will find the voice to match. For instance, he will automatically note whether this is an educated man with a cultivated voice, or a labourer with less refined vowels; whether he is excitable and eager and therefore likely to speak quickly, or heavy, pompous or pedantic, and consequently slower of speech. Basically I believe that all acting is re-creation through imitation, and certainly all actors should spend as much time as possible listening to and attempting to imitate the voices and speech patterns they hear about them every day. They should become avid eavesdroppers – on the bus or tube, in the supermarket, library and at public meetings, in the park, the launderette, the doctor's surgery – making a habit of listening not only to what people say but, much more important, how they say it. Radio and television are also invaluable sources of material, especially in their coverage of news and current affairs. If a tape-recorder is available it's a good idea to try to recapture the timbre and personal quality of an interesting voice that has been heard and to continue polishing and perfecting it until there is a marked improvement between the first recording and the last.

During a recent John Creascy play at Salisbury Playhouse the actor who played the part of Chief Inspector Isherwood stole the show with a perfect cameo performance. The way he stood and walked, the enquiring tilt of his head, the slightly guarded expression on his face, but, in particular, his tone of voice when he addressed his suspects, managing to combine a superficial impression of polite deference with devastating contempt, added up to a splendidly convincing characterisation. During an audience talk-out after the play he was asked how he had managed to recreate such a magnificently real police officer. 'No problem,' said the actor. 'He stopped me on the M1 one night and tore me off a strip for driving too fast. I looked at him, and I listened to him, and I thought – you'll come in useful one day. And he did.' Amateurs should always be ready to take a tip from the professionals. If they look, listen, and imitate, they'll create credible characters.

Two more specific problems which occasionally face the actor trying to find the right voice for his part are:
1 Capturing the sound of old age, and
2 Mastering dialect.

Various physical changes take place due to the ageing process, and several of these alter the voice. For instance, the timbre becomes thinner, the pitch is heightened, and the breath control becomes more erratic. As a result, the general sound is weaker with less body, and the rhythms of speech are less predictable. Again, the best method of capturing it accurately is to listen and imitate, and then to think and feel oneself into the skin of an old character.

## Exercise 6 – Ageing

The next two excerpts, from a Victorian melodrama called *Rose Ransome*, make a useful basis for practice. In the first, Ruby is a saucy young barmaid relishing the fact that she has been called to give evidence on behalf of her friend, George, who has been wrongfully accused of murder. In the second, she has disguised herself as an old gypsy in an effort to find a vital clue, and to protect and help the other innocent characters, especially George's wife, Rose.

1    CEDRIC: Now, Miss Hardy, perhaps you'll give us *your* account of the evening of the 13th. Take your time, and don't be in awe of any gentleman in this court. [*Looks at Black Jack*]

RUBY: In awe of him! That'd be the day. Blimey, I could tell you more stories about bad Black Jack and his little capers than you've had ...

CEDRIC: Quite. But at present we are more interested in the capers – or otherwise – of the gentleman in the dock. You do *know* the gentleman in the dock?

RUBY: Georgy Ransome? I should say so. A *real* gentleman, Georgy, wouldn't hurt a fly. Never took advantage of a girl's position, he didn't. Not so much as a pat upon the what-not. Not like some I could mention. [*Looks at Black Jack*] No. Georgy, he was different. Mind you, he did like a drop more than was good for him. Didn't seem as if he could help it, somehow. Seemed like a man with a curse upon him almost. But when he was sober – ah! a real gent.

CEDRIC: And on that particular night, was he drunk or sober?

RUBY: Drunk. No – sober. Well, both – if you see what I mean.

CEDRIC: Perhaps you'd explain.

RUBY: He came into the bar early on – the Star and Garter, you know, that's where I work – and he says, 'Ruby,' he says, 'I've got the black dog tonight, right enough. Give us a drink to drown it.'

RUBY: So he had one, – and then another ... you know how it is ... and after a while he seemed bright enough, chatting and laughing with his mates. Then, all of a sudden, he says, 'My little wife,' he says, 'must go home to my poor little wife.' And off he went.

CEDRIC: And what time was that?

RUBY: Near on ten o'clock, I should say.

CEDRIC: But you saw him again that same evening?

RUBY: Lor bless you, yes. He'd not been gone above half an hour but he was back again, sober as a judge (saving Your Grace) and miserable as hell. 'Ruby,' he says, 'Ruby, I am not fit to live. I am engulfed in guilt,' he says, 'and lost to heaven.' Those was his very words – like poetry they was.

CEDRIC: And what did you do, Ruby, in the face of this poetic outburst?

RUBY: Well, I offered him a drink, sir. 'Get this down you, Georgy,' I said, 'and you'll feel better.'

CEDRIC: And then?

RUBY: You'll never believe this, but he dashed the mug to the floor, spilled all that good ale. What a mess! 'Why do you want to go and do a thing like that, Georgy?' I said. And then he started again. 'Sweet temperance will I choose as my bright star,' he says. Well, you could have knocked me down with a beer mat! A real way with words he has, ha'nt you, Georgy love?

[*Ruby waves to George and blows a kiss. Rose weeps*]

CEDRIC: And at what time was this confrontation taking place?

RUBY: Oh, I know that well enough. 10.30 on the dot. 'Cos I says, 'Well, I'm not offering you another, that's for sure, 'cos we're closing now. You can just stay behind and help me clear up this mess.'

CEDRIC: And did he?

RUBY [*giggles suggestively*]: Not half. He didn't leave much before midnight, he didn't.

CEDRIC: One and a half hours – cleaning up?

RUBY: Oh no, sir. Not all that time. But you know how it is – he needed a little company, a little comfort. I thought it only neighbourly to see he got a bit of it!

[*Rose weeps, George groans*]

CEDRIC: I see! So, the defendant was with you from 10.30 p.m. till close on 12 p.m. You swear to that?

RUBY: Oh, I do sir. Yes. Definitely.

CEDRIC: So it is quite impossible that he was strangling the unknown girl at 11 p.m. when, as Sir Cecil has said, the church clock was striking. Thank you, Miss Hardy. There the defence rests.

2   [*Cecil staggers off stage downstage right. Rose kisses her baby passionately and puts her back in the pram. Enter Ruby, downstage left, heavily disguised as a gipsy*]

RUBY: Cross the gipsy's palm with silver, ma'am, and learn Dame Fortune's secrets. You have a lucky face.

ROSE: Do not mock me, I beg you. Once indeed I counted myself fortunate. Our little cottage was one smile of gladness. The sacred halo of a mother's blessing, the gentle benison of children's laughter – these were my daily companions. But now, now all is sorrow.

RUBY: Life has dealt harshly with you?

ROSE: Alas, alas, it has.

RUBY: And yet – you have a lucky face. Let me see your hand. Ah, it is as I thought. Your sufferings approach their end.

ROSE: But how? What must I do?

RUBY [*very confidential and mysterious*]: Listen to me carefully. Follow this road to the outskirts of the city. When you come to a lodging house called 'The End of the Rainbow', open and enter. At the third door, knock three times. Then, all that will stand between you and your happiness will be paper white as your pure mind, and ink as black as Black Jack's crime.

[*She begins to glide away, but Rose runs after her, offering her money*]

ROSE: Stay, oh stay. Who are you? What do you know of me? Destitute as I am, yet I would give you something for your pains.

RUBY: I don't want money, my dear.

See how much variety you can build into the two pieces, using your voice only. Make the barmaid Ruby as young and vigorous as possible, and the gypsy Ruby as old and frail as possible, while still retaining sufficient basic vocal characteristics to hint to the audience that they are, in fact, one and the same person. Remember that melodrama relies heavily on dramatic irony, letting the audience into secrets of identity which are hidden from the characters themselves.

Dialect is very difficult for any company to deal with so I would strongly advise amateurs to think very carefully before choosing a play in which it is absolutely essential. The problem is not as acute, of course, if the dialect is spoken locally because, even if it is not the natural speech of some of the members of the cast, at least there will be enough of the genuine article at hand for them to listen to, study and imitate until they have mastered its own particular music. And there are some dialect plays which, though set in one particular part of the country, can be translated to another without doing any damage to meaning or quality. However, if the dialect is not only alien to the cast but also absolutely essential to the play – and I really can't see how it is possible to produce O'Casey's *Plough and the Stars*, for instance, in anything other than a Dublin accent – there are only two ways to make a daunting task slightly less difficult.

The first is to find records and tape-recordings of the dialect required, to listen and listen and listen again, and then to practise and practise and practise again, until it has become almost second nature. This is not easy, but it does work if there is a will to make it work.

The second is to establish the dialect strongly at the beginning of the first act, and then to regulate it gradually until it becomes less dominant. Line by line the actors will be able to diminish a way of speech which is not natural to them so that they can grow into their parts more instinctively and convincingly, but the audience, having accepted that the action is set in Ireland, America, Italy or wherever, will barely notice the change in emphasis, provided that the accent does not vanish completely. This technique is often used very successfully in the professional theatre, and is a perfectly acceptable practice.

## The Body

When I review amateur dramatic productions I am often astonished to find that actors who can speak their lines with enormous sensitivity and understanding nevertheless move about the stage in a manner that is not only clumsy and unnatural but often totally inappropriate to the parts they are playing. Frequently they find their hands a great problem, if they are required to stand still for a long time they either fidget and shuffle or look as if they are in danger of over-balancing, and if they sit down they remain tethered in an artificial position, afraid either to move or to sit comfortably in case it doesn't look right.

Very often these stilted movements are caused by nervousness, and an inability to relax on stage which inhibits their behaviour. The first step to take to conquer this inhibition is to make a habit of doing the relaxation exercise, number 2 (p. 42), before each rehearsal and performance, and following up with a set of basic limbering movements. It's a good idea if these exercises are done as a group activity if possible.

### Exercise 7 – Limbering routine

1 Walk a few steps, then pause with the weight on the foot in front. Raise the arms gradually, stretching the hands and fingers upwards and forwards while bending the head backwards till the whole body is stretched. After holding the position for a moment relax gradually, lower the arms, bend the head and body forward, drop first into a kneeling, and then a crouching position, with the forehead touching the floor. Repeat five times for increased suppleness.

2 Stand on the right leg with hands on hips, bend the left leg at the knee and rotate five times. Stand on the left leg, rotate the right knee five times. Repeat the two movements, one after the other, five times. This exercise is designed to aid balance and weight distribution.

3 Stand upright, then bend the body from the waist till it is parallel with the floor. Stretch the arms forward and hold the head upright so that you can feel the neck and shoulder muscles working. Keeping the arms at shoulder level, bring them round in a circular movement to the side of the body, then back to their forward, outstretched position, the head remaining upright all the while. Repeat this stretching exercise five times to help reduce tension.

This routine, done regularly, should ensure that physically the actor is able to move about the stage competently. But the validity of his movements will, once again, depend upon his understanding of the character he is playing. This must be his pivot.

Just as skilled speech can be developed by concentrated, intelligent listening, so skilled movement can be developed by looking. The actor should constantly be watching the people around him to see how they use their bodies, their hands, their faces, and particularly their eyes, to communicate and to express themselves. The following exercise will help him to watch with greater awareness, and to imitate and re-create more precisely.

### Exercise 8 – Body language

Watch someone who is talking in an animated, engrossed manner but make sure that he does not know that he is being observed. Try to interpret his movements and facial expressions, then write down what you imagine to be the tenor of his conversation. Next ask a friend to watch you while you re-create the conversation without words, and to hazard a guess at what you have said. If he gets close to your intention you are watching and imitating well. If he totally misunderstands both the mood and content of your silent speech, you are probably not observing with sufficient care and need to work more diligently.

The movements which accompany conversation are *movements for a specific purpose*, in this case, communication. But people make two other types of movement: *instinctive movements*, as for instance in self defence; and *unconscious movements*, for example the nervous mannerisms which give a clue to their state of mind. These also should be observed and understood so that they can eventually be built into a characterisation. Watch a man blink rapidly, flinch, step backwards suddenly during a conversation, duck his head, or cover his face with his arm, and he is almost certainly demonstrating instinctive movements of self-defence. Watch a woman tapping a pencil on a desk, repeatedly smoothing her skirt, biting her nails, twisting a ring, and she is probably giving a physical indication of emotions of worry or apprehension.

It has been stressed that once a character in a play is totally understood an actor should be able, almost instinctively, to develop appropriate movements. Many professionals say that once they have got the feet and the walk absolutely right the rest follows easily.

Imagine the different walks of:

(*a*) a weary man who is feeling very depressed

(*b*) a happy, slender young girl, hurrying to meet her boyfriend, and

(*c*) an immensely fat, pompous official, consumed with a sense of his own importance,

and it immediately becomes apparent that walking can say a lot about character.

The important thing is that there should be a reason for each movement, and that it should arise from the actor's inner conviction about the part he is playing. To take two very straightforward examples, a nervous, timid character would probably move rather apologetically, with short steps and tiny, jerky gestures, finding it almost impossible to meet anyone's gaze directly. A secure, confident character would stand erect, move easily, and show no inhibitions about touching and looking at other people on the stage.

Old age affects movement as much as it affects speech, and this should always be taken into consideration when playing an elderly character. The actor must imagine, until he actually feels, a stiffening of the joints, a lack of suppleness, a general slowing down and weakening of all the functions of the body. He will not be able to sit down or stand up in one easy movement but will have to lever himself, using the chair, a companion or a walking stick for extra support. His eyes will probably move before his head turns, instead of at the same time. And there will be a stillness about him which will be much more effective than all the twitches and shakes that many young actors believe to be a necessary adjunct to old age.

The following exercise deals with three basic stage movements. Bear in mind while you are doing it that, even if the script is not specific, the actor should always know, as he enters or leaves the stage:

1 Where he has come from
2 Where he is going, and
3 Why,

otherwise his exits and entrances will lack conviction.

### Exercise 9 – Character in movement
Enter the stage, walk across it, and sit down as if you were:
(a) an old man/woman, walking in the park, who has just seen a convenient bench where he/she can rest in the sunshine;
(b) a distinguished and popular politician, walking on to the platform where he/she is to address an enthusiastic rally of keen party workers;
(c) a frightened and inexperienced drugs-smuggler, attempting to rendez-vous with a contact in a crowded café so that he/she can hand over a valuable package.

Good acting is based on authentic reaction. An actor should always be reacting to the circumstances in which he finds himself. He must react both to the character's *internal state* – his thoughts and emotions, and also to his *external state* – his relationship with other characters or objects on the stage. He must always be totally involved in whatever is happening in the script, whether it involves him in an active or passive role. Often the most difficult job of all is to support other actors merely by relating to them while keeping both quiet and still. The most brilliant example of this that I have ever seen was Janet Suzman's performance as Celia in a production of *As You Like It*. During Act 3, scene 2, when Orlando and Rosalind come face to face for the first time, no words or actions are required of Celia. All she has to do, according to Rosalind, is 'Slink by, and note him'. Most actresses playing Celia simply merge with the scenery at this point and leave the limelight to the lovers. Not so Miss Suzman. While remaining practically motionless, she reacted to her cousin's dashing performance as 'saucy lackey' with amazement, delight, incredulity and wry mirth, pointing the irony of the situation most eloquently while using only facial expressions and one solitary movement of her hand. As a result, this clever and crucial scene took on an extra dimension.

Though as a general rule movement on the stage should be as natural and unstructured as possible, there are three instances where this rule does not apply. The first is the *stage fall* which can be dangerous if not properly managed and controlled. It is most important that, when falling, the body should be totally relaxed, and the sequence of movements should be as follows.

1   Relax the body, sway first backwards, then forwards.
2   Drop into a kneeling position.
3   Twist the body and dip one hip till it touches the ground, then follow it by first one shoulder and then the other.
4   Finally, lower the head to the ground.

This should be practised quite slowly, then speeded up gradually till it looks realistic. The actor will not hurt himself provided that he remembers to round his shoulders, keeping his head well forward, until they have reached the ground.

The second rather specialised type of action is *period movement*. Women in particular have moved in different ways in different times and places. Compare the demure, restricted motion of a sixteenth century Puritan lady with the unfettered stride of a booted and mini-skirted girl of the early 1970s and the differences are immediately apparent. Sometimes they are born of social attitudes to do with class, sex, religion, and so on. More often they are created by the physical shape and weight of the costume and accessories of the period – by a constricting corset, perhaps, or a heavy wig, or high heels. All of these affect the movements of the wearer quite dramatically, and during the rehearsal period some approximation to the eventual performance costume should be used so that the actor can grow into the time as well as into the character, and learn how to manipulate both clothes and personal props.

The third type of action which needs to be carefully controlled is *stage fighting*. Unless great care is taken this can be either so realistic that it is dangerous, or so safe that it is unrealistic. Three rules should always be observed about fights of any sort.

1  They must look as real as possible.
2  They must be as safe as possible.
3  They must be kept short if possible.

If the fight is with swords or similar weapons it is essential:

(*a*) to use weapons that are blunt, and
(*b*) to get proper instruction and direction.

Since most actors are taught how to fight while they are at drama school it may be possible to persuade one to come along from your nearest professional theatre to advise you and help you to choreograph the movement. This choreography should be carefully noted, point by point, in 'the book', and repeated exactly at every rehearsal and performance. Contact the Artistic Director of your local theatre and tell him about your problem. He'll probably be very happy to recommend the right man – and suggest a small fee to make it worth his while.

You will notice during rehearsals that the sound of clashing weapons is just as dramatic as the sight of them, so you should make the most of this during the performance. It's safer, though, to keep the actors' physical grunts of effort and exhaustion to a minimum. If they get out of hand they either embarrass the audience, or remind them of wrestling on television. Either way, they're likely to react with laughter.

Similarly, it's difficult to simulate the actual piercing of the body on stage without descending into the realms of coarse acting and attendant mirth. The attacker should push his weapon past the *upstage* side of his enemy, and the attacked man should then clamp the sword to the side of his body with his arm so that it resists efforts to retrieve it. The manoeuvre must be rehearsed frequently, and watched carefully from all points of the auditorium, until it looks as realistic as possible from every angle. But remember that in the tension of the moment, and the speed of the action, these difficult incidents pass very quickly.

If the actor has to be stabbed, the action should be masked by the bodies of other people on the stage, or by his own body. If he is downstage, for instance, and his attacker approaches from upstage, the audience will not see the actual impact of the weapon. It's also very important to control the next moment or two with great care. If the victim staggers around the stage moaning for very long it looks ludicrous, but if he drops dead instantly it looks unrealistic. Timing is vital.

Fist fighting is, if anything, even more difficult to manage convincingly, and depends very much on sound. The movements have to be worked out very meticulously so that it looks as if a flailing fist has made contact, and it sounds as if it has made contact, while in fact it has done no such thing. Consequently the fight should be staged with one opponent facing upstage and the other downstage so that the audience cannot see very clearly what is happening between the two bodies. The sound of colliding flesh can be made either by one of the actors in the fight thumping his fist into his own palm, or by the stage manager doing the same thing in the wings, and making sure that the timing is immaculate. Again, the victim's reaction to the 'non-blow' must be convincing, and the tension of the confrontation must be maintained, otherwise the audience will see through the technicalities and lose concentration.

Kicking is very similar. If an actor is supposed to kick a prostrate body in the stomach the victim should lie on his side while the attacker ferociously kicks the floor very close to him. The actual movement is masked from the audience, usually by the victim's body, but the reaction to the kick, from all the actors involved, must be so accurate that it convinces the audience totally.

Note that all this demands very precise preparation and careful rehearsal if it is to succeed – otherwise it could destroy the production.

### Exercise 10 – In conclusion

You should now conclude this chapter by bringing together the three elements of good acting – *understanding* of character communicated through *speech* and *movement* – by acting out, as your final exercise, the two excerpts from *Rose Ransome*, on page 51.

This is not an easy task since both have their complications. In the first, Ruby is in the dock, unable to move freely. The actress must therefore convey her youth, energy, flirtatiousness, self-confidence, compassion, affection for George, scorn for Black Jack, and general lively good humour all through tone of voice, facial expressions, and gestures of the head, hands, arms and shoulders. In the second, she is a young woman pretending to be old, and therefore probably exaggerating her actions and voice, and though she is more mobile she is largely concealed by a large shawl – Figure 19 (p. 179) – so her body-language is comparatively limited.

# 4

# Direction

'One of the difficulties for the director is that, whereas the actor is able to learn his craft from watching and studying other actors, there is no specialised university or theatre, in the general sense, where a young person may learn the skills of direction. For the time being, until theatre direction becomes a general subject for study, the would-be director has a hard struggle to begin.

Many of my distinguished contemporaries – not all, I hasten to underline – began to exercise their obsession in the craft of direction while at their universities, and frequently to the disadvantage of their academic degrees. In my own case, I was more preoccupied with studying to be an actor, or at least that was my ambition when I left the army. I came to direction rather later in my life than many, and was generously helped on my way by the advantage of having belonged to a first-rate amateur company. This was, as is often the case, as much a matter of luck as of judgement; but the fact is, the director of this particular company was as good as, and sometimes better than, many a professional director I have worked with subsequently; and I learned from him, perhaps unconsciously, that it is not enough to manoeuvre actors from one side of the stage to the other, avoiding knocking each other, or alternatively the furniture over, but that qualities of leadership, decisiveness, and indeed scholarship are needed. And a casual familiarity with the *Penguin Book of Psychoanalysis* would not be unhelpful: for a good director has to be many things, none of them easy, and few of them acquired without scars.

For three years I worked as an actor, in repertory and television, and sometimes I wished I had perhaps trained for one year longer: because, if forced to display my hand, although the director has an obligation to interpret the dramatist, living or dead, as truthfully as he is able to, and to collaborate with designers, technicians, administrators, and above all, money-men (amateur or professional, budgets loom highly on one's list of priorities), at the end of the day – or, rather, the beginning of the evening – it is always the actor who has "to do it". He it is who has to confront a living audience with only his small self, frequently unprotected even by make-up, characterisation, or costume, to assist him. And the director's chief task, I believe, is to forge a secure relationship with that most sensitive, wayward, and vulnerable of humans, the actor. Each one is different, and in himself, if I may generalise, demands a life's dedication of study, but it is in the director's special rapport with the individual performer, from leading player, right down to walk-on, or understudy, that the particular flavour of every production will come across. This takes time, study, sensitivity, and a great deal of pain, as well as patience.

The theatre is ultimately a collaborative art, even when it is run as it sometimes is, by autocrats, nor should they ever forget it. The director constantly finds himself in the middle of warring, or at the least, antagonistic forces, and he has to find in himself that fine line between his own artistic integrity, or drive, and a skilful capacity for diplomacy. Because of the latter quality, direction often resembles politics, but because of the former, it has always seemed to me a profession infinitely more honest, and indeed, more honourable.'

**Patrick Garland**
*Director and writer*

The most important person connected with any dramatic production is the writer. Everyone else's primary concern must be the three-dimensional realisation of the writer's intention, for the benefit of the audience.

However, it is only on comparatively rare occasions that the writer can be, or wants to be, involved with a production of his work. And even when he can be present at some of the rehearsals or planning meetings his skills may not necessarily be those required to bring the written word to life, but rather those of representing life in the written word.

For this reason, the play needs a director who is, in fact, the writer's interpreter. He it is who must visualise the script in terms of characterisation, mood, sound and shape, evolve a coherent dramatic style, and re-create it.

There is often a degree of confusion between the meaning of the words 'director' and 'producer'. Twenty years ago most amateur companies would name the role I have just described as that of the producer. It was the producer who interpreted and visualised the play, ran rehearsals, organised the actors, and told his stage management, lighting and costume teams exactly what he required of them. Now the word 'producer' is rarely used and 'director' has taken its place and is largely preferred. 'Producer' is sometimes used in major professional ventures, especially in America, to describe the man responsible for the financial side of the production, the buying of the play or hiring of a writer, the renting of a theatre, and the formation of the company of actors and staff. In the United Kingdom it is more common for this job to be described as that of 'theatrical manager'. Throughout this book I will use the word 'director' as most amateur and professional companies now use it, to describe the central man responsible for any performance.

## The director's skills

Any director who hopes to achieve a successful production must possess several skills. The first, and most important, is *the ability to respond to a play-script* with (*a*) sensitivity, (*b*) imagination and (*c*) creativity:

(*a*) *Sensitivity* is the quality required to understand, almost instinctively, the total intention of the writer's work as regards meaning and mood.

(*b*) *Imagination* is the power required to visualise the script in terms of a thoroughly satisfying and honest production.

(*c*) *Creativity* is the talent required to embody that understanding and imagination on stage, in terms of people, movement, speech, sound, lighting – and, perhaps, scenery and props, though these are becoming, more and more, optional extras.

The second skill is the valuable personal quality of *being able to relate to each person involved* in the production, whether he is an actor, designer, or member of the stage management team, to explain coherently what is required, and to draw out of him the very best work of which he is capable.

The third skill is *group-management*. It is essential for the director to be able to weld together the highly individual members of his company into a harmonious team, prepared to submerge personal preferences and prejudices for the good of the production. This is a factor he should bear in mind when he is choosing his cast and backstage workers in the first place. Though some professional theatres might be strong enough to contain those egoists whose main consideration is the display of their own talent, they can be a major threat to amateur companies, creating both an unbalanced production, and an unhappy, demoralised group.

The final skill I would consider as absolutely essential is *the ability to audition perceptively*. Auditioning is never an easy task. Some very good actors read very badly. Others who read well at first sight never improve on their initial response to the script. Some competent actors refuse to accept direction and never come up with the performance the director requires from them. Some speak well but move badly, some are good with their own lines but cannot react convincingly to other actors on stage, some are very inhibited in emotional scenes, some don't look right for the part. Obviously the director's job is much easier if he has seen his potential actors performing in other plays. If not, he must devise casting techniques which illuminate the actor's potential talent as vividly as possible and also reveal something of his emotional make-up as well as his ability to respond imaginatively to the written word.

Only if a person feels that he already possesses, or can develop, these four skills should he offer himself as a director. Of course, no one is born a director – one becomes a director through consideration, observation, a dedicated enthusiasm for theatre, and through experience. It is up to a good amateur company to give the opportunity for that experience to those who ask for it.

Even in the professional theatre many brilliant directors look back at their first attempts at direction with horror, remembering the many errors of judgement and interpretation they made. Nevertheless this stage must be worked through so that they can learn from their mistakes. For the sake of the company arrangements should be made for fledgling directors to make their mistakes away from the glare of the public eye. There should be no recriminations if things go wrong. On the contrary, there should be an opportunity for constructive advice, and praise, from the more experienced members of the group.

### Exercise 1 – Director training (I)

Three members of the company who wish to direct plays should be asked to choose a short piece, either a one-act play or a section from a longer one, then to cast it and direct it to the best of their abilities. The three plays should be put on together as an evening performance for the rest of the company and a few invited friends. This should be followed by a *talk-out* in which the novice directors and their casts should discuss each production with the audience.

To be genuinely useful a talk-out of this kind needs to be well-organised by a strong chairman who will encourage helpful questions and comments, discourage trivial chatter, and make sure that the valid points are noted for future reference. I have been involved in many talk-outs, on both sides of the footlights, with professional and amateur companies, and have found that they serve a valuable double function. First of all, they give the director a chance to explain what he was trying to do, and why, so that the audience can judge whether or not he has achieved his aim. Secondly, any director who knows beforehand that he is going to be asked searching questions about his work tends to make sure that his interpretation is valid and coherent, and that the production contains no move, action or nuance which has not been carefully thought out.

## Exercise 2 – Director training (II)

While the company is working on a major production for public performance, directed by one of its most experienced and skilled directors, a trainee director should be invited to choose a cast from those actors not involved and, working quite separately without consultation or comparison, to prepare any one act of the same play for private performance, to the company only, during the week following the main production. Afterwards, the two directors, their casts, and other members of the group should get together to discuss and compare the two performances, analyse their differences and similarities, and find out not only what the new director can learn from his colleague's greater experience and techniques, but also what the more experienced director can learn from the novice director who may well have fewer preconceived ideas about what is required.

This sort of group analysis should always be a positive, constructive, and mutually helpful experience, never an excuse for negative criticism, self-congratulation, or point-scoring. This is demoralising, and invariably does more harm than good.

If the membership of the society is too small to allow two activities of this sort to be in preparation concurrently it may be possible to use the nearest professional theatre as a point of comparison. One of the plays on their programme should be chosen and as many members of the society as possible should make a point of going to see it. In the meantime a trainee director should be preparing a production of part of it, to be put on for fellow members within a few days of the professional performance, and to be followed by a talk-out.

I believe that it is very important for the amateur theatre and the professional theatre to keep in close contact with each other for their mutual benefit and support, and it is very possible that the professional director might be persuaded to come along to join in the discussion and give advice, if he understands the aim of the exercise, and is given sufficient notice to get his diary in order.

Once a director has been entrusted with the responsibility of producing a play for his amateur dramatic society he must first agree about the play which he is to do, making sure that it is right for the society, and for the audience, but, most of all, right for himself. I think that it is of vital importance that he should love and admire the play. If not, he should be firm and refuse to direct it. Any director must be in sympathy with his writer. If he is not totally convinced by the script he will not do it justice. He should be strong enough to say 'no', and the society should have enough sense and sensitivity to refrain from pressuring him against his better judgement.

Having agreed on the choice of play he must then be allowed a little time for reading and re-reading until he has completely mastered it, to his own satisfaction. With many plays, of course, there is no one correct and universal interpretation. *Waiting for Godot*, for example, is open to many. However, the director must always work out for himself a totally coherent interpretation which is completely consistent with the behaviour, mood, words and actions of the characters.

By the time he has had this period of consideration the director should know more about the play than any of the other people involved in the production. Whether they are actors, members of the stage management team, designers or whatever, they will have a slanted viewpoint. Only the director sees the play from an objective and comprehensive viewpoint. Only he can weave the various threads together into a unifying pattern of reactions and relationships.

While he is coming to terms with the play at this initial stage, these are the sort of questions the director should be asking himself:

1   What is the playwright trying to achieve?
2   What is the play about (*a*) on the surface level?
                                    (*b*) at a deeper level?
3   Is the play (*a*) tragedy?
                   (*b*) melodrama?
                   (*c*) comedy?
                   (*d*) farce?
                   (*e*) satire?
                   (*f*) a combination of two or more of these, or
                   (*g*) something quite different?
4   What sort of style is suitable for the production?
5   What is (*a*) the motivation, and
                   (*b*) the conditioning, of each character?

6 What previous (unseen) action led up to the present (seen) action of the play?

Unless the playwright is still alive, accessible, and prepared to talk, or has gone on record as stating the aims of his work, the director has to decide for himself what he is trying to achieve.

Some plays have helpful introductions or prologues which provide most of the answers. For instance, Ben Jonson laid all his cards on the table in his prologue to *Every Man In His Humour*, insisting that he wanted to portray:

> 'deeds and language, such as men do use:
> And persons, such as Comedy would choose
> When she would show an image of the times,
> And sport with human follies, not with crimes,
> Except we make 'em such by loving still
> Our popular errors, when we know they're ill.
> I mean such errors, as you'll all confess
> By laughing at them, they deserve no less:
> Which, when you heartily do, there's hope left, then,
> You, that have so grac'd monsters, may like men.'

Clearly, his aim was doubly didactic, in terms of both human behaviour and theatre. He wanted to mirror men's follies in comic terms so that those follies should be recognised and consequently corrected. He also wanted to develop a more realistic and credible form of drama, removed from what he considered the theatrical excesses and contrivances of the contemporary stage. Handed such an explicit brief, any director must find his task easier.

Modern writers are often less explicit. Beckett and Pinter, for example, strongly resist efforts to persuade them to explain what their plays are about, preferring their audiences to work it out, and perhaps leaving the door open for several interpretations instead of opting for one definitive one.

It sometimes happens though that a writer feels that his work has suffered either by errors of judgement in the first production, or by the lack of sensitive response from the critics, and consequently comes to the conclusion that his play will fare better if he makes a few useful explanatory comments. These the director should note with great respect.

Here is John Arden's rueful account of the reception of his play *Live Like Pigs* at the Royal Court Theatre, London, in 1958.

## INTRODUCTORY NOTE

When I wrote this play I intended it to be not so much a social document as a study in differing ways of life brought sharply into conflict and both losing their own particular virtues under the stress of intolerance and misunderstanding. In other words, I was more concerned with the 'poetic' than the 'journalistic' structure of the play. The reception of the production at the Royal Court seemed to indicate that I had miscalculated. On the one hand, I was accused by the Left of attacking the Welfare State: on the other, the play was *hailed* as a defence of anarchy and amorality. So perhaps I had better declare myself. I approve outright neither of the Sawneys nor of the Jacksons. Both groups uphold standards of conduct that are incompatible, but which are both valid in their correct context.

The Sawneys are an anachronism. They are the direct descendants of the 'sturdy beggars' of the sixteenth century, and the apparent chaos of their lives becomes an ordered pattern when seen in terms of a wild empty countryside and a nomadic existence. Put out of their fields by enclosing landlords, they found such a existence possible for four hundred years. Today, quite simply, there are too many buildings in Britain, and there is just no room for nomads. The family in this play fails to understand this, and becomes educated in what is known as the 'hard way', but which might also be called the 'inefficient way'.

The Jacksons are an undistinguished but not contemptible family, whose comparative cosiness is not strong enough to withstand the violent irruption into their affairs that the Sawneys bring. Their natural instincts of decency and kindliness have never been subjected to a very severe test. When they are, they collapse. I do not regard them as being necessarily typical in this. They are the people I have chosen for the play, because they illustrate my theme in a fairly extreme form.

To any producer interested in presenting *Live Like Pigs* may I offer one or two suggestions?

(i) The play is in large part meant to be funny.

(ii) The Old Croaker-Blackmouth-Daffodil group have much the same effect upon Sailor's household as the Sawneys in general do upon the Jacksons.

(iii) The singing of the ballads should be in some way integrated into the action or else cut out. At the Court they were unsuccessful because the singer was put on the stage between the scenes and quickly taken off again so that no one was really clear whether he was in the play or out of it.

(*Copyright 1961 John Arden, published by Penguin*)

Alan Bennett's brief note at the beginning of the Faber edition of *Getting On* shows similar regrets, and an apprehension that directors will mis-understand his play. The most worrying factor in both these cases is that it is evident that their directors have not recognised the comedy or tragedy which is implicit, the mood has been totally misinterpreted. *Getting On* is essentially a play about failure and disillusion. It is a sad reflection on the contemporary theatre that all too often it plays up comedy and turns a blind eye to the undeniably tragic undertones of much of the work of contemporary writers.

### Author's Note

The text here printed differs in some respects from that first pre-sented at the Queen's Theatre. That version had been clumsily cut without my presence or permission and some small additions made: the jokes were largely left intact while the serious content of the play suffered.

I have removed the additions and largely restored the cuts. This makes the text overlong. But in the event of further productions I would ask that the play be cut with an eye to its seriousness as well as its humour. Otherwise it becomes a complacent light comedy with sad and sentimental moments.

The play was originally entitled *A Serious Man*.

(*Copyright 1972 Alan Bennett, published by Faber, 1972*)

## Exercise 3 – Interpretation of author's intention
In the light of what the authors say about their plays, work out the most effective and accurate way of directing the three following scenes.

### EVERY MAN IN HIS HUMOUR *by* BEN JONSON

(*Note:* Mr Stephen is listed in the Dramatis Personae as 'a country gull' or rural fool, Brainworm is a sharp-witted teasing servant, Edward Knowell is the hero of the play, and one of its few admirable characters.)

### ACT I   SCENE II

[*A room in* KNOWELL'S *house. Enter* ED. KNOWELL, *with a letter, followed by* BRAINWORM.]

ED. KNOWELL: Did he open it, sayest thou?

BRAINWORM: Yes, o' my word, sir, and read the contents.

ED. KNOWELL: That scarce contents me. What countenance, prithee,
made he, i' the reading of it? Was he angry, or pleas'd?

BRAINWORM: Nay, sir, I saw him not read it, nor open it, I assure
your worship.

ED. KNOWELL: No? how know'st thou, then, that he did either?

BRAINWORM: Marry, sir, because he charg'd me, on my life, to tell
nobody that he open'd it: which, unless he had done, he would
never fear to have it reveal'd.

ED. KNOWELL: That's true: well, I thank thee, Brainworm.

[*Enter* MR STEPHEN]

STEPHEN: O, Brainworm, did'st thou not see a fellow here in a
what-sha'-call-him doublet/ He brought mine uncle a letter e'en
now.

BRAINWORM: Yes, master Stephen, what of him?

STEPHEN: O, I ha' such a mind to beat him – Where is he? canst
thou tell?

BRAINWORM: Faith, he is not of that mind: he is gone, master
Stephen.

STEPHEN: Gone? Which way? When went he? How long since?

BRAINWORM: He is rid hence. He took horse at the street door.

STEPHEN: And I stayed i' the fields! whorson scanderbag rogue!
O that I had but a horse to fetch him back again.

BRAINWORM: Why, you may ha' my master's gelding, to save your
longing, sir.

STEPHEN: But I ha' no boots, that's the spite on't.

BRAINWORM: Why, a fine wisp of hay, roll'd hard, master Stephen.

STEPHEN: No, 'faith, it's no boot to follow him, now: let him e'en
go, and hang. 'Pray thee, help to truss me a little. He does so
vex me –

BRAINWORM: You'll be worse vex'd when you are truss'd, master
Stephen. Best keep unbrac'd; and walk yourself till you be cold:
your choler may founder you else.

STEPHEN: By my faith, and so I will now tell'st me on't: How
dost thou like my leg, Brainworm?

BRAINWORM: A very good leg, master Stephen! But the woollen
stocking does not commend it so well.

STEPHEN: Foh, the stockings be good enough, now summer is coming
on, for the dust: I'll have a pair of silk, again' winter, that I go
to dwell i' the town. I think my leg would show in a silk-hose.

BRAINWORM: Believe me, master Stephen, rarely well.

STEPHEN: In sadness, I think it would: I have a reasonable good leg.

BRAINWORM: You have an excellent good leg, master Stephen, but
I cannot stay to praise it longer now, and I am very sorry for't.

STEPHEN: Another time will serve, Brainworm. Gramercy for this.

[*Exit* BRAINWORM]

ED. KNOWELL: Ha, ha, ha!

[ED. KNOWELL *laughs, having read the letter*]

STEPHEN: 'Slid, I hope he laughs not at me; an' he do –

ED. KNOWELL: Here was a letter, indeed, to be intercepted by a man's father, and do him good with him! He cannot but think most virtuously both of me and the sender, sure – that make the careful costermonger of him in our *familiar Epistles*. Well, if he read this with patience, I'll be gelt, and troll ballads for Mr John Trundle, yonder, the rest of my mortality. It is true, and likely, my father may have as much patience as another man; for he takes much physic and oft taking physic makes a man very patient. But would your packet, master Wellbred, had arriv'd at him in such a minute of his patience; then, we had known the end of it, which now is doubtful, and threatens – What! my wise cousin! Nay, then, I'll furnish our feast with one gull more to'ard the mess. He writes to me of a brace, and here's one, that's three: O, for a fourth; Fortune, if ever thou'lt use thine eyes, I entreat thee –

STEPHEN: O, now I see who he laughed at. He laughed at somebody in that letter. By this good light, an he had laugh'd at me –

ED. KNOWELL: How now, cousin Stephen, melancholy?

STEPHEN: Yes, a little. I thought you had laugh'd at me, cousin.

ED. KNOWELL: Why, what an' I had, coz, what would you ha' done?

STEPHEN: By this light, I would ha' told mine uncle.

ED. KNOWELL: Nay, if you would ha' told your uncle, I did laugh at you, coz.

STEPHEN: Did you, indeed?

ED. KNOWELL: Yes, indeed.

STEPHEN: Why, then –

ED. KNOWELL: What then?

STEPHEN: I am satisfied, it is sufficient.


## LIVE LIKE PIGS *by* JOHN ARDEN

[*Angry knocking at the back door in the kitchen*]

MRS JACKSON [*off*]: Let me in. Let me in. [*She storms into the hall through the kitchen, very angry indeed*] The last straw. Oh I've stood enough. Stood enough. But By, I'm not taking this. Where are they?

SAILOR: What the hell are you on about?

MRS JACKSON: My washing. All my washing hanging out on the line in the back garden and it's gone! I want it back, I tell you, I want it back!

SAILOR: We don't have your bloody washing. Now you get out o' here and keep out. It's not your place, no, and never will.

MRS JACKSON: I'm going to find my washing. And my little cat. My little cat. Took her and eaten her. Took her and eaten her.... [*She hurries about the ground floor rooms, routing about in the piles of junk*] You'll not stop me. I'll find my washing. I know you've got it here.

   [RACHEL *tries to stop her, with an angry shout; but* SAILOR *holds her*]

SAILOR [*restraining Rachel*]: Let her rummage if she wants. We've nowt o' hers. Can't ye sees she's – [*He taps his forehead*] Let her be. She'll soon be tired of it.

MRS JACKSON: Where is it? Where is it? [*She goes upstairs into the big bedroom*]

RACHEL: You keep out o' there!

SAILOR: Let her be. We're wanting no more trouble *this* day.

   [MRS JACKSON *goes into the small bedroom.* DAFFODIL *follows her in*]

DAFFODIL [*quietly*]: My room, this is.

MRS JACKSON: I don't care.

DAFFODIL: Is it your husband: red face, hairy legs? Eh?

MRS JACKSON [*briskly*]: Don't you talk about my husband's legs. There's enough and all to talk about without that like o' rudeness. I want my washing!

DAFFODIL: My mam the Croaker, she saw his legs when he wor with Big Rachel. She says, hairy.

MRS JACKSON [*taking it in*]: Eh? ... When he wor with –

DAFFODIL: Big Rachel? Oh aye. [*She giggles*] Last afternoon. In there. Croaker knows what they did. I wor asleep though. I thought he wor Blackmouth, but he warn't.

MRS JACKSON [*stunned*]: With Big Rachel...

DAFFODIL: In that room: *there*. They lay down. Lovely.

MRS JACKSON: That's not true.

DAFFODIL: Ent it?

MRS JACKSON: You're wanting to frighten me.

   [DAFFODIL *grins*]

MRS JACKSON [*in a whisper*]: Oh no. It's not right. Ben wouldn't do that. Never. No. [*She comes down the stairs, and meets Rachel in the hall*] Are you – are you – you're Rachel.

RACHEL [*nods*]: Have you found your washing yet, missus?

MRS JACKSON: He wouldn't do that? Would he? Would he? [*She looks at Rachel, then turns and runs out of the house, through the kitchen door*]

   [RACHEL *laughs*]

DAFFODIL [*laughs*]: That sent her, didn't it? Oh –

[*She sings:*]

> Up and down the road we go
> He comes fast and she comes slow
> Slowly slowly wait for me
> Oh – I'm so blind that I can't see.

What can't you see?

> Twenty fingers holding tight
> Twenty toes in the middle of the night
> Four lips. Four eyes. Four ears.
> And all the rest as goes

SALLY: With his long red nose.

DAFFODIL: With his long red nose.

SALLY }
DAFFODIL: } With his long red, *nose!*

[*The* OLD CROAKER *cautiously puts her head in at the front door*]

CROAKER: I tear them all up, don't I?

[*She comes inside. She has her arms full of washing, all in rags and tatters, and streamers of it are trailing behind her. She continues to rip the fabrics up.*]

SAILOR [*strides furiously towards her*]: Why, you old –

CROAKER [*terrified*]: Oh *no*, Sailor, don't.

[*She throws the washing at his feet and cowers away. He looks at it and her, then bursts into laughter.*]

SAILOR: By God. Her bloody washing! Let 'em all come. We've got the washing –

[*They all start in, tearing the washing up and shouting:* 'We've got the washing.' *Up and down the house they dance throwing the washing all around and over each other.*]

(*Copyright 1961 John Arden, published by Penguin*)


## GETTING ON by ALAN BENNETT

[POLLY *and* GEORGE *now prepare for bed.* POLLY *clearing up the house.* GEORGE *is also tidying up:* POLLY *has a transistor with her which is playing chamber music.*]

[*A recurrent theme in the play should be* GEORGE *switching off this transistor whenever he can and* POLLY *switching it back on again when she notices. She should come back in her nightdress, with transistor and do some incongruous job that suddenly strikes her, like polishing some brass ornament or touching up a picture frame with paint. She goes out eventually turning the lights off, but* GEORGE *comes back, turns one of them on, now in his pyjamas. He looks at himself in the mirror.*]

GEORGE: When does it happen? When did I turn into this? This sagging cistern, lagged with an overcoat of flesh that gets thicker and thicker each year. The skin sags, the veins break down, more and more galleries are sealed off. And you never notice. There is no pain. No warning shots. No bells ring back at base to indicate that another section of the front line has collapsed. This is the body I live with and hoist into bed each night. I heave it desperately from place to place, dump it with less and less enthusiasm on someone else's body, then lug it off again and go about my business as a representative of the people. Save me, O God, from the Car Wash and the lawn-mower on Sundays, the steak house and the Whisky a Go Go. Deliver me from leisure and salmon pink trousers. Give me the Roman virtues, O God. Dignity, sobriety. And at the last, let my heart not be whisked across London preceded by fourteen police cars, sounding their klaxons, the transfer of my liver not be discussed by trendy surgeons (who consent willingly to make up) on late night television programmes. May I die, as I have lived, just about in one piece and my carcase not be scavenged as soon as the breath can more or less safely be said to have left my body. Shovel me into the dustbin, O Lord, without reducing me to offal in some sterile and gleaming knackers yard. And make me a decent man, O God.

[*He turns off the light, and for a second or two the stage is dark. During the last speech the sound of chamber music from* POLLY's *transistor can be heard*]

(*Copyright 1972, Alan Bennett, published by Faber*)

The playwright may be trying to achieve any one, or several, of many possible aims. On the simplest level he may be aiming at pure entertainment – laughter, if he is a comic writer, bafflement, if he writes 'whodun-its', a thrill of fear, if he specialises in horror stories. In such a case the director must be true to the writer's intention and make sure that the comedy is totally hilarious, the mystery completely intriguing, the horror thoroughly spine-tingling.

If, however, the comedy, mystery or terror is a means to a dramatic end, a method of expressing a philosophy of life or attempting to teach some sort of lesson, it must never be allowed to supercede this aspect of the play as a whole. The director must make absolutely sure that the significance is not sacrificed for an easy laugh.

Another scene from *Getting On* can be used to illustrate this point.

[GEORGE *enters breathless*]
GEORGE: Where's the bucket?
POLLY: What bucket?
GEORGE: The bucket. Quick, quick, for God's sake, where's the bucket?

POLLY: What bucket?

GEORGE: The *bucket*. The bowl, anything. Come *on*. It's the dog. It's there.

POLLY: What? Oh, no, George, you can't.

GEORGE: Yes, I bloody well can. [*He rushes out with the dripping pail. Shouts outside as he throws the water. He returns, satisfied*] Got it. Purple in the face as it was passing some particularly recalcitrant stool. It leaped out of its skin. Sodden.

POLLY: It's not the dog's fault.

GEORGE: Maybe. Sometimes I think St Francis of Assisi was barking up the wrong tree. Of course it's the dog's fault. If it will choose our step.

[*He is about to throw another one, when there is a knocking at the door.* GEORGE *opens it, bucket in hand, sees who it is, turns round smartly and comes away from the door, followed in by* MRS BRODRIBB]

MRS BRODRIBB: One moment, young man. Some person on these premises has just thrown a bucket of water over my dog. I have just met him running down the street soaked to the skin.

GEORGE: Your dog, Mrs Brodribb?

MRS BRODRIBB: My dog, Mr Oliver.

POLLY: What makes you think it was here?

GEORGE: Polly. If by dog, Mrs Brodribb, you mean that polka-dotted sewage machine on legs, yes. It was me.

MRS BRODRIBB: So, you admit it ... he admits it. You ought to be ashamed of yourself, a man in your position, an unprovoked assault.

GEORGE: Unprovoked? Unprovoked? Mrs Brodribb, I have lost count of the number of times that creature has fouled our doorstep. It's every time he shoves his arse outside your door.

MRS BRODRIBB: Arse! Oh!

POLLY: It does happen rather often, Mrs Brodribb. I'm sure my husband didn't mean to harm him, only to teach him a lesson.

MRS BRODRIBB: If you wanted to attack a defenceless dog why didn't you choose one your own size? They have to go somewhere.

GEORGE: Then why not on your own doorstep then?

MRS BRODRIBB: Because he needs the walk. Besides, you should be flattered.

POLLY: Flattered!

MRS BRODRIBB: When Max ...

GEOFF: Max!

MRS BRODRIBB [*silencing him with a look*]: ... pauses by your door-step he is not simply relieving himself. He is leaving a message, a sign, a note.

GEORGE: A message, is it? Then I wish he wasn't quite such a frequent correspondent. Your dog, Mrs Brodribb, is a proper little Mme de Sévigné. Besides, who is it leaving a message for, for God's sake? Not for anybody at this address. We haven't any dogs. We have a goldfish and a hamster. Surely he's not contemplating starting up a deviant relationship with them?

MRS BRODRIBB: Don't you be sarcastic with me. I don't want any of your House of Commons manners here. I know one thing. I shan't ever vote Socialist after this. Not that I ever did.

GEORGE: And another thing, Mrs Brodribb. This leaving notes business. Presumably it's to do with ... I'm sorry to have to mention this word ... but it has to do with sex, hasn't it?

MRS BRODRIBB [*who has been circling round the company, stares long and deep into* BRIAN'*s face*]: I've seen you on television, too. You're all the same.

GEORGE: Sex, Mrs Brodribb. But Max can go on leaving little notes for other dogs on our step until he's blue in the face, but I bet you never let him out to back them up, do you? Except once a year with some other equally spotted bitch under medical supervision at forty guineas a time in some foul kennels in Hounslow. So what's all this message leaving, Mrs Brodribb? What are all these notes? I'll tell you what Max is, Mrs Brodribb. He's all talk and no trousers. But for future reference I am not going to have my doorstep used as a post-restante by frustrated dalmatians who never come. And I mean come, Mrs Brodribb.

POLLY: We have got a bit fed up of it.

MRS BRODRIBB: It? It? What you call it, Mrs Oliver, is an extremely sensitive creature, twice champion in his class at Crufts and a thoroughbred dalmatian. That dog, as you call it, has ten times more breeding than you have.

GEORGE: Mrs Brodribb. Shit has no pedigree.

MRS BRODRIBB: Did you hear that? Did you hear that? Such ... language, and from one of our elected representatives. But I give you fair warning, if there is any repetition of this incident, if you ever interfere with Max again, I shall be forced to fetch my husband, diabetic though he be. And that's my last word.

GEOFF: Aw, piss off, you old cow.

[ENID *comes in with a jug just as* MRS BRODRIBB *is going out*]

MRS BRODRIBB: If we had a real Conservative government I should have you horsewhipped.

[ENID *is mystified,* GEOFF *bursts out laughing, and there is a general hubbub*]

[ENID *goes upstage into the kitchen with* GEORGE *and* BRIAN *and is told about* MRS BRODRIBB *in half-heard dialogue which goes on under the action, from various people*]

ALL: She's a silly woman from the other end of the road. George just

threw a bucket of water over her dog. The dalmatian. Ought to
have thrown it over her. Quite. Who wants beer? How many are
we? I hope the chicken'll be big enough. Where's salt and pepper,
etc. etc?

It seems to me that this scene can be played in one of two ways,
depending upon the director's interpretation of Alan Bennett's intention.
Mrs Brodribb can be played as pure caricature, totally comic. In this
case the director will probably give her a high-pitched, affected, middle-
class accent, dress her in shapeless tweeds, and ask for an exaggerated
rather than a naturalistic performance. Alternatively, she can be played
absolutely straight, with conventional but not unattractive clothes, and a
voice that is not in itself a matter for mirth.

The first approach will undoubtedly get more laughs. The second, I
believe, makes more sense taken in the context of the play as a whole.
Mrs Brodribb's views may seem comic in the eyes of the Oliver's and
Bennett's audience. But she is the only person in the play who appears
entirely satisfied with her own particular political viewpoint, her philosophy, and her personal relationships – even if these are canine rather
than human. Unlike Polly, George, Brian, Enid, Geoff, and even Andy,
she is beset by no doubts and uncertainties. Consequently, if she is
depicted as a real person, and not as a figure of fun, she provides the
key to understanding the theme of the play through this effective contrast
in characterisation.

Once a director has understood what the writer is trying to achieve,
it should be a comparatively simple step to work out what the play is
about. Of course, this must be examined on at least two levels. For
instance, on the surface level *Macbeth* is about a man who murders
ruthlessly to achieve the throne for himself and his heirs. On a deeper
level the play is about the nature of kingship and the corrupting power
of ambition.

On the surface Alan Ayckbourn's *Norman Conquests* trilogy is about a
man's unsuccessful attempt to go away for an illicit weekend with his
sister-in-law. On a deeper level it is about the destructive claustrophobia
of middle-class marriage and family life. It is a frequent mistake on the
part of professional and amateur directors alike to treat Ayckbourn as a
comic writer. The laughter is there, of course, in abundance. But so are
the tears. They must be given equal weight.

### Exercise 4 – Discovering what the play is about

Work out to your own satisfaction what the following plays are about, on as many levels as are relevant, then discuss your conclusions with other members of your group who have been reading the same scripts.

(*a*)   *Look Back In Anger* – John Osborne
(*b*)   *Roots* – Arnold Wesker
(*c*)   *Move Over Mrs Markham* – Ray Cooney and John Chapman
(*d*)   *How The Other Half Loves* – Alan Ayckbourn
(*e*)   *The Cherry Orchard* – Chekhov
(*f*)   *Loot* – Joe Orton

To help you analyse the theme of each play you should consider:

1   What each character does and says – and whether these two are consistent with each other.
2   Whether the dramatist portrays him as funny, tragic, admirable, contemptible, important, insignificant, etc.
3   How he reacts with other characters in the play.
4   How he fares in the final *denouement*.
5   What sort of pattern all these characters make when studied together as part of the shaped action which is the play.
6   Whether this pattern conforms with, or reacts against, the prevailing standards, aims and values at the time when it was written.

At this stage it is valuable for the director to try to decide what type of play he is dealing with, so that he can come to some conclusions about the appropriate style of his production.

This is not an easy task. There are several named compartments plays can be slotted into – satire, melodrama, farce, etc. – but most of them are too subtle to allow of simplistic pigeon-holing, and this is their strength. However, it is necessary to decide whether a play is supposed to be tragic or comic, otherwise the balance and emphasis of the production can be quite wrong.

The old definition of a tragedy was 'a play of a serious or sorrowful character with a fatal or disastrous conclusion'. A comedy was defined as 'a stage play of a light and amusing character with a happy conclusion to its plot'. Neither of these seems to me a totally satisfactory definition of modern writing techniques. The best contemporary analysis I have heard is as follows – 'a play can be described as a man's journey from A to B. If he reaches B it is a comedy. If he doesn't, it is a tragedy'.

It is also important to consider the nature of related dramatic forms still seen on the stage. Though *melodrama* is often given broad comic overtones in contemporary productions, it was originally conceived as 'a dramatic piece characterised by sensational incident and violent appeals to the emotions, but with a happy ending'. The strange thing is, it is often more effective and surprisingly moving – though, paradoxically, even funnier – if played absolutely straight. For instance, if any dramatic society attempts to play *Sweeney Todd* strictly for laughs it runs into difficulties, for the power of the climax defies attempts to belittle it, and the audience, uncertain as to whether it should laugh or cry, leaves the theatre feeling oddly dissatisfied and cheated. Though morals and mores change, suffering is always 'relevant', and rarely a matter for mirth.

When considering comedy a director should be able to differentiate between straight comedy, farce and satire, all of which remain as popular with contemporary audiences as they ever were, and all of which demand their own particular style.

*Farce* is a type of comedy in which the main object is laughter, usually at the expense of probability or realism. It is a very ancient form of theatre. The names most closely connected with modern farce are those of Ben Travers, Georges Feydeau and Brian Rix, the latter being responsible for the famous and highly successful Whitehall farces.

Though there are many farces available for production by amateur companies it is wise to think very carefully before choosing one for the repertoire because they present enormous difficulties to both director and actors, and often to the stage staff too. Their success depends almost entirely upon split-second timing and skilful stage business – if they are allowed to become slow and heavy for even a minute or two they are destroyed. And though nothing is funnier and more enjoyable than a well-produced farce, nothing is more tedious and boring than a bungled one. Consequently this genre should only be attempted by a highly experienced, competent and confident group.

*Satire* is essentially a critical comic form which uses the weapon of laughter to ridicule the behaviour of men. It is a sharp, sophisticated type of theatre which derives from intellectual or philosophical concepts, though it may well use slapstick or farcical techniques to embody its message. It has a long history and has recently enjoyed renewed popularity both on television and in live theatre, especially alternative theatre which tends, of its nature, to be critical of, or at least irreverent towards, the Establishment. In general terms satire does not present any overwhelming stylistic difficulties. Its successful staging depends, however, on a certain awareness on the part of the audience, and the possibility of a latent sympathy, among some of them at least, with the views of the writer.

## Exercise 5 – Identifying the type of play
Try to classify which type of drama each of the following plays belongs

to remembering that some of them may be composite, containing characteristics of several different types:

(*a*)  *Charley's Aunt* – Brandon Thomas
(*b*)  *Little Malcolm and His Struggle Against the Eunuchs* – David Halliwell
(*c*)  *Maria Marten and the Red Barn Murder* – Brian J. Burton (version)
(*d*)  *All My Sons* – Arthur Miller
(*e*)  *Blithe Spirit* – Noel Coward
(*f*)  *Forget-Me-Not-Lane* – Peter Nichols

Having decided:

1  What is the author's intention
2  What is the play about, and
3  What is its dramatic type

the director is ready to consider the *style* of his production.

Style is the director's personal visualisation of the play. It evolves from his success in unifying:

1  His interpretation of the main theme
2  His assessment of the pattern of characterisation
3  His view of how the play should look, and
4  His judgement of how the play should sound.

The first of these is all-important, of course, because the physical staging of the play will depend largely on whether the director sees it as a sombre tragedy, a soufflé-light comedy, a social comment, or whatever.

Presumably the director will want to make a statement of his own views of life and/or theatre through his production of a specific play, and this will be most clearly demonstrated through style. It is to be hoped that his approach to the characters will be a fresh and imaginative one. There seems to me no valid point in simply repeating a characterisation which has already been thoroughly explored in a previous production. Unless a director feels he has something new and valuable to say about Macbeth, or Archie Rice, or Mrs Malaprop, or Beatie Bryant, for instance, he should not opt to direct the plays in which they appear. Again, it's a lesson to be learnt from the professionals. Lord Olivier made stage history when he played Othello as aggressively Negroid in appearance and behaviour, thus giving a new dimension to the character's significance.

Another way of making a useful new statement is through imaginative casting, avoiding the obvious or commonplace. Type-casting should be shunned. The most successful amateur performance of *The Crucible* that I have seen cast as John Proctor's wife, a woman who was obviously some years older than he, verging on middle-age. This unexpected choice of actress not only gave an added poignancy to the character of Elizabeth but also tied in logically with her feeling of physical inferiority, her difficult pregnancy, and also her husband's remorse at his sexual betrayal of her.

A director can also make his own personal comment by re-appraising who is the dominant character in the play. The answer is not always as obvious as it seems. It is possible to argue that the most significant character in *Hamlet* is not Hamlet but Gertrude, or that *The Taming of the Shrew* says more about Petruccio than his victim. The sheer weight of time and familiarity tends to close our eyes to the intrinsic meaning of some plays, and therefore they should always be re-examined with fresh vision before each new production if they are to have that essential spark of vitality.

Though the director must discuss the final look of the play with his designer, wardrobe mistress, lighting engineer and stage manager, and must be prepared to compromise if necessary to come to terms with the limitations of existing facilities, manpower and the budget, nevertheless the visual impact of the production will depend upon the picture he has in his head. This picture will have been created from his analysis of the play. It may be based upon a significant metaphor. I saw a production of *The Glass Menagerie* which was set within an open wooden framework to represent the actual exterior of the house in which the Wingfield family lived. In effect, the frame looked like a cage and thus subtly underlined the feeling of trapped impotence experienced by the people inside.

Sometimes a director will base the look of his production on a picture. *Love's Labour's Lost*, for example, looks superb when conceived in terms of a Watteau painting. The lyrical pastoral elegance of the artist's style lends itself perfectly to the mood of Shakespeare's youthful play. The fact that Watteau belonged to a later century than Shakespeare does not make their stylistic marriage invalid, for the form of Watteau's painting and the content of Shakespeare's play blend perfectly, and this harmonious blending of form and content is the essence of style.

Many directors realise that it is not necessary to restrict the style of a play to the period in which it was either written or set provided that there is some valid reason for the time change. It is perfectly acceptable to set Shakespeare, or any other writer from a previous age, in contemporary England – but only if contemporary values and ideas are revealed and explored through the script. If modernisation is used just as a whim or gimmick the results can be disastrous.

When contemplating the sound pattern of a production the director must consider such matters as pace, rhythm and intonation. The shaping of a sentence, the stress given to the ending, and the tone in which it is delivered, can determine whether it is received seriously or with laughter. The sound of comedy, especially farcical comedy, tends to be quite different from that of tragedy; altogether faster and lighter.

Take this simple sentence – The house is full of strangers. First, imagine it as it would be said in a farcical comedy by a young, shy bridegroom leading his wife into the idyllic honeymoon retreat he had imagined would be totally private and secluded. Now imagine it as it would be said in a serious drama by a young, escaping RAF pilot reaching the farmhouse in occupied France where he had expected to meet only a known contact.

The same sentence would sound totally different. Both young men are in a similar situation. Both are in a strange place, in unnerving circumstances, confronted by the unexpected. Both see the strangers as ominous. Yet the disaster facing the bridegroom is *comic* and his tone of voice must signal to the audience that this complication holds in store a host of comic possibilities, embarrassments, frustrations, confusions and mistaken identities. The disaster facing the pilot is *tragic* and he must signal to the audience that the complication could give rise to tragic possibilities, betrayal, torture, imprisonment and death.

Often there is no hard and fast rule about how a specific effect should be achieved. Intense emotion can be denoted either by a combination of noise and emphatic movement or, even more effectively, by quiet and stillness. The choice is a stylistic decision. A pause and change of pace can emphasise part of the script and indicate that certain sections of dialogue are being highlighted in order to underline their significance. Alternatively a director might prefer to maintain the pace and reveal significance through movement and facial expressions instead.

To maintain the interest and attention of the audience there must be constant variety in the sound quality of the dialogue, with effective use of varying rhythms and the colouring, or range, the actors give to their voices. A director should listen carefully to the conversations he hears around him and notice which ones catch the attention of their listeners and which ones bore them. The sounds on stage should never be boring. They should be orchestrated into a totally satisfying and effective pattern of balanced sound which will be yet another mark of the director's personal style.

When a director has worked through the period of thought and study that is the initial essential of a good production, he is almost ready to begin auditioning for the play. But before then he must apply himself to three practical tasks.

First of all he must hold *a production meeting*. This is crucially important since it is the occasion when the director gets together with his team of designers, stage-managers, and lighting and sound technicians, and works out exactly what he wants and how it is to be achieved. Taking into account the money and resources available, the talent and skills of the team, and the facilities of the theatre, they must decide together, at this early stage,

1 What needs to be done,
2 How it should be done,
3 When it should be done, and
4 Who is to do it.

Once this meeting has been held the practical team must go into action very quickly so that scenery, props, costumes, lights and recordings will be constructed, hired or otherwise acquired in sufficient time.

Publicity and front-of-house organisation may be discussed at a separate meeting. The director may well want to make his views known on this subject though he will probably play a subsidiary role and leave the decisions to the publicity team.

Secondly, he must make out a rehearsal schedule so that anyone wishing to take part in the play can be sure that he will be able to attend the required number of rehearsals before he commits himself. It is a good idea to give every aspiring actor a copy of the schedule before he even reads for a part.

The timetabling of a rehearsal schedule is quite a complicated affair since it is obviously undesirable to ask all the actors to be present at every rehearsal. The action must be split up into sections in such a way that no actor has to turn up more often than necessary, and none is kept sitting around for hours just to say a few lines. Bored actors tend to deliver boring acting. If, on the other hand, they know that the director only calls them when he really needs them, and that he is genuinely concerned about not wasting their time, they will repay him by working very hard and willingly when they are called. The director of an amateur group must always be aware that most of his actors have full-time jobs and family commitments, and that their time is at a premium so should be used as a valuable commodity. Of course, on those occasions when a complete run-through is called for some of the small-part actors in particular will have to spend some time sitting around just waiting for their cue, but if the general timetable has been sensibly organised they will expect and accept this.

Professional actors know all about the amount of time they have on their hands both during rehearsals and the run of play, and they learn to use it effectively, writing, reading, working at handcrafts, and so on. For amateur actors it often comes as a surprise. Their director should warn them that this is an inescapable part of the job and persuade them to be prepared for it.

Printed in Figure 1 is a rehearsal schedule for an amateur open-air production of *Love's Labour's Lost*.

*Note:*

1   The director has decided beforehand how many rehearsals he will need;
2   He has worked out how long each will last;
3   He has gauged the length of the complete rehearsal period;
4   He has divided up most rehearsals so that some actors need not stay for the full two hours;
5   He has divided up the action so that few actors need to be present at all three of the week's rehearsals, especially during the early stages of the rehearsal period;
6   He has laid down quite specifically that actors must have disposed of their books by a certain date, having allowed them approximately two weeks to learn at least some of their lines, and three weeks to learn them all;
7   He has also timetabled
   (*a*)  The costume-measuring session
   (*b*)  The delivery of props
   (*c*)  The set up and technical rehearsals
   (*d*)  The dress rehearsal, and
   (*e*)  The performances;
8   He has taken the precaution of arranging a reserve rehearsal in case extra time is needed to cope with unforeseen problems.

Given this sort of information at the casting session no actor can be justified in failing to learn his lines on time or missing rehearsals. He knows what the commitment involves right from the beginning, and can decide whether he can offer the amount of time and work that is required, depending upon which part he auditions for.

### Exercise 6 – Making out a rehearsal schedule
Work out a rehearsal schedule for Shakespeare's *As You Like It* or Thornton Wilder's *Our Town* or any other large-cast play you would

LOVE'S LABOUR'S LOST
REHEARSAL SCHEDULE

**Notes**
1. I hope not to exceed rehearsal periods of 2 hours, 3 nights a week Monday, Wednesday and Thursday.
2. Timings for various characters to appear for rehearsal have been worked out and are shown in the remarks column of the schedule. The aim is to avoid unnecessary 'hanging about' but will only be achieved with your cooperation.
3. Please, therefore, be punctual and have a pencil and rubber with you.

**Key**
K–King   D–Dumain   B–Berowne   L–Longaville   P–Princess
Ma — Maria   Ka — Katherine   R — Rosaline   By — Boyet   A — Armado
C — Costard   Mo — Moth   Mc — Mercade   J — Jaquenetta   H — Holofernes
Dl – Dull   N – Nathaniel   BB – Blackamoor

| Date | Act | Scene | Characters required | Remarks |
|------|-----|-------|---------------------|---------|
| Mon 8 May | All 5 Acts | All Scenes | All | Cutting and measuring for costumes and read through. |
| Wed 10 May | 1 | 1 & 2 | K D B L BB C Dl J Mo A | Required 7.20 pm. J Mo A at 8 pm. |
|  |  |  | P Ka Ma R By (K D B L) | Required at 8.30 pm. |
| Thu 11 May | 3 | 1 | A Mo C B | Required at 7.20 pm. |
|  | 4 | 1 | P R Ma K By (C) | Required at 8 pm. |
|  | 4 | 2 | Dl H N J (C) | Required at 8.30 pm. |
| Mon 15 May | 4 | 3 | K B D L | All required at 7.20 pm. |

*Figure 1*   Rehearsal schedule for *Love's Labour's Lost*

| Date | Act | Scene | Characters required | Remarks |
|------|-----|-------|---------------------|---------|
| Wed 17 May | 5 | 1 | H N Dl C A Mo | Required at 7.20 pm. |
|  | 5 | 2 | P R Ma Ka By K B D L (Mo) | Line 1-483 inc. Required at 8 pm. |
| Thu 18 May | 5 | 2 | Whole Cast | Line 484 to end. Required at 7.20 pm. Mc at 8 pm. |
| Mon 22 May | 1 | 2 | A Mo Dl C J | Required at 7.20 pm. NO BOOKS. |
|  | 3 | 1 | (A Mo) C B | Required at 8 pm. |
|  | 1 | 1 | K (B) D L BB (C) Dl | Required at 8.30 pm. NO BOOKS line 1-179. |
| Wed 24 May | 4 | 1 | P R Ma Ka By C | Required at 7.20 pm. |
|  | 2 | 1 | (P R Ma Ka By) K B D L | NO BOOKS line 1-89. Required at 8 pm. |
|  | 4 | 2 | H N Dl J C | Required at 8.30 pm. |
| Thu 25 May | 5 | 1 | H N Dl C A Mo | Required at 7.20 pm. |
|  | 4 | 2 | (H N Dl C) J | Required at 8 pm. NO BOOKS line 1-82. |
|  | 4 | 3 | K B L D (C J) | Required at 8.30 pm. |
| Mon 29 May | 5 | 2 | P Ka R Ma By K B D L Mo | Required at 7.20 pm. |
|  |  |  | (P Ka R Ma By K B D L Mo) C A J N H Dl Mc | Required at 8.30 pm. |
| Wed 31 May | 1 | 2 | A Mo Dl C J | Required at 7.20 pm. NO BOOKS. |
|  | 3 | 1 | (A Mc) C B | Required at 8 pm. NO BOOKS. |

*Figure 1*   Rehearsal schedule for *Love's Labour's Lost*

| Date | Act | Scene | Characters required | Remarks |
|------|-----|-------|---------------------|---------|
| OPEN AIR REHEARSALS WEATHER PERMITTING, 9 DE VAUX PLACE. ALL BOOKS DOWN PLEASE. All props, Bench and Swing to be ready. | | | | |
| Thu 1 June | 1 | 1 | P R Ma Ka By C | Required at 7.20 pm. |
| | 2 | 1 | (P R Ma Ka By) K B D L | Required at 8 pm. |
| | 4 | 2 | H N Dl J C | Required at 8.30 pm. |
| Mon 5 June | 5 | 1 | H N Dl C A Mo | Required at 7.20 pm. |
| | 4 | 2 | (H N Dl C) J | Required at 8 pm. |
| | 4 | 3 | K B L D (C J) | Required at 8.30 pm. |
| Wed 7 June | 5 | 2 | P Ka Ma R By K B D L Mo | Required at 7.20 pm. |
| | | (twice) | (P Ka Ma R By K B D L Mo) C A J N H Dl Mo | Required at 8.30 pm. Scene will be run twice. |
| Thu 8 June | 1 | 2 | A Mo Dl C J | Required at 7.20 pm. |
| | 3 | 1 | (A Mo) C B | Required at 8 pm. |
| | 1 | 1 | K (B) D L BB (C) Dl | Required at 8.30 pm. |
| Mon 12 June | 4 | 1 | P R Ma Ka By J | Required at 7.20 pm. |
| | 2 | 1 | (P R Ma Ka By) K B D L | Required at 8 pm. |
| | 4 | 2 | H N Dl J C | Required at 8.30 pm. |
| Wed 14 June | 5 | 1 | H N Dl C A Mo | Required at 7.20 pm. |
| | 4 | 2 | (H N Dl C) J | Required at 8 pm. |
| | 4 | 3 | K B L D (C J) | Required at 8.30 pm. |
| Thu 15 June | 5 | 2 | P Ka Ma R By K B D L Mo | Required at 7.20 pm. |
| | | (twice) | (P Ka Ma R By K B Dl Mo) C A J N H D L Mc | Required at 8 pm. |

| Date | Act | Scene | Characters required | Remarks |
|------|-----|-------|---------------------|---------|
| Mon 19 June | 1 2 3 (twice) | All | K D B L BB C Dl A Mo J P Ka Ma R By | Required at 7.20 pm. Straight run through twice. |
| Wed 21 June | 5 (twice) | Sc 2 | P Ka Ma R By K B D L Mo | Required at 7.20 pm. Straight run through twice. |
| | | | C A J N H Dl Mc | Required at 7.45 pm. |
| Thu 22 June | 4 & 5 (twice) | Sc 1 | P R Ma Ka By C Dl H N J C | Required at 7.20 pm. Straight run through twice. |
| | | | B K D L | Required at 7.45 pm. |
| | | | A Mo | Required at 8 pm. |
| Sun 25 June | Whole Play Everyone | | | Required at 2.30 pm. Make up. |
| Mon 26 June | Reserve rehearsal hopefully not required. | | | |
| Tue 27 June | LIGHTING REHEARSAL | | | Required at 7 pm. Director Lighting Design, SM, ASM. |
| Wed 28 June | SET UP AND TECHNICAL | | | Details to be issued by Stage Manager. |
| Thu 29 June | Whole Play Everyone | | | First Dress Rehearsal 6.30 pm OLD SARUM. |
| Fri 30 June | Whole Play Everyone | | | Second Dress Rehearsal 6.30 pm OLD SARUM. |
| Sat 1 July Mon 3 July Sat 8 July | PERFORMANCES | | | |

*Figure 1*  Rehearsal schedule for *Love's Labour's Lost*

like to direct. Base it upon the model given here, calculating that you have two months from the auditions to the performance dates.

Before he conducts the auditions the director can make his job easier by drawing up a set of 'character-cards', one for each character in the play. The card should carry, on one side,

1  Any given facts about the character which are *recorded in the text* e.g. name, age, significant physical characteristics, intellectual qualities, emotional qualities, choice of clothes, type of voice, and anything else that is relevant.

2  Any supposed facts about the character which are *implied in the text* through dialogue and action.

3  Brief notes about other characters in the play with whom this character must react and whom he must complement.

On the other side of the card he should list the name of everyone who auditions for that part, outlining:

1  How he/she correlates physically with the character,
2  The quality of his voice,
3  The quality of his movements,
4  The sensitivity of his interpretation of the role,
5  His general acting ability and stage presence,
6  His previous dramatic experience.

## Exercise 7 – Casting

Do the first half of a set of character-cards for *The Crucible* and/or *Getting On*. If this can be worked upon as a group exercise, with several directors making out separate sets of cards and then comparing them in a discussion session, a lot will be learned about what the script says explicitly, what is implicit, and what is simply assumed intuitively by the director. It is valuable that such assumptions should be challenged in order to discover how strong are the foundations upon which they are built.

*Casting* is probably the most important activity in any production – everything depends upon it being done properly – so the process should never be rushed, and it should never be completed without massive consideration. The final word about who is to act in each part must rest with the director for it is his responsibility to see that style of the acting matches up with the picture that he already has in his head. But to help him, and to make sure that he isn't later accused of favouritism, the society should appoint a casting committee of two or three of its established members who:

1  Know and like the play

2   Are themselves experienced in acting or direction or both, and
3   Don't want a part themselves.

All members of the society should be notified of the auditions in good time so that they can arrange to be present if they want to read for a part. If new talent is being sought – and this should be part of every society's regular activities – the auditions should also be advertised in the local paper and potential new members invited to take part.

When anyone auditions he should be given two forms:
1   The rehearsal schedule discussed earlier, and
2   An audition sheet similar to the one reproduced in Figure 2.

*Note:*
1   It gives, and requests, membership information;
2   It requests that all those seeking parts should ensure that they will be free for the rehearsal and performance period, and asks them to state, from the beginning, if and when they will be unavailable;
3   It asks (*a*) which part he wants, and
           (*b*) whether he will accept some other part;
4   It asks which backstage activity can be offered by any actor who is not selected for the cast;
5   It requests details of name, address and telephone number.

As soon as a casting decision has been made the information should be filed away for future use, and any offers of help taken up at the earliest opportunity, before he loses interest and finds some other club to join.

It is a good idea to begin with informal individual auditions. This ensures that each would-be actor gives the reading an original and personal interpretation, and is not influenced by hearing other actors at work. Later, group auditions will solve problems of balancing personalities, orchestrating voices, and matching up physical requirements.

The material for the auditions can be:
1   A prepared piece from the play to be produced, or some other play;
2   An unseen piece from the play to be produced, or some other play;
3   A piece of improvised speech and action;
4   A combination of some or all of these;
      for each tells a different story about an actor's talents and resources.

The director and his committee should make sure that they do not audition too many people at any one sitting, because judgement rapidly becomes impaired if too many fine distinctions have to be made. Several short auditions are much more useful and constructive than one or two lengthy ones.

## STUDIO THEATRE — AUDITIONS

1. All new members are welcomed — Subscriptions:—
   Full Members     £3.50 )
   Husband and Wife   £5.00 ) Minimum
   Full-time Student      75p

2. Please study rehearsal schedule to make sure that you will be available over the rehearsal and performance period.

3. If you are offered and accept a part, or backstage post, you will have to become a member. Those with parts will be expected to pay for their script.

4. Are you prepared to accept any part offered?   YES/NO
                                          (delete as necessary)

NAME ........................................................................................................

Address ....................................................................................................

Telephone ...............................................................................................

Dates unable to attend rehearsal ........................................................

Are you a member?   YES/NO

Those auditioning: Please state below in which characters you are interested


Backstage:          Please tick your particular interest
Stage Management
Publicity
Sound
Lighting
Prompt
Costume
Props
Stagehand
Front of House

*Figure 2*    Audition sheet

The final choice of actors is an important factor in the eventual style of the play – how it looks, how it sounds, how its theme is interpreted. To make sure that the style is fresh, and not a re-hash of a previous production, the director should avoid preconceptions about which actor can do what, and who 'looks right' for the part. Most competent actors are capable of playing a wide range of parts. Type-casting only serves to blunt their ability. Recently I saw a repertory performance of *Move Over Mrs Markham* in which the actress who usually played comic character parts was given the straight role of the glamorous and charming Joanna Markham, while the one who usually played the lead female was asked to act the eccentric, doggy, children's writer, Olive Harriet Smythe. It was an experiment which paid dividends, since both women revealed skills that had lain dormant, and the audiences, who thought that they had seen the full range of their acting ability, were delighted with these new insights.

A well-judged element of surprise is one of the hallmarks of the good director. He should take particular care not to be too influenced by physical characteristics. Good acting – plus subtle make-up – can make a plain woman beautiful, a young man old, an old woman middle-aged, a handsome man ugly.

On the other hand, it is sometimes important to match characters up with each other physically. For instance, give a large lady a little husband and you'll find it difficult to avoid unwanted laughs. And in a play like *Love's Labour's Lost*, which revolves around two quartets of young people, there is much to be said for making each group a cohesive whole by ensuring that the individuals are approximately the same size, shape and age. This not only gives the production a satisfying look, it also underlines the significance of the theme.

Consideration should also be given to the quality of the actors' voices. The director must choose these very carefully, looking for a variety of timbre and type so that they complement each other as do the instruments of an orchestra. Voices that are too similar can be both boring and confusing for the audience.

Even more important than physical qualities is the quality of the personality. Actors must be part of a team, prepared to submerge themselves in the play. If one of them has an over-powering stage presence, and either can't or won't discipline it, he can ruin the balance and distort the relationships as drawn in the script. He might excel as Lear, Luther or Tamburlaine, but will spell disaster to any play without a main protagonist. He should be handled with care, and only cast if he can be controlled.

Many amateur dramatic societies agonise over the perennial problem of whether they should give parts to their less-experienced or less-talented members, even if they are not the best actors available, just to be fair to them and give them some encouragement.

Having been involved in this sort of decision-making for several years, I have reached the conclusion that, when mounting a major production for a paying audience, it is the director's duty to assemble the best possible combination of actors, regardless of personal diplomacy. Untried or inexperienced actors should be given parts in play-readings and one-act plays for private performance until they are sufficiently accomplished to be a credit to the society in public. If they are really lacking in talent they should be gently persuaded towards some of the other, equally important, theatrical skills in the hope that they will be able to contribute to the society as part of the design or stage management team, or front-of-house group.

It is worth remembering that the British Theatre Association not only recommends teachers to help dramatic societies with their internal training programmes, it also holds Residential Summer Schools which include movement, voice and acting classes in their programme, as well as tuition in production and stage management. It can play a vital part in improving the standards of any group.

As soon as the director has chosen his cast he should make his decision known without delay both by individually contacting everyone who has won a part, and also by putting up a cast list on the society's notice board.

Those who have not got parts should have been told beforehand that if they don't hear from the director within a week they will not be needed, but it is to be hoped that they will involve themselves in some other area of the production.

The short period between the publication of the cast list and the first rehearsal read-through will be a very busy one for everyone concerned with the production. The chosen actors will be occupied in reading the play and considering their own parts in relation to the general pattern of action and characterisation. The stage management team, the designers of scenery, props and costumes, lighting technicians and sound engineers, as well as the front-of-house team and publicity people, will be holding their second production meeting with the director to discuss the progress of their own work programmes and to iron out any difficulties which have arisen. And the director will be envisaging, step by step, the movement and shape of the play, depending upon the nature of his stage and the way he has decided to utilise it.

The stage will depend very much on the facilities of the hall to be used for the production, and will usually be a raised, curtained platform at one end of a rectangular room. But amateurs are too often timid and conventional in their use of space. Variations can be employed even within this arrangement – some possibilities are outlined in the chapter on Design (pp. 153–68). As a general rule, if the director decides upon a conventional box set with curtains, he is limiting his options. If he is content to rely upon a few simple props, clever lighting, and the imagination of his audience, the possibilities are immense.

Not all directors are agreed about the desirability of *blocking* the movements of their production before beginning rehearsal. My own opinion is that it is certainly wise to have some idea of how each actor will make every entrance and exit, and of the way in which they will move around the acting area when they are on it. This first tentative shaping should be pencilled on to a blank page interleaved with each page of script. A combination of the diagrams and numbered notes will ensure that none of the planning will be overlooked in the bustle of the rehearsal.

Reproduced in Figure 3 is a director's diagram and accompanying notes for a page of the script of John Bowen's *Heil, Caesar!*, an interesting modern interpretation of Shakespeare's *Julius Caesar.*

The director should be prepared to alter his first ideas if they prove unwieldy, or if better ideas are thrown up during rehearsal, but this period of adjustment should be strictly limited. Changes made in the last week or two of the rehearsal period only serve to confuse and upset the actors and the stage manager, and undermine their confidence in the director's competence.

When the director is blocking his production he should always be aware of the main purposes of movement and grouping.

The first is the *functional* one of moving the characters around so that they can further the action of the story, and occupy the most desirable position for any specific speech or piece of stage business.

The second is the *practical* one of focusing and maintaining the concentration of the audience which will become bored if the characters are too static.

The third is the *aesthetic* one of giving the visual satisfaction of a well-composed picture, with skilled grouping and shaping.

Having these three considerations firmly in mind, the director must then discipline himself to make the characters appear to move according to their inner compulsions and not as if they are puppets attached to his strings. Unless the play is a fantasy or musical their actions should seem realistic and logical. For instance, if a man is leaving a room in a hurry he will normally take the most direct route, not indulge in a circular tour of the room to avoid masking the leading lady. If he is downstage and wants to talk to somebody upstage he will naturally turn his back on the audience, and there is no reason why he shouldn't provided that he can manipulate his voice so that it remains audible.

Heil, Caesar!

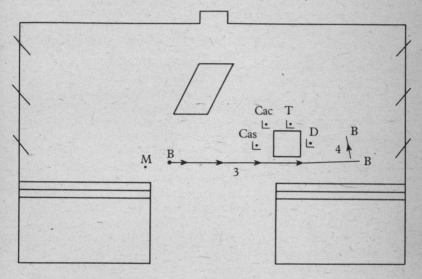

1. Cassius turns to the others — that 'Ah!' is 'Got him' to the others. When Messala and Brutus have moved down all eyes have been on them. Now all eyes are turned on one another with satisfaction. When Brutus and Messala pick up the dialogue eyes turn to them again. We need a pause after 'Ah!' for impact.
2. Brutus executes definite body turn to Cassius.
3. Brutus crosses below table, beyond Decius.
4. Brutus upstage to behind Decius again — not too close in.

Notes _____

*Figure 3*    Director's blocking diagram

# HEIL, CAESAR!

MESSALA: By?

BRUTUS: Me. And these gentlemen.
*[Brutus has now committed himself, to the relief of the conspirators]*

1    CASSIUS: Ah!

2    MESSALA: May one ask why?

BRUTUS: There is a plot to make him Emperor.

MESSALA: So?

BRUTUS: Government of the people by one man — one man and his friends. Laws made and unmade, not by the elected Assembly, but by the will of one man, the whim of one man! Advancement through the favour of one man!

MESSALA: Yes, well, the general answer to your question is that the Army will do what it's told, as long as it's paid and fed and given a reasonable excuse for whatever dirty work it's asked to do. Provided you don't actually intend to get rid of any Army Area Commanders, myself, included . . .

BRUTUS: We don't plan to get rid of anyone except Caesar himself. And that reluctantly.

CASSIUS: Er . . .

2    BRUTUS: Yes?

3    CASSIUS: Antony.

BRUTUS: No.

CASSIUS: But you've got the proof of his guilt in your hand.

BRUTUS: You said yourself, without Caesar there's no plot.

DECIUS: But . . .

4    BRUTUS: If we're to say to the people: 'This was a cruel necessity', how shall we justify it, how shall they believe us, if we simply set about killing everyone who might be dangerous? It's that kind of thing we're acting to prevent.

CASCA: It's not safe to leave Antony alive.

BRUTUS: It's not safe to kill Caesar, but it seems we must do it.

CASSIUS *[after a pause]*: Agreed.

## Exercise 8 – Blocking

Reproduced here are two dramatic scenes, one a modern comedy with many characters and much required movement, the other an old tragedy with only two characters and little movement. Draw the outline of a stage on several pieces of blank paper, mark on it any furniture, scenery, exits and entrances that you consider necessary – using the symbols given in the chapter on Design (p. 162) – and then block out the action for each scene as effectively as you can. You might like to use chessmen as characters to help you visualise the movement. Bear in mind what has been said about functional movement, visual variety, visual satisfaction, and logical realism.

Finally, add numbered direction notes using the *Heil, Caesar!* example to guide you.

### Excerpt 1 – from *Blonde on the Bonnet*

*As the action begins George and Marge Gubbins are at home in their living room. Marge is sitting on the settee, knitting, George is in his armchair opposite her, reading his paper. There is a loud knocking, and "They" begin to arrive, following each other in quick succession, though ignoring each other totally, and building up to a chorus of interference. Enter Daphne, very giggly, very gushing.*

DAPHNE: Hello there. Mind if I come in?

GEORGE: Who're you when you're at home?

DAPHNE: Daphne, that's me. I don't suppose you'll have heard of me . . .

GEORGE: No.

DAPHNE: . . . but I'm from the Happy Housewives Hello Club. – Hel*lo*. [*she giggles*]

MARGE: Hello.

    [*More knocking. Enter Smythe, very dapper, cultivated voice*]

SMYTHE: Good morning, good morning, Mr . . . mm . . . er . . . Gubbins. Yes, yes, quite. And *Mrs* . . . mm . . . mm . . . Gubbins too! Splendid.

GEORGE: That's us. And who the hell are you?

SMYTHE: Smythe. S–M–Y–T–H–E. Got it? Good, you've *got* it. Man from the council, that's me.

MARGE [*horrified*]: I told you, George. Did I, or did I not, *tell* you?

GEORGE [*dismissively, returning to his paper*]: Good morning.

SMYTHE: But you don't understand. I . . .

GEORGE: No reps, no callers, no men from the council. Sorry, rules of the house. Good morning.

DAPHNE [*to Marge*]: Yes. The Happy Housewives Hello Club. I'm the secretary, actually. [*giggles*]

MARGE: Did you hear that? George? She's the secretary. Isn't that nice?

DAPHNE: Thank you. You're probably wondering what I'm doing here ...

GEORGE: Yes.

DAPHNE: Well, the thing is ...

[*There's a tremendous knocking. George groans. Enter P.C. Billings*]

BILLINGS: Hello–hello–hello.

GEORGE [*crossly*]:
DAPHNE [*thrilled*]:  Hello.

BILLINGS: And what *exactly* is going on here then?

GEORGE: Funny you should ask that, Constable. Amazing how you chaps smell 'em out – dens of vice, sinks of iniquity, wherever they might be. Actually, I'm reading my paper – or trying to – and Marge here is knitting a tonsil warmer for a passing giraffe. Do you happen to *know* of any passing ...?

BILLINGS: Now then–now then–now then. It doesn't pay to jest with the law, you know. The law doesn't take kindly to jesting with.

MARGE: I *told* you, George. I *told* him, Daphne. There'll be trouble, I said, as soon as They ...

BILLINGS: Your car, sir. I take it that *is* your car parked outside your front door – the low-slung, scoop-backed, raked-screen, fully-automatic convertible?

GEORGE: What about it?

SMYTHE [*interrupting to press forward his case*]: Mr ... er ... Gubbins, this matter is extremely serious, you mark my words.

MARGE: Yes. You mark his words, George.

SMYTHE: You see, you seem to have acquired – for want of a better word – a sub-tenant. Now, may I point out, according to our rules governing housing in the public sector, section 4, para 6, council tenants may not, definitely Not, with a big, big, N, sub-let their property or any part of the aforesaid property. Have I ... ?

GEORGE: She's not.

SMYTHE: What?

GEORGE: NOT.

SMYTHE: Not WHAT?

GEORGE: A sub-tenant.

SMYTH: Ah!

DAPHNE: *As* I was saying, we started our club especially for the women of our community, to make sure no lonely house-wife was sitting at home when she could be coming along and having a bit of a giggle. I mean, if you haven't got friends and neighbours, the world can be a very sad place.

MARGE: Oh, I do agree there. Don't *you* agree, George?

DAPHNE: After all, the way we see it, the mobile society is breaking down our rural living patterns, plucking up our deepest roots.

GEORGE: Nasty, that.

DAPHNE: *Yes.* I mean, the ancient traditions of kith and kin have become obsolete, the extended family a thing of the past. And we women are the losers, Marge, the *losers.*

MARGE: Do you know, Daphne, you've taken the words right out of my mouth. That's just what I was saying to Edna. Isn't it, George? Edna, I said, woman is the unhappy *serf* of the nuclear family situation.

DAPHNE: Go on – did you really.

MARGE: My very words.

DAPHNE: That's astonishing. Perhaps we're telepathic.

GEORGE: Perhaps you've been watching the same programme on telly!

MARGE: Open University?

DAPHNE: Sociology?

MARGE: Second Level?

DAPHNE: The role of women in a changing society.

MARGE: *Yes.* Well, it just goes to show, doesn't it?

DAPHNE: Isn't the world a small place – that's what *I* always say.

MARGE: That's what *I* always say, too.

[*They both giggle hilariously, and* GEORGE *sighs.* BILLINGS *takes the opportunity afforded by the brief pause*]

BILLINGS: Illegally parked, sir.

GEORGE: You what!

BILLINGS: The car.

GEORGE: Pull the other one. That's a legal parking street, that is. Has been for years.

BILLINGS: Yes. Legal for parking *cars.* [*pause*] But not blondes.

MARGE: I *told* you, George.

BILLINGS: It's down in black and white, sir. The parking of blondes on bonnets in minor roads and side streets is specifically forbidden. Causes an obstruction, you see. Not to mention a distraction to passing motorists.

[*More knocking. Enter* VIOLET JAMES, *very middle class, professionally charming and liberal-minded*]

VIOLET: Mr Gubbins? So glad to find you at home. I'm Mrs (do-call-me-Violet) James.

MARGE: Oh yes?

VIOLET: Your neighbourhood health visitor.

GEORGE: Oh Christ!

(*Copyright Jennifer Curry 1979, published by New Playwrights Network.*)

## Excerpt 2 – from *Macbeth*

SCENE VII   *Macbeth's castle*

[*Hautboys and torches. Enter a Sewer, and divers servants with
dishes and service over the stage. Then enter* MACBETH]

MACBETH: If it were done, when 'tis done, then 'twere well
It were done quickly; if th'assassination
Could trammel up the consequence, and catch
With his surcease, success; that but this blow
Might be the be-all and the end-all – here,
But here, upon this bank and shoal of time –
We'd jump the life to come. But in these cases
We still have judgment here; that we but teach
Bloody instructions, which, being taught, return
To plague th'inventor. This even-handed justice
Commends th'ingredients of our poisoned chalice
To our own lips ... He's here in double trust:
First, as I am his kinsman and his subject,
Strong both against the deed; then, as his host,
Who should against his murderer shut the door,
Not bear the knife myself. Besides, this Duncan
Hath borne his faculties so meek, hath been
So clear in his great office, that his virtues
Will plead like angels, trumpet-tongued, against
The deep damnation of his taking-off;
And pity, Like a naked new-born babe,
Striding the blast, or heaven's cherubin, horsed
Upon the sightless couriers of the air,
Shall blow the horrid deed in every eye,
That tears shall drown the wind ... I have no spur
To prick the sides of my intent, but only
Vaulting ambition, which o'erleaps itself,
And falls on th'other——

[*Enter* LADY MACBETH]

How now! what news?

LADY MACBETH: He has almost supped. Why have you left the
chamber?

MACBETH:   Hath he asked for me?

LADY MACBETH:   Know you not he has?

MACBETH:   We will proceed no further in this business:
He hath honoured me of late, and I have brought
Golden opinions from all sorts of people,
Which would be worn now in their newest gloss,
Not cast aside so soon.

LADY MACBETH:                    Was the hope drunk,
            Wherein you dressed yourself? Hath it slept
                since?
            And wakes it now, to look so green and pale
            At what it did so freely? From this time
            Such I account thy love. Art thou afeard
            To be the same in thine own act and valour
            As thou art in desire? Wouldst thou have that
            Which thou esteem'st the ornament of life,
            And live a coward in thine own esteem,
            Letting 'I dare not' wait upon 'I would',
            Like the poor cat i'th'adage:
MACBETH:                              Prithee, peace!
            I dare do all that may become a man;
            Who dares do more is none
LADY MACBETH:                  What beast was't then
            That made you break this enterprise to me?
            When you durst do it, then you were a man;
            And, to be more than what you were, you would
            Be so much more the man. Nor time nor place
            Did then adhere, and yet you would make both:
            They have made themselves, and that their
                fitness now
            Does unmake you. I have given suck, and know
            How tender 'tis to love the babe that milks me –
            I would, while it was smiling in my face,
            Have plucked my nipple from his boneless gums,
            And dashed the brains out, had I so sworn as
                you
            Have done to this.
MACBETH:                    If we should fail?
LADY MACBETH:                        We fail!
            But screw your courage to the sticking place,
            And we'll not fail. When Duncan is asleep
            (Whereto the rather shall his day's hard journey
            Soundly invite him) his two chamberlains
            Will I with wine and wassail so convince,
            That memory, the warder of the brain,
            Shall be a fume, and the receipt of reason
            A limbec only. When in swinish sleep
            Their drenchèd natures lie as in a death,
            What cannot you and I perform upon
            Th'unguarded Duncan, what not put upon
            His spongy officers, who shall bear the guilt
            Of our great quell?

MACBETH:                                Bring forth men-children only!
For thy undaunted mettle should compose
Nothing but males. Will it not be received,
When we have marked with blood those sleepy
      two
Of his own chamber, and used their very daggers,
That they have done't?

LADY MACBETH:                            Who dares receive it other,
As we shall make our griefs and clamour roar
Upon his death?

MACBETH:                                I am settled and bend up
Each corporal agent to this terrible feat.
Away, and mock the time with fairest show:
False face must hide what the false heart doth
      know.

                                            [*Exeunt*]


By now the director has covered a lot of the groundwork of his production. To his own satisfaction he has:

1   defined the purpose of the author,
2   interpreted the meaning of the play,
3   isolated its theme,
4   visualised an appropriate style,
5   discussed its staging, publicity, front-of-house arrangements, and so on with his production teams,
6   cast his actors, and
7   completed his initial blocking.

He is now ready to begin rehearsals.


## Rehearsals

There are several stages in the rehearsal process, for all of which adequate time should be found. They are as follows:

1   Initial read-through
2   Blocking
3   Initial run-through
4   Detail-building
5   Run-throughs
6   Technical rehearsals
7   Dress rehearsals.

## Rehearsal discipline

It cannot be repeated too often that though the director should not be bossy and self-important he must always be firmly in control of the rehearsal. He will set the mood of concentrated discipline which is absolutely essential if progress is to be made, and will rely on his stage manager to help him to maintain it.

It is true that many people join amateur dramatic groups for the social contacts, friendship and companionship they offer, but it is a mistake to think that rehearsals should therefore be relaxed events with plenty of time for chat. Three points need to be made to those who come along in this frame of mind. The first is that often the closest relationships are built through working together towards a mutual goal and achieving excellence. The second is that though amateurs, by definition, give their time for love rather than money, the audiences are normally expected to pay for the privilege of watching the results of their labours, and they will only get their money's worth if the entire company has made a consistent and disciplined effort to put on the best show of which they are capable. Thirdly, there is time for socialising after and between rehearsals, but not during them. So the director should ensure that the rehearsal itself is a period of consistent endeavour for every individual concerned, whether or not he is on stage at the time.

## Duration of rehearsals

Because of the high level of concentration and effort required the director must time and pace his rehearsals very carefully. If it is a full-length play that he is preparing the read-through may be a lengthy business, and the actors should be warned beforehand. Similarly the dress rehearsals, and especially the technical rehearsal, will be extremely time-consuming and, of necessity, open-ended, so no one should be allowed to expect to get home early.

For the other rehearsals, however, a fixed duration should be set, and they should start and end promptly. My experience has led me to the conclusion that, for amateurs who have already done a day's work before they begin rehearsal, two hours is the optimum length. However, they should be asked to arrive a quarter of an hour before the beginning of the formal work so that they have time to relax and get into the mood of their part. This brief period can be spent in any of several ways, probably in limbering and relaxation exercises, or in quiet consideration of the script. There will also need to be a pause somewhere in the middle of the two hours for a brief respite, but this should only last for about five minutes and should not be used as a coffee break, for nothing is more damaging to the rhythm of the work. Treat the occasion as if it were a championship tennis match – a bottle of squash and a jug of water can be kept on one side in case anyone is flagging, but sociable drinking should be kept until the end, when the pleasure has been earned. With this sort of firm timetabling it is absolutely essential for the director to keep the rehearsal moving along – if at the end of the evening only a quarter of the planned programme has been covered everyone begins to feel panic-stricken and demoralised, and the production suffers as a consequence.

### Siting of rehearsals
The read-through is the only rehearsal in which the actors can expect to do their work sitting down in comfort. From then on they will be on their feet and moving.

The best place to rehearse is on the stage where the actual performances will take place. This is very rarely possible though. Amateur actors usually find themselves working in private houses, hired rooms, village halls, pubs, even barns and garages, often to the dress rehearsal stage. But it is up to the stage manager to make that place measure up literally to the actual stage from the beginning of the rehearsal period. He must take the measurements of the acting area that is to be used for the performance and recreate them in the rehearsal venue by means of chalk or, preferably, tape. With the cooperation of the designer he must also indicate where there are exits and entrances, windows, fireplaces, stairs or any other significant features.

### Familiarisation with the set
By this time the designer will have created a three-dimensional model of the set which should always be available so that the actors can see and familiarise themselves with the environment in which they will be acting, and will have no new problems to solve when the set is actually built.

The stage manager should also furnish the area for each rehearsal with orange boxes, stools, rostra, or whatever is available, as substitutes for the actual furniture that will eventually be used for the performance, so that the actors can actually sit down, lie down, climb up, or do whatever the script requires of them, right from the beginning of the rehearsal period. Many amateur actors find it frightening enough to have to remember their words and put on a convincing performance before an audience without having the extra burden of trying to work out how to cope with the hazard of an unfamiliar piece of furniture.

## Familiarisation with props and costumes

This striving towards familiarity at an early stage should also extend to costumes and personal props. For instance, if the women are to wear long skirts or elaborate hats in the performance they should use them to rehearse in as much as possible – probably not the actual costume, but a substitute which will feel the same weight and affect their movement in the same way. Similarly, if an actor has to be dressed to appear grossly fat, the sooner he gets used to his padding the better. It will affect the way he walks and stands, the way he gets up and sits down, and these changes from the norm must become second nature to him long before he is subjected to the scrutiny of an audience.

The same applies to personal props. Whether it is a crossbow or a cigarette lighter, a fan or a flick-knife, if an actor has to use something in the play he should have it, or a very good substitute, as soon as possible. This is one of the reasons for holding the first production meeting well before rehearsals begin. Well-organised stage management and wardrobe teams will have worked out then not only what is required for the run of the play, but also what will be needed to make absolutely sure that the rehearsals are as useful as possible.

It is not normally practicable to have stage lighting for rehearsals before the actors move on to their proper stage, but it is essential to provide it as soon as possible. Just as unfamiliar props can confuse an actor and make him forget a line or movement, so unexpected lights can completely unnerve him. He must be given a chance to get used to them before the actual performance.

*The initial read-through* is extremely important because it is on this foundation that the actors build their relationships with the play, and with the director.

Either from previous knowledge of the play, or from their preliminary reading of the script, the actors will probably have their own ideas of what it is about and how it should be approached. But not until they have read it as a group and listened to the director's analysis of its theme and mood will they be able to visualise the individual essence of this particular production. Therefore it is up to the director to have done his homework thoroughly so that he can answer any questions adequately, justify his artistic decisions, and assure the actors that his view of the staging of the play is practicable. A director's talent lies not only in seeing creative possibilities but also in knowing that, with the help of his stage-management team, he can make them work.

The read-through should be at the same time serious and informal, and should be composed of three main activities. Sitting in a circle with the actors, the director should give a very brief resumé of the play, and then begin the reading without delay. This is the first phase of the read-through. It is not a good idea for him to elaborate on his view of the characters at this stage – it is a much better idea for him to listen and note very carefully what the actors bring to their parts. They may have a fresh and imaginatively attractive interpretation which will be lost if the director inhibits them by announcing his own view too forcefully.

The best plan is to have a discussion about characterisation, interpretation and style immediately after the first reading, in the second phase of the read-through. At this stage everyone should be given a chance to air his opinions, and there should be a helpful exchange of ideas. The director must have the last word, but he shouldn't give it until he has listened and thought very carefully. Nor should he impose it too dogmatically. In the case of a divergence of opinion it is his job to woo the actors into a willing acceptance of his point of view – even to persuade them, if possible, that it is their point of view as well, since it is obviously difficult to play convincingly a part one isn't convinced by. When a fair measure of agreement has been reached – bearing in mind that this is only the beginning, and that ideas will change and grow during the rehearsal period as new layers of meaning are discovered beneath the surface of the words – the director should take the opportunity to give the actors any cuts or alterations that he has made in the text, and see that they are also passed on to the stage-manager.

The third and final phase in the read-through is a second reading of the script, preferably quite fast and without interruption, so that the actors can build into it the extra understanding they have acquired from discussion, even though at this stage it will be in a very rudimentary state.

It is worth noting that this 'sandwich-technique' of practical work-discussion-repeated work is very effective, since it normally produces instant and visible improvements which build up the morale and self-confidence of the actors and help them to remember the lessons that have been learned.

### Exercise 9 – Initial read-through

The director should select a group of actors and arrange an initial read-through of the beginning of *An Ideal Husband*, using the sandwich-technique of reading then discussion, followed by final re-reading. Given here are the opening pages of the play, but those groups planning to use it as an exercise are recommended to use the whole of the first act with its many complicated moves and groupings.

## ACT I   SCENE I

*The octagon room at Sir Robert Chiltern's house in Grosvenor Square.*

*The room is brilliantly lighted and full of guests.*

*At the top of the staircase stands* LADY CHILTERN, *a woman of grave Greek beauty, about twenty-seven years of age. She receives the guests as they come up. Over the well of the staircase hangs a great chandelier with wax lights, which illumine a large eighteenth-century French tapestry – representing the Triumph of Love, from a design by Boucher – that is stretched on the staircase wall. On the right is the entrance to the music-room. The sound of a string quartette is faintly heard. The entrance on the left leads to other reception-rooms.* MRS MARCHMONT *and* LADY BASILDON, *two very pretty women, are seated together on a Louis Seize sofa. They are types of exquisite fragility. Their affectation of manner has a delicate charm. Watteau would have loved to paint them.*

MRS MARCHMONT: Going on to the Hartlocks' tonight, Margaret?

LADY BASILDON: I suppose so. Are you?

MRS MARCHMONT: Yes. Horribly tedious parties they give, don't they?

LADY BASILDON: Horribly tedious! Never know why I go. Never know why I go anywhere.

MRS MARCHMONT: I come here to be educated.

LADY BASILDON: Ah! I hate being educated!

MRS MARCHMONT: So do I. It puts one almost on a level with the commercial classes, doesn't it? But dear Gertrude Chiltern is always telling me that I should have some serious purpose in life. So I come here to try to find one.

LADY BASILDON [*looking round through her lorgnette*]: I don't see anybody here to-night whom one could possibly call a serious purpose. The man who took me in to dinner talked to me about his wife the whole time.

MRS MARCHMONT: How very trivial of him!

LADY BASILDON: Terribly trivial! What did your man talk about?

MRS MARCHMONT: About myself.

LADY BASILDON [*languidly*]: And were you interested?

MRS MARCHMONT [*shaking her head*]: Not in the smallest degree.

LADY BASILDON: What martyrs we are, dear Margaret!

MRS MARCHMONT [*rising*]: And how well it becomes us, Olivia!
[*They rise and go towards the music-room. The* VICOMTE DE NANJAC, *a young attaché known for his neckties and his Anglomania, approaches with a low bow, and enters into conversation*]

MASON [*announcing guests from the top of the staircase*]: Mr and Lady Jane Bartford. Lord Caversham.

[*Enter* LORD CAVERSHAM, *an old gentleman of seventy, wearing the riband and star of the Garter. A fine Whig type. Rather like a portrait by Lawrence*]

LORD CAVERSHAM: Good-evening, Lady Chiltern! Has my good-for-nothing young son been here?

LADY CHILTERN [*smiling*]: I don't think Lord Goring has arrived yet.

MABEL CHILTERN [*coming up to* LORD CAVERSHAM]: Why do you call Lord Goring good-for-nothing?

[MABEL CHILTERN *is a perfect example of the English type of prettiness, the apple-blossom type. She has all the fragrance and freedom of a flower. There is ripple after ripple of sunlight in her hair, and the little mouth, with its parted lips, is expectant, like the mouth of a child. She has the fascinating tyranny of youth, and the astonishing courage of innocence. To sane people she is not reminiscent of any work of art. But she is really like a Tanagra statuette, and would be rather annoyed if she were told so.*]

LORD CAVERSHAM: Because he leads such an idle life.

MABEL CHILTERN: How can you say such a thing? Why, he rides in the Row at ten o'clock in the morning, goes to the Opera three times a week, changes his clothes at least five times a day, and dines out every night of the season. You don't call that leading an idle life, do you?

LORD CAVERSHAM [*looking at her with a kindly twinkle in his eyes*]: You are a very charming young lady!

MABEL CHILTERN: How sweet of you to say that, Lord Caversham! Do come to us more often. You know we are always at home on Wednesdays, and you look so well with your star!

LORD CAVERSHAM: Never go anywhere now. Sick of London Society. Shouldn't mind being introduced to my own tailor; he always votes on the right side. But object strongly to being sent down to dinner with my wife's milliner. Never could stand Lady Caversham's bonnets.

MABEL CHILTERN: Oh, I love London Society! I think it has immensely improved. It is entirely composed now of beautiful idiots and brilliant lunatics. Just what Society should be.

LORD CAVERSHAM: Hum! Which is Goring? Beautiful idiot, or the other thing?

MABEL CHILTERN [*gravely*]: I have been obliged for the present to put Lord Goring into a class quite by himself. But he is developing charmingly!

LORD CAVERSHAM: Into what?

MABEL CHILTERN [*with a little curtsey*]: I hope to let you know very soon, Lord Caversham!

MASON [*announcing guests*]: Lady Markby. Mrs Cheveley.

[*Enter* LADY MARKBY *and* MRS CHEVELEY. LADY MARKBY *is a pleasant, kindly, popular woman, with grey hair à la marquise and good lace.* MRS CHEVELEY, *who accompanies her, is tall and rather slight. Lips very thin and highly-coloured, a line of scarlet on a pallid face. Venetian red hair, aquiline nose, and long throat. Rouge accentuates the natural paleness of her complexion. Grey-green eyes that move restlessly. She is in heliotrope, with diamonds. She looks rather like an orchid, and makes great demands on one's curiosity. In all her movements she is extremely graceful. A work of art, on the whole, but showing the influence of too many schools.*]

LADY MARKBY: Good-evening, dear Gertrude! So kind of you to let me bring my friend, Mrs Cheveley. Two such charming women should know each other!

LADY CHILTERN [*advances towards* MRS CHEVELEY *with a sweet smile. Then suddenly stops, and bows rather distantly*]: I think Mrs Cheveley and I have met before. I did not know she had married a second time.

LADY MARKBY [*genially*]: Ah, nowadays people marry as often as they can, don't they? It is most fashionable. [*To* DUCHESS OF MARYBOROUGH]: Dear Duchess, and how is the Duke? Brain still weak, I suppose? Well, that is only to be expected, is it not? His good father was just the same. There is nothing like race, is there?

MRS CHEVELEY [*playing with her fan*]: But have we really met before, Lady Chiltern? I can't remember where. I have been out of England for so long.

LADY CHILTERN: We were at school together, Mrs Cheveley.

MRS CHEVELEY [*superciliously*]: Indeed? I have forgotten all about my schooldays. I have a vague impression that they were detestable.

LADY CHILTERN [*coldly*]: I am not surprised!

MRS CHEVELEY [*in her sweetest manner*]: Do you know, I am quite looking forward to meeting your clever husband, Lady Chiltern. Since he has been at the Foreign Office, he has been so much talked of in Vienna. They actually succeed in spelling his name right in the newspapers. That in itself is fame, on the continent.

LADY CHILTERN: I hardly think there will be much in common between you and my husband, Mrs Cheveley! [*Moves away*]

VICOMTE DE NANJAC: Ah, chère Madame, quelle surprise! I have not seen you since Berlin!

MRS CHEVELEY: Not since Berlin, Vicomte. Five years ago!

VICOMTE DE NANJAC: And you are younger and more beautiful than ever. How do you manage it?

MRS CHEVELY: By making it a rule only to talk to perfectly charming people like yourself.

VICOMTE DE NANJAC: Ah! you flatter me. You butter me, as they say here.
MRS CHEVELEY: Do they say that here? How dreadful of them!
VICOMTE DE NANJAC: Yes, they have a wonderful language. It should be more widely known.

(*From 'An Ideal Husband' by Oscar Wilde*)

After the read-through the rehearsal schedule will move on to the second stage for the blocking. The director will have marked out on the inter-leaving of his playscript the rudimentary moves he wants his actors to make, and over a period of one to three rehearsals the actors must walk through them so that he can make sure that they are practicable, and that they look right. Every actor must always equip himself with pencil and rubber so that he can make a note of his own moves as he is given them. The stage-manager, who should be at every rehearsal, will also make a note of every move, and of every alteration. When a change is given he should see to it that the actors walk through the change straight away and amend their copies so that the old move is eradicated and there are no arguments or confusions at a later date.

While he is supervising the blocking rehearsals the director should be watching very carefully and critically to make sure that the grouping and movements of the actors fulfil all the requirements already outlined (see p. 94). He should also be watching their reactions to see if they are quite relaxed and secure about what they are doing. If he notices any uneasiness or discomfort he should try to find out what is wrong, and, if necessary, put it right. He should not, however, be too open to requests for changes to be made, otherwise his individual picture will be spoiled and valuable rehearsal time lost.

### Exercise 10 – Blocking
Still working with the opening scene from *An Ideal Husband*, block out all the necessary movements, paying particular attention to exits, entrances, and grouping.

After the blocking has been completed it's a good idea to have an *initial run-through*, preferably uninterrupted. This will consolidate the various aspects of the play in the actors' minds, give the director a chance to see how well it works, and reveal whether there are any snags to be smoothed out before the next stage of rehearsals. It will also give the stage manager the opportunity to gauge what his team will need to do during the performance, and how long they will have to do it in. And finally, it will give some idea of how long the separate acts and the performance as a whole will run, so that plans can be made for organisation of the intervals, and so on. Do bear in mind though that while the actors still have their books in their hands and are a little uncertain about their moves they will be comparatively slow, and that performances are almost always faster than rehearsals anyway.

The next phase of the rehearsal period, the *detail building*, is often the most important and satisfying for the actors, though it can be extremely time-consuming, demanding rigorous attention to the minutiae that go together to make for excellence.

At this stage the director and actors together must examine, scene by scene, each sentence, each movement, each facial expression, to make it live with a reality of its own in such a way that the audience will be totally convinced that these are not characters in a play but real people with lives of their own. In fact, what is required is more than simply an illusion of reality. The director should be striving to build in to his production a quality of imaginative creativity which will make the audience catch their breath with delight and surprise even while they recognise the validity and honesty of the action.

It is during the detail-building that the timing of lines and the inflection given to key words should be examined, pauses should be built in to speeches, reactions should be clarified, especially from those who have little to say. This is the time when movements should be made significant and expressive – though never needlessly exaggerated – and when the manipulation of props and costumes should be practised to perfection. This is the time, above all, when pace should be controlled, when the decision should be taken as to which sections of the play should be moved along with speed and dynamism and which should be allowed to be slower and more reflective.

In short, this is the stage of rehearsals when the 'business' should be perfected. Stage business includes:

1  Gestures of head, shoulders, hands and arms,
2  The manner of walking and moving,
3  The manner in which personal props are manipulated, and
4  The use made of large props and scenery.

There are two kinds of stage business:

1  *Functional*, i.e. necessary to the advancement of the plot, and therefore normally written in to the script, and
2  *Superimposed*, i.e. added by actor, director or writer to enrich the production by:
   (*a*) setting the scene,
   (*b*) revealing character and relationships,

(*c*) heightening the significance of the action,

(*d*) building interest into potentially static scenes.

As a general rule, the audience's enjoyment of a play depends to a large extent upon the success of its business, since this is what gives it its dramatic vitality. In fact, many a director has found that the only way to bring a pedestrian script to life is to deck it out in vivid business. While this is no excuse for bad writing, it does offer an escape route for those faced with producing a play which lacks substance or satisfaction. What is more, when combined with a good script the effect can be sensational. A splendid example of this was Michael Blakemore's scintillating production of Ben Travers' *Plunder* at the National Theatre in 1976, when the comic business of Frank Finlay and Dinsdale Landen had the audience torn between continuous spontaneous applause and helpless mirth, so meticulous was its devising and execution.

It sometimes happens that a play contains a set piece which is extremely difficult to rehearse. This may be a stage fight, or a dance, in which the movements are very complicated and special choreography is required. Or it may be a scene like the famous dual-time dinner party in Alan Ayckbourn's *How The Other Half Loves* in which split-second timing is essential. As far as blocking and detail-building rehearsals are concerned, it is usual better to deal with these separately, otherwise they slow down the general progress and those actors not directly involved tend to get very bored and restless.

At the beginning of the detail-building stage of the rehearsal schedule the actors will still be using their books, but they should be encouraged to have their parts learnt by the time they are half-way through, otherwise the holding of scripts will inhibit their movement and concentration, and much of the value of the rehearsals will be lost.

By this stage the director and his group of actors should have had experience of a read-through of part of *An Ideal Husband* as well as blocking it.

## Exercise 11 – Detail-building

Now try building in the detail and business necessary to transform this same section of script into a polished performance. If it can be organised, let other members of the society watch the work in hand and then join in a general discussion about the preparation of the piece, the aims and achievements, as well as the problems encountered in preparing it.

When the interpretation and characterisation of the play has evolved satisfactorily, the detail and business has been built into the production, and the first performance is beginning to loom large, it is very important that some rehearsals should take the form of *run-throughs*. In other words, the rehearsal should begin at the beginning of the play and continue to the end without interruption except for brief interludes between acts. Only in this way can the actors get the feeling of the development of their parts, the pattern of reactions with other characters, and the organic growth and interweaving of plot and sub-plot. And only in this way can pace and timing be accurately gauged and adjusted.

During each run-through the director should watch and listen with objective attention and make notes of anything that requires more work. At this stage it is too late to make major changes. It is also too late to be highly critical of the actors' achievement. As the performance becomes imminent they need their confidence boosted, as a rule, not diminished by a director who is beginning to panic.

As well as assessing the validity and effectiveness of each actor's performance, the interaction of the cast as a whole, the pace, verbal rhythms and general 'look' of the play, the director should be aware of two absolutely basic requirements. He must make quite sure that the actors:

1  Can be seen, and, even more important,
2  Can be heard.

Nothing infuriates and alienates an audience more than actors who mumble or whisper inaudibly.

At the end of the run-through the actors should be called together to listen to the notes, be advised as to how any problems can be solved, and then act the difficult sections again straight away. The practice adopted by some directors of giving notes at the end of one rehearsal to be tried out in the process of the next rehearsal is not a sound one. Changes and improvements need to be tried out immediately if they are to work. If there is a time-lag it invariably leads to confusion.

At the *lighting rehearsal* the lighting designer, in conjunction with the director, makes a final decision about the settings of the lanterns that will be used to create the desired lighting effects throughout the show. Further details are given in the chapter on Lighting p. 136.

The *technical rehearsal* is a vitally important part of the rehearsal schedule, but primarily it is for the benefit of the stage management and technical teams rather than the actors. It is therefore dealt with in much greater detail in the chapter on Stage Management (p. 122), and only outlined here.

Though the actors have been rehearsing for weeks and are almost to performance level by this stage, in most cases the stage staff will not yet have had the opportunity for a rehearsal since they can't work properly until they gain access to the actual performance area. So, as soon as the stage is ready – usually about three or four nights before the show – they must be given the chance to have a thorough technical rehearsal.

This is the occasion when all the props, scenery and lighting are at last assembled together, tried out and timed, and lights and sound effects cued exactly. The assistant stage manager responsible for the props is able to see that they are in the right place for the actors both on and off stage, the stage manager can supervise that any stage effects or scene changes are being coordinated correctly by his stage crew, and finally, the deputy stage manager, or whoever is on 'the book', is able to check that he is giving their cues to all the back stage staff at exactly the right time.

When these checks have been worked through, and the technical problems satisfactorily solved, the stage manager can rest assured that the technical part of the production will be working smoothly for the dress rehearsal.

As a rule the technical rehearsal should be supervised jointly by the stage manager and the director who must work in very close partnership to ensure that both of them are satisfied with the way things are going, and that both technical and artistic requirements are being met.

If there is time, and the stage is available, I think that two *dress rehearsals* are better than one. They should be exactly like performances and should be run by the stage manager without interference from the director. The director's role is simply to watch and discover how effective the work of the previous weeks has been in translating the play from a two-dimensional script into a three-dimensional reality. He will, of course, be able to give notes to the cast at the end of the rehearsal provided that they can be implemented without confusion or worry. What the cast will need most at this stage will be encouragement and reassurance, unless they have gone past their peak and become complacent. A certain amount of tension, or 'stage nerves', is desirable because it tends to trigger off a sparky and exciting performance.

The first dress rehearsal will be an uninterrupted run, on the stage to be used, in which the actors will have the make-up, props, costumes, sets, and stage-lighting of the actual performance. If another can be arranged, there should be one extra ingredient – a live audience. This can be enormously helpful to an amateur cast in that they will learn how to cope with the distraction of an audible response from the auditorium, and, especially if it is a comedy, how to time their lines so that they are not drowned by laughter. Inexperienced actors often find it almost impossible to remain silent while an audience laughs. Terrified that their flow of ideas and activity is being temporarily halted, and that the break in rhythm might have an adverse effect upon their memorising of the lines, they rush on regardless with the result that sections of the script are lost for ever. Even if the stage management team has provided some laughter during rehearsals, and the director has warned them of this extra hazard, they will still not be adequately prepared, for audiences are notoriously unpredictable in their responses and often laugh, or refrain from laughter, in the most unexpected places.

Many amateur dramatic societies get 'audience experience' by inviting a local group like the Darby and Joan Club to their second rehearsal, with happy results. The visitors know that the occasion is a preview, are happy to be given complimentary or cut-price tickets for this sort of occasion, and boost the actors' morale considerably by being a relaxed, appreciative and responsive audience. The actors learn from the experience, their guests have a pleasant outing, and everyone gains. At the end of it the cast should be as ready as they ever will be for their first night.

## The director and actor-training

Though the preceding section of this chapter has given some idea of the activities required of the company as a whole during the rehearsal period, extra work may be necessary if the actors are very inexperienced. Either this should be fitted in to the period before the rehearsal schedule begins, or an extra half hour should be tacked on to the beginning of each rehearsal, or an extra training session should be timetabled into the schedule each week, for those who need it.

The purpose of the work done in this extra time will be to develop and improve the actor's technique, especially with regard to the way:

1 He uses his voice
2 He uses his body
3 He expresses emotion
4 He memorises his lines.

1 As far as an actor's voice is concerned the director must see that it is audible to the whole audience, and it is appropriate to the part he is playing.

A good actor does not make himself heard simply by shouting louder. In fact, shouting often blurs the sound of the words and makes them more difficult to hear. He makes himself heard by concentrating on relaxation, articulation, and pitch.

Good speech depends a great deal upon breath and muscle control, and these are only achieved in a state of *relaxation*. As soon as breathing becomes erratic – and stage fright is one of the commonest factors which causes this to happen – the voice cannot be disciplined effectively. This is one of the reasons why actors should be encouraged to practise relaxation exercises regularly, but particularly before rehearsals and performances.

Competent *articulation* is also essential if the actor is to make himself heard, and he must learn to form his words in the front part of his mouth where he can use his teeth, tongue and lips to produce the required sounds.

He must also be encouraged to experiment with *pitch*, raising and lowering the level of his voice to the stage where it is comfortably heard in a variety of environments without ever sounding too loud or too quiet.

The type of voice an actor will assume to fit the character he is playing will, of course, depend upon his understanding of his part and his discussion of it with the director. It is useful for any actor to get into the habit of listening to radio plays whenever possible, to discover how much is revealed about a character simply by the way he speaks – by variety of pitch, by the shaping he gives to his sentences, the stresses he places on specific words, the inflections, tone of voice, and significant pauses.

### Exercise 12 – Use of voice

Director and actor should work together on evolving two entirely different interpretations of the following speech, one straight, one ironic. The actor should then tape-record both versions and play them to a small audience, asking them to make a note of their understanding of the character as it is revealed not only through the words, but also through the way they are spoken.

Alternatively, choose a speech from the play you are currently working on and treat in a similar way.

The frequent use of a tape-recorder is of great value in voice training. Many amateur actors find it difficult to recognise the strengths and weaknesses of their own voices until they have listened to them objectively in this way.

## THE TAMING OF THE SHREW –
## WILLIAM SHAKESPEARE

KATHERINE:

Fie, fie! unknit that threatening unkind brow,
And dart not scornful glances from those eyes,
To wound thy lord, thy king, thy governor:
It blots thy beauty as frosts do bite the meads,
Confounds thy fame as whirlwinds shake fair buds,
And in no sense is meet or amiable.
A woman mov'd is like a fountain troubled,
Muddy, ill-seeming, thick, bereft of beauty;
And while it is so, none so dry or thirsty
Will deign to sip or touch one drop of it.
Thy husband is thy lord, thy life, thy keeper,
Thy head, thy sovereign; one that cares for thee,
And for thy maintenance commits his body
To painful labour both by sea and land,
To watch the night in storms, the day in cold,
Whilst thou liest warm at home, secure and safe;
And craves no other tribute at thy hands
But love, fair looks, and true obedience;
Too little payment for so great a debt.
Such duty as the subject owes the prince,
Even such a woman oweth to her husband;
And when she's froward, peevish, sullen, sour,
And not obedient to his honest will,
What is she but a foul contending rebel,
And graceless traitor to her loving lord? –
I am asham'd that women are so simple
To offer war where they should kneel for peace,
Or seek for rule, supremacy, and sway,
Where they are bound to serve, love, and obey.
Why are our bodies soft, and weak, and smooth,
Unapt to toil and trouble in the world,
But that our soft conditions and our hearts
Should well agree with our external parts?
Come, come, you froward and unable worms!
My mind hath been as big as one of yours,
My heart as great, my reason haply more,
To bandy word for word and frown for frown;
But now I see our lances are but straws,
Our strength as weak, our weakness past compare,
That seeming to be most which we indeed least are.

Then vail your stomachs, for it is no boot,
And place your hands below your husband's foot:
In token of which duty, if he please,
My hand is ready; may it do him ease.

2  Just as speech can be made more powerful if actors can practise separating their words from facial expressions, bodily activities and gestures, so *movement* can become more effective if it is separated from language. Any actor will learn a lot about technique through practising mime. In this art form every movement must speak. Any movement which adds nothing to understanding is not only irrelevant but also damaging to communication. The essence of mime is to express meaning through movement. There is a very good exercise which actors can use to develop this side of their craft without feeling at all inhibited or embarrassed by it. In fact, it is a popular party game.

### Exercise 13 – Use of body

Each actor in turn should be given an adverb – e.g. surreptitiously, timidly, nonchalantly, aggressively – and asked to illustrate it by action alone, while the rest of the group attempts to guess what the word is. Since on this occasion it is work and not play it is a good idea to follow up the mime by discussion in which the group says what was good and clear, and what was misleading or confusing, and works on the action until it is as specific as possible.

3  The best way for a director to develop the emotional range of the actor's technique is to set the group exercises in improvisation. Many people find this difficult at first, but once the barriers of shyness have been broken down they discover that it is a great release and gives them a strength and self-assurance that they can carry over into their work upon a script.

Quite simply, the actors should be given the beginning of a situation, a thumb-nail outline of the characters involved, and a few known circumstances, and should then concentrate on developing that situation, and the characters, as honestly and realistically as possible. It is better if the improvisation does not take place on a stage, which has connotations of 'performing' rather than 'being', and that any audience should be absolutely silent and passive. If they join in, even by applause, the actors tend to become self-conscious and lose concentration, and the improvisation becomes less honest.

The material that is used in improvisation is the basic experience of the actors rather than the written imaginative experience of a playwright. For this reason the director should choose situations which might spark off some degree of recognition or understanding on the part of the group rather than those which are totally beyond them. Note, however, that this does not mean that they must have lived through it all themselves, rather that they are capable of making the imaginative leap necessary to work out what it feels like.

## Exercise 14 – Improvisation

Improvise upon these given situations with members of your society. It might be interesting if two or three groups improvise upon each separately, without seeing each other's work, in order to discover in what different directions the same set of starting conditions can lead.

(a) John, Jane and Eva meet in a pub, by chance, after a long separation. Jane was John's first wife. He left her twenty years earlier to marry Eva who was at that time pregnant. Jane, who was childless, agreed to a divorce for the sake of the expected baby, despite the fact that she still loved John. She has not seen him since that time, and it is her first meeting with Eva.

(b) Julie has travelled from the north to pay an unexpected visit to her twenty-two-year-old son, Nigel, in his London flat. She had been led to believe, by his rare letters, that he had a good job and was happy and successful. She finds him out of work and living in what she considers squalid conditions with Louise, to whom he is not married.

(c) Charles, middle-aged and prosperous, imagines that he has a successful marriage to Yvonne who, for many years, has been a superb home-maker and cook as well as hostess to his business acquaintances. He arrives home one evening to find her packing her cases, preparing to leave him, not for another man but for a high-powered job and a new life as a career woman.

After the actors have worked on this material they might like to evolve some of their own situations for further exploration. Improvisation classes can very usefully become part of the regular activity of an amateur dramatic society, giving great pleasure as well as invaluable training. They can also become the starting point for material written by the group for performance.

4 One of the most frightening things about acting for many people is the business of having to memorise their lines. It is particularly nerve-racking since actors depend upon each other for receiving the

correct cues, and there is the dreadful feeling that if a speech is confused the rest of the cast is being let down.

There are several things a director can do to help actors to be word-perfect and secure. First of all, he should insist that the books are down early in the rehearsal schedule so that there is plenty of time to get used to being without them.

Sometimes it's a good idea to dispense with the prompt for one or two rehearsals so that the actors have to get themselves out of their own messes. If they must rely on their own ingenuity they will develop a degree of self-help, by putting the right words into each other's mouths, and by learning to paraphrase the gist of what should be said even if they can't remember the exact words. Some schools of thought maintain that, for this very reason, it is better to dispense with the prompt for the performances themselves. Nothing is more amateurish than to hear actors being prompted, and the play invariably loses its pace and rhythm, as well as the attention of the audience, if it is subjected to this sort of traumatic interruption. It is true that professional actors forget their lines more often than one would imagine from watching them, but they are adept at covering their tracks, hiding their mistakes, and helping each other. Amateurs would do well to learn from their example.

If the company is sufficiently experienced and confident to dispense with a prompt, do so, especially if it is a theatre in the round production in which it is difficult to conceal his presence. If, on the other hand, it is felt that a prompt is absolutely vital to their peace of mind it is very important that he should be competent. A good prompt will have attended all the rehearsals so that he is familiar with the silences as well as the sounds of the play, totally understands the rhythms of the dialogue, and is acquainted with all the movements and 'business' that have been built in. He will also know exactly how to pitch his voice so that it can be heard the first time by the actor in need, but will not boom around the auditorium. And he will know exactly how many words, and which ones, to feed. During performances he must be seated where he has a good view of the entire acting area but is invisible to the audience.

Secondly, the director can help his actors by insisting that every one should practise relaxation and concentration. Stage fright is as bad for the memory as it is for the voice. On the other hand, if an actor is deeply involved in his part, and totally immune to the fact that his family and friends are in the audience scrutinising his every move, he is more likely to say the right words at the right time.

Thirdly, if he has made sure that the actor totally understands the part he is playing and the meaning of the play as a whole, as well as each separate sentence, the director has put him in a position in which he will be able to work out a logical sequence to his speeches and not spend his time blankly grasping for unrelated words.

Of course, whether the actor learns his part by listening to it over and over again on a tape-recorder, by reading and re-reading it section by section, or by repeatedly practising his words, and his cues, with a friend, depends entirely upon his own preferences and circumstances. The one imperative is that he realises he has a serious commitment to make himself word-perfect by a certain, agreed date and works at it. The actor who makes excuses and refuses to discipline himself to make an effort should be dropped and replaced if possible, otherwise he will completely destroy the production.

# 5

# Stage Management

'The first essential for good stage management is to be the right sort of person. The right sort of person will find the necessary skills quite easy to learn. The wrong sort of person will make life hell for himself and all around him – particularly for the misguided enthusiast who talked him into taking on the job.

The right sort of person has organising ability, tact and patience, a way of understanding both artistic and technical problems, and a capacity for hard work and thorough preparation. It is preparation that keeps the gremlins at bay. Nothing should be left to chance. Every detail should be thought out and tested while there is still time. If you think of all the disasters that can possibly happen, they won't happen, and you'll know what to do about them when they do!

The other thing about the right sort of person is that he or she actually finds stage management fun.'

David Ayliff
*Head of Stage Management Training, RADA*

The stage manager is the lynch pin of any production: the director's right-hand man. The stage manager is responsible for the technical organisation of a production, and should complement the director's responsibility for artistic direction.

His duties are as follows. He must:
1  Read the play until he is thoroughly familiar with it;
2  Attend the production meetings;

3  Liaise closely with the director, the scenic designer, the lighting designer, and the sound technician;
4  Allocate staff to the various tasks;
5  Supervise the acquisition and organisation of props, and mechanical effects for the production;
6  Supervise the preparation of the prompt copy ('the book');
7  Prepare the acting area for rehearsals;
8  Keep a list of names and addresses of the actors and backstage staff involved and be responsible for issuing rehearsal calls;
9  Be responsible for discipline at rehearsals, including prompt beginnings;
10  Supervise the 'fit-up';
11  Be responsible for the technical rehearsal;
12  Run the dress rehearsal;
13  Run the show, for which he is the ultimate authority;
14  Supervise the 'get-out', the clearing of the stage after the final performance.

The stage manager's task starts at the first production meeting and continues until the stage is empty after the last performance. Nowadays it is common in the theatre for the stage management team to be responsible for the provision of all properties, including stage furniture, and the separate 'properties man' has almost disappeared. If, however, an amateur company has someone responsible for props I would suggest that he should come under the jurisdiction of the stage manager.

The stage manager is also responsible for any moveable scenery which can be flown from a fly gallery above the stage or stacked in the wings to be set during the production. This means that he should know, after the production meetings, how the scenic designer is going to set the production, and how the lighting designer is going to hang his lanterns above the stage. This information will ensure that, with proper pre-planning, there should be no conflict between scenic, lighting and stage management departments at the fit-up.

At this point the stage manager should allocate jobs to his staff, deciding who is going to do props, who is going to borrow or hire the furniture required for the production, who is going to be responsible for 'the book' during the rehearsal period, and how the stage management staff are going to share out the tasks during the production.

It is important to realise that careful planning at this stage of the production can save hours of work and effort at a later date. It is also important that the stage manager should have complete confidence in his own ability and that of his team. Although his basic task is to provide the technical requirements of the production, occasionally he may have to suggest to the director or the scenic designer that a particular requirement cannot be met because of technical or economic difficulties.

The stage manager should plan the work of his team so that he himself is completely free of any specific job during the dress rehearsals and performances. Someone has to supervise, and be available for any emergencies that may occur, and who better than the stage manager? By this stage he will have an overall mastery of the play and its technicalities which will be second to none.

The person chosen to be 'on the book' is usually the deputy stage manager (DSM), or at least someone who has a reasonable amount of stage management experience. His first job will be to prepare a prompt copy. This consists of interleaving a script with pages of plain paper. It can be done in several ways:

(a)  by sticking sheets of paper, slightly smaller than the pages of the script copy, down an inside margin;

(b)  by taking a copy apart, punching with a two-hole punch, and interleaving the printed pages with plain paper, in a ring binder; (If this method is chosen I would suggest you strengthen the holes with linen reinforcing rings which can be bought from stationers.)

(c)  by taking *two* script copies to pieces and sticking each page to alternate pages of an exercise book. (Two copies are needed as the underneath side of the printed script cannot be used);

(d)  by cutting a rectangular hole, which is slightly smaller than the printed pages of the script, in alternate pages of an exercise book, and then taking a script to pieces and glueing it around the margins to the edges of the hole.

Whichever method is used, it is essential that alongside of each page of printed script there is a blank page on which to make notes, because, by the end of the play, the prompt copy is going to be, effectively, a map, guide book, and history of the production.

### Exercise 1 – Making the prompt copy

With an old play script, or scripts, make yourself a prompt copy using one of the methods outlined above, experimenting until you find which seems most convenient to you.

The DSM will attend all the rehearsals and mark in the book all the movements that the director gives the actors and will annotate against the script at which line the move occurs. The moves can be plotted either by making small ground plans and using arrows to indicate the direction of the move, or by using the convention of naming parts of the stage, for example, 'DSL' for a move downstage left. The convention is that stage left is on the actor's left hand side as he faces the audience, stage right is on his right hand side, downstage is towards the audience, and upstage away from the audience. Each of these moves is numbered, and that same number is written against the printed line at which the move takes place.

At a later point in the rehearsals, when the lighting designer and the sound designer have plotted their cues, these too are noted in 'the book' prior to the technical rehearsal. As soon as the lighting designer has decided when he wants the lights to change, the cue number is written in the prompt copy with the work 'GO' beside it – e.g. LXQ21GO – so that in the event of a new operator having to take over, the lighting design can still be effective, and cue changes occur on time by instruction from the DSM. A similar process is used for sound cues.

It is usual to mark a warning about a page or so of script before the cue change takes place so that the sound or lighting operator can prepare himself to carry it out (see Figure 4). This warning is written in a similar way – e.g. WARNLXQ21. The warning and the go for each cue are connected with a vertical line so that the DSM is aware of which are related to each other. It is possible to give the warnings for several cues at the same time – e.g. WARN FXQs 4, 5, 6 & 7 – if a series of cue changes are going to occur in quick succession.

The final item to go into the prompt copy is the cast calls. Although it is the responsibility of the cast to ensure that they are in the wings ready for their entrance cues, it is common to give them a call as an extra safeguard. In a theatre equipped with intercom this will usually be done by the DSM from the prompt corner desk. Alternatively an assistant stage manager (ASM) must go to the dressing rooms. Do make sure that the calls are given in sufficient time to enable actors to make their entrance without having a panic-stricken rush that can cause havoc even with the most meticulously prepared production.

At the technical rehearsal minor adjustments may have to be made to the precise time at which the director wants a cue change to be made, but these should only be a matter of a couple of words, or a line of script, as the pre-planning has ensured that the work has been scrupulously done and all the cues carefully worked out.

During rehearsals the DSM should also note any changes to properties or furniture that the director may introduce, and report these to the stage manager after the rehearsal to make sure they are provided.

The person allocated to properties should see to it, right at the outset, that a complete list of required props is made out. A list is sometimes

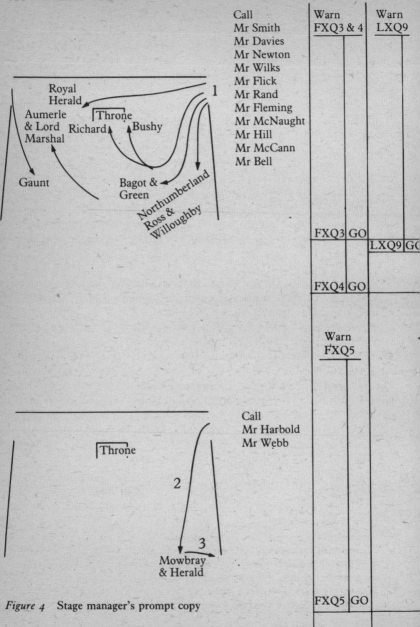

Figure 4 Stage manager's prompt copy

AUMERLE:
Yea, at all points, and longs to enter in.

LORD MARSHAL:
The Duke of Norfolk, sprightfully and bold,
Stays but the summons of the appellant's trumpet.

AUMERLE:
Why then, the champions are prepared, and stay
For nothing but his majesty's approach.
    *[The trumpets sound and the King enters with his*    1
    *nobles, including Gaunt, and Bushy, Bagot, and*
    *Green. When they are set,* enter Mowbray, Duke of    2
    *Norfolk, in arms, defendant; and a Herald]*

KING RICHARD:
Marshal, demand of yonder champion
The cause of his arrival here in arms.
Ask him his name, and orderly proceed
To swear him in the justice of his cause.

LORD MARSHAL *(to Mowbray):*
In God's name and the King's, say who thou art
And why thou comest thus knightly-clad in arms,
Against what man thou comest, and what thy quarrel.
Speak truly on thy knighthood and thy oath,
As so defend thee heavens and thy valour!

MOWBRAY:
My name is Thomas Mowbray, Duke of Norfolk,
Who hither come engaged by my oath, —
Which God defend a knight should violate! —
Both to defend my loyalty and truth
To God, my King, and my succeeding issue
Against the Duke of Hereford that appeals me;
And by the grace of God and this mine arm
To prove him, in defending of myself,
A traitor to my God, my King, and me.
And as I truly fight, defend me heaven.        3

given in the printed script. Look at this, but do not consider it as the final word on props for the play, rather as a guide. I would suggest that the play should be carefully read, and every reference to a prop, whether it occurs in a stage direction or in the dialogue, be noted down.

Don't be afraid to borrow props from shops. Often they will be gladly lent in return for an acknowledgement in the programme. If props are lent make sure that they are taken back promptly and in the same condition as you received them. The names of hiring firms can be obtained from Stacey Publications' *Theatre Directory*, or from the theatrical press. Often firms specialise in a particular type of prop, so do save yourself time by going to the one which seems likely to have what you require. Nor should you hesitate about asking for the help of your local professional theatre. Apart from the fact that it may be able to help you from its own props store, it will undoubtedly have a wealth of experience in knowing which firm to go to for particular props.

The job of getting all the props together can be a long one, and it may be that the cast will want to use props during rehearsals before the actual props have been obtained. If this happens, a substitute prop can be used by the actor. Almost anything will do provided the size and weight is comparable, for instance, a broomstick can substitute perfectly well for a lance, but the actor should always know what the prop is supposed to be.

When all the props on the list have been acquired they can be divided into two groups, those that are set on the stage, and those that are personal to the actor.

## Exercise 2 – Making up the props list

Carefully note down every prop that is required for the first act of *Getting On* by Alan Bennett, whether it is mentioned in the stage directions or referred to in the dialogue, or both. (It will help if you can persuade someone else to do the same exercise so that you can check your list and find out whether it is thoroughly comprehensive.)

Once the props list has been completed, checked and double-checked, the time-consuming task of collecting them together can begin. Some props will have to be made, some can be borrowed, some will have to be hired or bought. Since there are plays which use hundreds of props it is necessary to have some sort of organisation to ensure that they are returned safely to their rightful owners at the end of the run. The form printed in Figure 5 shows one way of coping with the problem. Note that it makes provision for:

1  The name of the production;
2  A description of the prop;

# PROPS FOR RICHARD II

| Item(s) | Borrowed or rented | From whom? (with address) | By whom? | Date | Condition | Date returned (with initials) |
|---|---|---|---|---|---|---|
| Gold chain | B | J. Smith Winterslow | J.C. | 30/5 | Good | |
| Pewter tray | B | Swan Hotel | P.B. | 2/6 | Good, but dents at edges | |
| Riding whip | B | D. Greville Downton | J.C. | 3/6 | Good | |
| Carved chair | B | Y. Cory | B.C. | 3/6 | Good, left rear leg chipped | |
| Hand mirror | B | Batten Antiques | P.B. | 5/6 | Good | |
| Two swords | R | R. White & Sons 25 Shelton Street London | J.C. | 6/6 | Slightly tarnished | |
| Dagger | R | R. White & Sons 25 Shelton Street London | J.C. | 6/6 | Good | |
| Wicker basket | B | P. M. Jones Wilton | B.C. | 8/6 | Beginning to fray at rim | |

*Figure 5*  Props collection list

3   A description of the condition of the prop;
4   The name of the lender and the borrower;
5   The date it was returned and the initials of the person who returned it.

Consequently it provides a useful safeguard against vagueness, negligence, and subsequent recriminations and ill-feeling.

Stage management is responsible for ensuring that the former group are positioned correctly on stage, and a group plan should be made which will detail exactly where props are to be set. If the setting is changed during the play a separate ground plan should be made for each setting, and a list made of all the changes.

Personal props can be considered in two parts: those that the cast carry about their persons all the time, such as cigarettes and handkerchiefs, and those that will be on the backstage props table ready for the actor to take on at a specific entrance. It is as well to insist that actors return props to the table as soon as they make an exit. However the actor organises his personal props it is up to stage management to check them all before he goes on stage. Nothing looks worse than an actor opening an empty cigarette case on stage because he smoked the last one the previous night and it has not been re-stocked. Incidentally, if smoking is part of the play, don't forget to have some damp sand in the bottom of the ashtrays so that cigarettes do not continue to burn when they are put down.

At this point the stage manager should also consider what mechanical effects will be required during the production. These can include smoke, flashes, explosions, and so on, all of which are usually produced at the appropriate time by a member of the stage management team.

Many of these mechanical effects involve the use of pyrotechnics, and it should always be borne in mind that *all pyrotechnics are dangerous*. It may also be necessary to get the permission of your local fire officer to use them on stage if the conditions of your theatre licence require it.

Smoke or fog can be made in various ways. Two common methods are by using dry ice, or smoke powder or pellets. Dry ice vaporises on contact with water so all that has to be done is to drop some pieces of dry ice on to warm water in order to produce clouds of smoke. Since dry ice has to be kept very cold, once it has been bought it should be wrapped in thick layers of newspaper and kept in a freezer. To avoid the possibility of freeze burns it should be handled only when wearing gloves. If some control of the smoke is required it is a good idea to hire a machine which will vaporise the dry ice and disperse it through a hose pipe.

Smoke powder can be ignited by using a flash box for small quantities of smoke, or by using slow burning smoke powder – which is heated on a hot plate – for large quantities of smoke. Smoke pellets can be placed in a tin and simply lit with a match. Determine the amount of smoke you produce by the number of pellets you use. It is wise to test all these methods well before the final rehearsals as disaster can occur when the audience is reduced to a coughing, blinded mass as the auditorium relentlessly fills with smoke.

Flashes can be produced by using flash powder or flash pots. Flash pots are simple to operate as they have their own firing device and only need to be connected to a supply – but they are expensive. Flash powder needs a flash box to ignite it. A flash box consists of a fireproof insulated box with terminals between which a fuse wire can be placed. Wires are taken from the terminals to a switch away from the box. A small quantity of flash powder is placed over the wire, and when the switch is operated the powder burns, giving a white flash and a puff of smoke. Keep the boxes away from any combustible material on stage. One disadvantage of the flash box is that the fuse wire has to be replaced every time it is used.

For rifle shots and explosions it is usual to use stage maroons. Maroons come in various sizes and are fired electrically by being connected to a switch which is operated when required. Maroons should always be placed in metal bins, the tops of which are covered with fine chicken wire.

Pyrotechnics should never be left lying around a stage. They should be kept in a strong box which can be locked, and this should be the responsibility of one member of the team who should ensure their safety. In addition, when flash boxes have been charged, the lids of the smoke or flash powder containers should be immediately replaced before returning them to the strong box.

Further advice and information about all kinds of mechanical effects can usually be obtained from the firms which supply them. Look them up in Stacey Publications' *Theatre Directory*.

The stage manager should mark out the floor of the rehearsal room according to the designer's ground plan before rehearsals begin. This can be done with tape or chalk. Furniture, or substitute furniture, is placed in position, and entrances marked, so that the cast knows precisely what stage area is available to them. If you are lucky enough to have your own rehearsal room, the marking-out can be done at the beginning of the rehearsal period and left until the end. If you are in borrowed premises, stage management should arrive early for rehearsals so that the floor can be marked out in readiness for a prompt start. It is the lot of the stage manager to be first at a rehearsal, and last away from it!

It is also the stage manager's responsibility to ensure that the cast is called for the rehearsal, and that the rehearsal starts on time. As soon as the play has been cast he should see that the names, addresses and telephone numbers of the cast go into the front of the prompt copy so that they can be easily contacted. Any actor who cannot attend a rehearsal for which he is needed should let the stage manager know well in advance so that, if need be, the schedule can be changed, in consultation with the director, or, if that is not necessary, someone else can stand in to read the part.

During rehearsals the stage manager should note scenery and furniture changes which occur during the play, and should plan how any scenery is to be stacked in the wings, and how his team is going to make the changes in the most efficient way. With difficult changes it is a very good idea to rehearse the ASMs beforehand. A generally helpful rule that can usually be observed in scene shifting is – carry something on before carrying something off.

When the scenic designer and the carpenters have finished their scenery, the lighting designer has completed his design, the sound designer is prepared, and the props and furniture are all available, the day of the 'get-in' arrives. This is when the company gets in to the theatre to prepare it for their play. The stage manager is responsible for the overall supervision of the '*fit-up*', getting the stage into a state of readiness for the performance, when the sets are erected, the lights put up, focused and their levels set, the sound equipment fitted and sound levels set, and the props and furniture placed in position.

The time is now ripe for *the technical rehearsal*. Although the actors will have been rehearsing for weeks, the technical rehearsal is the only opportunity the backstage staff are given to get their parts right. The technical rehearsal is usually run by the stage manager, and gives him a chance to see that scene changes can be made in the time available, that sound cues can come in on time, and that any rapid costume changes can be mastered. If things go wrong it is up to the stage manager to stop the technical rehearsal and go back so that it can be put right. Although this can be very boring for the cast, nevertheless, if there is a tricky scenery or lighting change, the stage manager must be satisfied that it is being done correctly before he allows the rehearsal to go on, even if it means going over the same change four or five times.

The dress rehearsals should be run as performances, with the stage manager taking responsibility, and the whole play run through without a break. The director can give the cast any notes that he may have made at the end. Thirty-five minutes before curtain-up the cast should be given the 'half-hour call', at twenty minutes the 'quarter-hour call', at ten minutes the 'five minutes, please', and five minutes before curtain-up the cast is given 'Act One, beginners, please', which is the signal for all those on stage at the beginning of the play to go down into the wings.

For the actual *performances* there should be some arrangement between front-of-house and stage management so that the house manager can signal that the audience is in and seated, whereupon the stage manager can start the show. He should warn the cast on stage that the play is about to start, and tell the DSM in the prompt corner. It is he who will then get the show in motion by giving cues to the various people for house lights to go down, stage lights to come up, introductory music to fade, and the house tabs, or curtains, to go up.

From then on the DSM will remind all the backstage departments of their cues until the play ends. Although some people consider that lighting and sound operators should take their cues for changes visually, from the action on the stage, I think that it is just as well for the DSM to give them their cues so that they receive a reminder that a change is due. A play with only four lighting changes in two hours, for instance, can be very boring for the lighting operator, and he may well have a lapse of concentration.

After the interval the stage manager will go through the same routine to start the second half before handing over to the DSM.

As well as cueing, the DSM gives the actors prompts if they are required. If a prompt has to be given it must be given clearly and sufficiently loudly for the actor to hear. To avoid giving a prompt when the actor is only making a dramatic pause, ensure that all such pauses are clearly marked in the prompt copy during rehearsal.

From the first night on, it is the stage manager's entire responsibility to run the show. He is the ultimate authority. The director's job is now finished and the cast must understand this. If all the planning has been done properly, the team will click smoothly into action for a fault-free performance. Incidentally, it's a good idea for the stage manager to have a first aid box easily available in the wings to cope with any minor accidents that occur during the play.

The final responsibility of the stage manager is to ensure that the stage is cleared after the final performance, and that equipment borrowed or hired is returned to its owners.

The stage manager's main job is to tie together all the technical organisation that the play requires. It is made easier by meticulous planning of every smallest requirement. In the amateur theatre the stage manager, like so many others of the production team, is often battling against time to complete his work. It is a wise precaution, a sort of safety belt, to aim to do everything at least one week before it is necessary – that way, with luck, you'll meet your deadlines.

### Exercise 3 – Stage manager's schedule
Imagine that you are going to stage manage one of the plays from which excerpts are reprinted in this book, and compile a detailed and comprehensive list of all the duties you would have to undertake, in the order in which you would expect to have to carry them out. Work out how many assistants you would need to help you, and which jobs you could allocate to them.

Imagine that your society possesses its own rehearsal room but puts on its plays in the village hall.

# 6

# Lighting

'Of all the changes in the theatre in the last twenty-five years, the change in stage lighting is one of the most dramatic. A quiet revolution has taken place that has advanced lighting's role from that of merely providing illumination of the stage, to where it has become a potent element in the director's scheme of things, that assists in his interpretation of the playwright's intentions. Indeed, going further, the new way in which light can be employed has had a profound impact upon the shape of stages themselves and has heavily influenced the drama's move out of the proscenium and on to the "open stage".

In an obvious way the changes in technology and equipment have been very considerable. Perhaps surprisingly these changes are still only beginning. The explosive development of the microprocessor is, without doubt, going to bring the memory control of lighting into even the smallest theatre and within reach of the most modest budget. But it is not technology alone that has brought about this changed appreciation of the role that lighting has to play in theatrical production, and for the fundamental reasons one has to look back further in time.

Until the early years of the twentieth century and the moment where, through electricity, the spotlight and the dimmer came into use, the principal task of lighting had been to illuminate the stage. Of course, considerable efforts were made to achieve effects such as sunsets, flames, night, day, fire and snow, but, with the limitations of the candle, oil and gas lighting of each period illumination was the prime problem. Fundamentally, the light that issued from one of these sources was at its brightest around that source. As one moves further away from, say, a candle or a gas jet, the brightness of the light rapidly decreases. Rows of light sources above and around the stage, crude reflectors and lenses and other devices did everything they could to amplify the light, but the stages of previous ages were, by comparison to today, very dim indeed. The electric spotlight made possible, from a comparatively small lantern, a beam of light to a point remote from the source, and thus a multiplicity of spotlights can fill a space with light that is distant from the actual fittings themselves. Add to these devices dimmers so as to allow the distribution of light to be remotely changed as the director wishes and one has an entirely new weapon in the theatrical 'armoury' – the ability to fill a space with light, and light of any desired "character".

Why is this of any import? Light enables the human being to see. Without light, we are blind. The sense of sight is a primary one and fundamental to our perception of the world around us. Furthermore, the quality of light has a direct physiological and psychological effect upon the subconscious. Not only is the eye inevitably drawn to the brightest object within its field of vision, but our emotions and perception of our environment are directly affected by the character of the light that surrounds us. A glorious, fresh sunrise or a grey, overcast, rainy morning certainly determine how quickly and with what sense of feeling we leap out of bed in the morning! Light affects our lives continuously and now, for the first time in human history, we can, even at night, create a variable quality of light upon the stage that appears to have no direct connection to the light sources from which it, in fact, emanates.

So this is the "new lighting" forecast by men such as Adolph Appia and Gordon Craig, pioneered between the wars principally, perhaps, in the United States, and now, although still in its infancy, having an increasing impact upon theatrical production. Its development has led to the emergence of a specialist professional, the lighting designer. His job: to employ lighting to the fullest extent in support of the drama. His qualifications: imagination, an awareness of the subtleties of the behaviour of light, a sympathy for the author's and director's intentions, and more imagination. He must possess a knowledge of the technical facilities at his command, but his technical knowledge is, in fact, secondary to his need for creativity. More can often be achieved with more equipment, but a great deal can be conjured up with quite modest facilities, provided the lighting designer employs his resources intelligently and imaginatively.

Of course, his first duty is still to illuminate the actors in their performance, but it can be tremendously satisfying to the designer to both achieve visibility and create an atmosphere upon the stage that amplifies and supports the playwright's and director's intention.'

Richard Pilbrow
*Director of Theatre Projects, lighting designer
and theatre consultant*

We need stage lighting for three main purposes:
1   To light the actors;
2   To light the set; or create the setting; and
3   To create mood.
To help us there is a great variety of equipment available.

## Lanterns

There are various types of lantern, and these can be divided into *spotlights* and *floodlights*. Of the different sorts of 'spots' the most versatile are probably the 'profile' or 'mirror' spots which are used when a high-definition beam is required on the stage, and most front-of-house spots are of this type. They can vary from 250 watts to 2 kilowatts in size and consist of a lamp almost entirely surrounded by a mirror which focuses the light at 'a gate', so that anything that is placed in the gate is projected by the lantern. As a consequence, the beam projected on to the stage can be shaped by having adjustable shutters in the gate, or by making a *'gobo'* for the required beam shape. Gobos that slide into the gate runners must be made of heat-resistant material such as mica or metal because of the high temperatures. A useful piece of equipment is a flexible aluminium pie dish which can be cut with scissors to any shape. Thus it becomes very easy to project those leafy glades on to the stage simply by cutting a gobo to give the patches of light and shade, and coupling with an appropriate green colour.

*Profile spots* usually give a hard edge to the beam which means that there is a sharp cut-off on the stage between where there is light and where there is no light. This can be undesirable if you are graduating from one lighting area to another. However, the beam can be softened either by adjusting the lens in the tube – this varies the beam size so both the gate shutters and the lens have to be adjusted at the same time – or by having two sets of shutters. The latter arrangement is sometimes called a 'bi-focal spot' and in addition to the usual gate shutters it has a second set of shutters with serrated edges just behind the gate. This arrangement makes it possible to have mixtures of hard and soft edges in the same beam.

Whereas with profile spots the lamp remains stationary and the lens moves, with *Fresnel spots*, the lens remains stationary while the lamp moves to adjust the focus. Fresnel spots are characterised by the stepped lens which gives an even beam of light with very soft edges. These blend easily with the edges of other similar spots and are often used to give a smooth spread of light over the stage. The light beam is a cone of light. This means that the size of the beam on the stage increases as the lantern is placed further away from the stage, but it can be compensated for by adjusting the position of the lamp relative to the lens. As the lamp is moved away from the lens so the beam narrows, and vice versa. One disadvantage of the Fresnel spot's soft edge is its tendency to spill light outside the main beam. This can be controlled by a *barn door* which is a device having four rotatable shutters that can be slid into the runners on the front of the lantern.

Although *focus spots* are no longer made, there are still quite a lot around in older installations. They consist of a moveable lamp and reflector behind a plano-convex lens, give a hard edge, and can be uneven unless care is taken in setting the reflector. The lens has the disadvantage that it is usually heavy, tends to project a filament image in the middle of the beam with a colour spectrum at the edge, and, unless great care is taken, breaks very easily.

The simplest form of lantern is the *floodlight* – a lamp and a reflector in a box with colour filter runners which can be moved from side to side or up and down. There is no means of controlling the beam so the size of the area covered by light depends on the distance of the flood from the stage. Floods vary in size from 200 watts to 1000 watts. In amateur companies where budgets are limited, floodlights can be made fairly readily by a competent handyman from large household tins combined with reflector spotlight bulbs whereas is it impracticable to make do-it-yourself spotlights.

If a series of floods are combined into one unit, usually 1830 mm long and wired in three or four circuits, this is called a *compartment batten*. Each different circuit can be given a different colour filter to make colour mixing possible. Battens are given various names, depending upon where they are used. If they are being used on the front edge of the stage they are called *footlights*, if on any other part of the stage, *electrics groundrows*. Although compartment battens were used for practically all stage lighting in the early days of lighting by electricity, nowadays they tend to be used for lighting large areas of scenery, such as cloths, skies and borders.

These types of lanterns are the ones that are most generally used in the theatre, but for special effects and requirements there are others available.

*Effect projectors* are used for projecting slides on to a background. The slides cover a range of optical effects such as cloud, snow, rain and fire.

*Follow spots* are usually associated with the 'star' of a show and are high-intensity lanterns capable of picking out small areas on the stage. Strictly speaking, any profile spot that can be fitted with an *iris diaphragm* can be used as a follow spot, but in modern theatres, with their general high-intensity overall light, it is more common to use a lantern which is fitted with a special lamp known as a *compact source iodine (CSI) discharge lamp*. Unless you are lucky enough to use a large, well-equipped theatre, it is common practice to hire effects projectors and follow-spots as and when they are needed.

## Lamps

Apart from the CSI lamp mentioned earlier, there are two different types of lamp in common use. *Tungsten lamps* work on the same principle as the more familiar domestic lamps. To ensure that the filament relates correctly to the lens of the lantern, modern spotlight lamps have a special pre-focus cap. A disadvantage of tungsten lamps is that as the metal of the filament evaporates with the heat, the glass is blackened and the light output decreases during the life of the lamp. This difficulty is overcome by the newer *tungsten halogen (T/H) lamps* which maintain the light output throughout their life. In general, lamp design is a compromise between greater light output and longer life. As output goes up, life goes down. But most T/H lamps give a longer life and brighter light than the corresponding tungsten lamps. They are usually more expensive to buy, but if lanterns are used extensively then the greater cost is outweighed by the longer life.

## Lighting controls

Nowadays the operation of lighting control boards is a much simpler operation, thanks to the introduction of electronic dimmers which have entirely displaced resistance dimmers in the manufacturers' catalogues.

However, there are many resistance dimmers still around and these will continue to be in use for some considerable time to come.

The purpose of lighting control is to distribute the electricity to the lanterns, and to change the stage picture by varying the amount of electricity going to each one. Directly-operated resistance dimmers made it necessary to have the control panel immediately adjacent to the stage area so that the cable runs to the lanterns should be short. Electronic dimmer control makes it possible to have the distribution part of the control system (i.e. the dimmer racks) near the stage while the varying part of the system is mounted remotely, and connected to the dimmer racks by low-voltage cables. This has the advantage of allowing the lighting operator to be seated in a part of the auditorium from which he can see the action on stage. It is common practice in modern theatres to have the control room at the back of the auditorium.

Two further advantages have accrued from the use of electronic dimmers. The first is that, unlike resistance dimmers which are built to vary a specific load and are not effective at any other loading, electronic dimmers can effectively vary any load from about 60 watts up to its maximum capacity which is usually 1 or 2 kilowatts, although some have a maximum of 5 kilowatts. Secondly, it is possible to build the remote control desk with more than one control lever for each dimmer and so enable the operator to 'preset' his cues.

A *lighting cue* (Q) is any change to the intensity settings of lanterns. On preset control desks each set of control levers is called a *preset*, and each preset is controlled by a master lever.

When a master lever is at zero, its preset levers do not affect the dimmer and so they can be moved without affecting the intensity setting of the lantern. This means that the operator can set the levels that he requires for each lantern prior to the cue, and then, when the cue occurs, the entire change is effected by the movement of one master lever. The next change can be set on another preset with its master at zero, and so on for as many presets as are available, sometimes two, commonly three, and occasionally four. So, any cue change becomes a simple matter of moving master levers instead of having to move each individual dimmer at the time of the cue. This enables the operator to concentrate on the timing of the cue – that is, whether it is a sudden change as when a light is switched on, or a slow change, as for a sunset, for example – without having to bother with the settings at the cue.

Electronic dimmers have enabled *memory dimmer systems* to be built, using the memory storage that was developed for computers. Since the maximum number of presets that can be handled manually in comfort is about four, when more than this are needed the necessary information is stored as a lighting state number, and can be retrieved by the touch of a switch. Effectively it operates like a board with an infinite number of presets.

## Lighting rig

The problem of many amateur companies is obtaining sufficient lanterns and control equipment to achieve a comprehensive lighting rig. Before a start can be made to lighting design a certain minimum number of lanterns is needed. This minimum will vary depending upon the size of the stage, but my suggestion for the average small theatre/hall would be:

1  Six profile spots for Front of House;
2  Six presnel spots for the no. 1 bar, immediately behind the proscenium;
3  Two Fresnel spots for downlighting on the no. 2 bar further upstage; and
4  One or two lengths of two circuit compartment batten for lighting backcloths.

This equipment can be bought, hired or borrowed. If you are going to buy, make sure that the lenses are not cracked, and that shutters work satisfactorily. Occasionally, hiring firms will sell second-hand lanterns. Hiring firms are listed in the Yellow Pages of the telephone directory, advertised in theatrical magazines, and are also entered in the invaluable *Theatre Directory*, an amateur stage handbook published by Stacey Publications. (This little publication is worth its weight in gold since it contains the names and addresses of all the suppliers, associations and organisations which can be of help to the amateur group in any area of production, ranging from publishers to drama festivals.) Incidentally, hiring firms can be relied upon not only to hire out lanterns and equipment in good condition, but usually to back up the service by giving sound advice and assistance in overcoming specific problems.

Borrowing equipment is a good idea when there are several amateur groups in the same area who can arrange to pool equipment for their shows. It can be most effective where local drama associations are formed so that each theatre group knows what is available from others nearby.

Nowadays it is standard theatre practice to use 15 amp BESA round-pin plugs for circuits rated at up to 2 kws. Smaller installations sometimes use 5 amp plugs where only 1 kw circuits are used, but it is useful to follow the standard practice so that all equipment, whether owned, hired or borrowed, can be used with ease. One of the most dangerous theatrical malpractices is to do electrical work 'against the clock', because it is then that short cuts are taken and jobs are not finished correctly. Nowhere other than in the theatre can the old adage 'electricity is a good servant but a bad master' be more easily demonstrated. When a circuit fails in the middle of a show because a plug has been changed incorrectly there is often little that can be done to correct it, and the whole of the lighting design can be made to look ridiculous.

A company should always make sure that it has a competent man or woman as the electrician, someone who will be aware of the maximum loads that circuits will take and what ratings fuses have, so as to avoid overloading cables. He will also know that he should treat his equipment carefully. Theatre electrical fittings are expensive, and the possibility of a company having to replace lantern bulbs which have been broken through carelessness can mean the difference between a profit and loss on a show.

## Lighting design

Ideally, the lighting designer should be involved right from the beginning of the production planning. He should attend the production meetings where, very often, he will be able to make a positive contribution not only as to what can be achieved by lighting alone, but also as to how lighting might affect the scenic design.

The components that make a good lighting design will come from the script, so the first step is to read the play. The designer should note from the text and the author's stage directions any references to lighting, as well as those points at which lighting can change the atmosphere, such as time of day, time of year, or weather. He should find out how the director intends to direct the play, on what he is placing emphasis, whether he intends it to be staged in a stylistic or naturalistic manner. He should also find out what sort of scenic design is contemplated, examine the set model, and make sure that the scenic design does not conflict with the lighting design he is planning. Remember that lighting should complement the scenery and action, and should not dominate them, or distract from them.

The lighting designer should then attend rehearsals. Although by this stage he will have some idea as to how the director intends to use the stage, it often happens that, when actors start rehearsing, changes from the original plan are made to individual moves or to whole scenes, and these should all be carefully noted.

Every production has limitations on the amount of equipment available, whether it is an amateur show in a village hall or a glossy West End musical, and obviously the lighting designer has to work within his budget, but he must start his design by deciding what lanterns he would like to provide lighting where and when he needs it. It has been found that, to light actors without creating harsh shadows, it is best if they are lit from each side at an angle of 45°, with the lantern placed in such a position that the beam of light shines down at 45° (Figure 6a). Obviously we cannot provide two lanterns for each different position of every actor, so what we do is divide the stage into rectangular areas and ensure that two lanterns light each area. The size of the areas will depend on the lanterns we are using since different lanterns have different beam widths. In addition, the further the lanterns are from the stage, the greater will be the area covered. Suppose we say a beam is 2.5 m in diameter and we have a 8 m wide proscenium arch on a stage 5 m deep. We divide the stage into six areas and, for the sake of convenience, letter them A to F. We then ensure that we have two lanterns to cover each area. This is the basic principle adopted to make certain that actors are lit adequately (Figure 6).

However, it may be that the director is using his space in such a way that much of the action takes place in one area at three different times of the day. In this case we will need to use more than two lanterns to cover the particular area as we have to create mood as well as light the actors. It may be that there is bright sun shining out at one time of the day, so we will use a no. 3 straw colour or a no. 5 pale yellow filter. Colour filters are known by numbers which do not follow in any particular sequence, but the whole range is usually found in the manufacturer's catalogue. Later on, at night when the moon is shining, we may want no. 17, a steel blue colour.

When we have finally decided where we want to place the lanterns, and what colours we are going to use, it is essential to put it down on paper in a *layout plan*.

The *layout plan* is a plan of the stage showing the set, the furniture, and the lights. It is usual to show on the plan the type of lantern, and the colour each will have.

There are two methods of indicating types of lantern – one uses a diagram of the actual lantern to the same scale of the floor plan, and the other uses international symbols which indicate whether the lantern is a profile spot, a Fresnel spot, or whatever (Figure 7(a) and (b)).

It is also essential to have a *lighting schedule* (Figure 8) which numbers each lantern, states what type it is, what it is doing, what colour filters will be used with it, and into which circuit it is plugged.

Having got this far, the lighting designer should, during the final

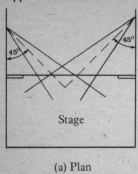

Stage

(a) Plan

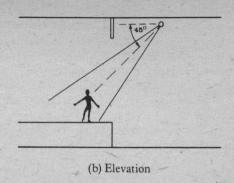

(b) Elevation

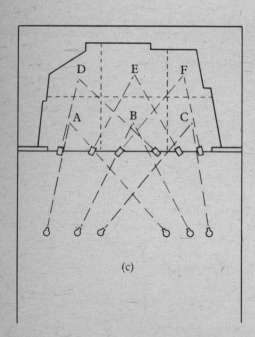

(c)

*Figure* 6  Lighting the actor

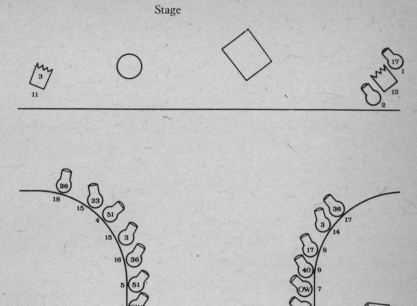

*Figure 7a*   **Lighting layout plan**

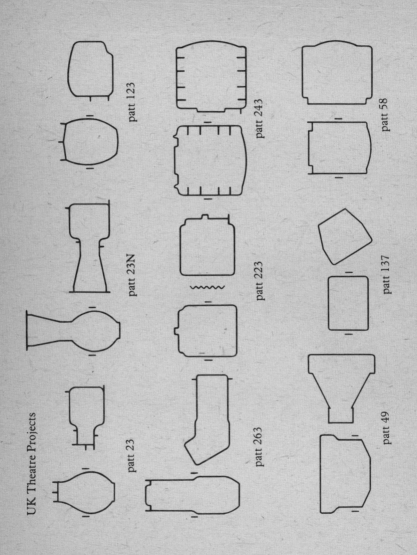

UK Theatre Projects

patt 123

patt 243

patt 58

patt 23N

patt 223

patt 137

patt 23

patt 263

patt 49

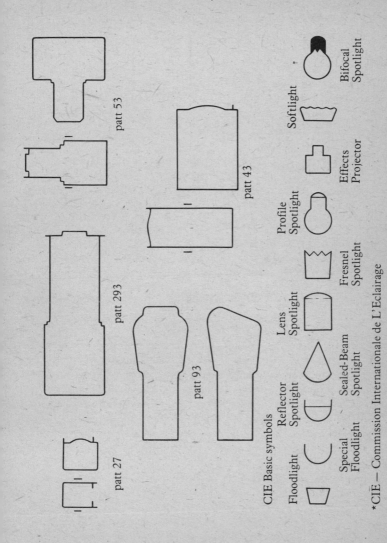

patt 53

patt 43

patt 293

patt 93

patt 27

Softlight

Bifocal
Spotlight

Effects
Projector

Profile
Spotlight

Fresnel
Spotlight

Lens
Spotlight

Sealed-Beam
Spotlight

CIE Basic symbols

Reflector
Spotlight

Special
Floodlight

Floodlight

*Figure 7b* Lantern symbols

*CIE — Commission Internationale de L'Eclairage

"WHERE THERE'S A WILL"

| No. | Type | Purpose | Colour | Circuit |
|-----|------|---------|--------|---------|
| 1 | patt 23N | Elizabeth effect | 17 | 1 |
| 2 | patt 23 | Miss Andrews | 10 | 2 |
| 3 | patt 23 | Diarist | OW | 3 |
| 4 | patt 23 | Douglas final effect | 51 | 4 |
| 5 | patt 23 | Douglas lectern | 51 | 5 |
| 6 | patt 23 | Girl reading | OW | 8 |
| 7 | patt 23 | Girl reading | OW | 8 |
| 8 | patt 23 | Dorothy L. Sayers | 17 | 7 |
| 9 | patt 23 | Nurse writing | 40 | 6 |
| 10 | patt 43 | Gallery effects | 3 | A |
| 11 | patt 123 | Acting area | 3 | 9 |
| 12 | patt 123 | Acting area | 3 | 9 |
| 13 | patt 23 | Acting area | 3 | 10 |
| 14 | patt 23 | Acting area | 3 | 10 |
| 15 | patt 23 | Nurses | 23 | 6 |
| 16 | patt 23 | Staff | 36 | 12 |
| 17 | patt 23 | Acting area | 36 | 11 |
| 18 | patt 23 | Acting area | 36 | 11 |

*Figure 8*   Lighting schedule

rehearsals, decide on his *cue synopsis*. A *lighting cue* refers to the moment when the lights change, a *cue state* refers to which lanterns are lit and at what dimmer setting after the cue has taken place. A cue synopsis can give the page number on which the cue occurs, what action is taking place on the stage, the cue number, the time it takes to carry out the cue, plus a note about the lighting effect you are trying to achieve (Figure 9).

It is a good idea to have a couple of spots shining on the front curtains when the audience comes into the auditorium. These dressing lights, or 'tab warmers', do just what the name implies – give a pleasant warm glow to the curtains and immediately put the audience into a receptive mood.

Now that the lighting is designed, all that is left to do is to rig it and get it operating! The majority of amateur theatre companies will get in to their theatre only a short time before the first performance, and it is only then that the designer's theory will be turned into practice. The lanterns can be rigged in position from the lighting layout and roughly

| Cue | Speed | Effect |
|-----|-------|--------|
|  | ½ hour | Preset on stage Houselights |
| 1 | 20 secs | Build to Chorus |
| 2 | Snap | Gallery effect on Constable |
| 3 | 3 secs | Build to Diarist |
| 4 | Snap | X-fade Constable to Elizabeth |
| 5 | Snap | FBO |
| 6 | 5 secs | Build to Diarist and Elizabeth |
| 7 | 2 secs | X-fade to girls |
| 8 | 3 secs | X-fade to announcer |
| 9 | Snap | Fade announcer |
| 10 | Snap | Build to Elizabeth |
| 11 | 10 secs | X-fade to Andrews |
| 12 | 3 secs | Fade Andrews |
| 13 | Snap | Build to Elizabeth and Douglas |
| 14 | 10 secs | FBO |
| 15 | 4 secs | Build to Diarist |
| 16 | 10 secs | X-fade to Lectern |
| 17 | 5 secs | Build to Girls |
| 18 | 5 secs | X-fade to reading Girls |
| 19 | 3 secs | Build to Douglas |
| 20 | 10 secs | Build to Girls |
| 21 | 15 secs | X-fade to Diarist |
| 22 | 10 secs | X-fade to Girls chorus |
| 23 | 10 secs | FBO |
|  |  | Houselights and preset |
|  |  | Interval |

*Figure 9*    Cue synopsis

focused from the lighting schedule. If the lanterns over the stage are rigged first the lighting men can usually move on to rig the front-of-house lanterns when the scenery arrives. Where temporary cables are being used to carry power to the lanterns, take care that they are out of the way of the audience, and tied off neatly. Always keep temporary cables tidy as it is surprising how easily even as few as half a dozen begin to get out of hand, especially near to the point at which they are plugged in. Remember that spilled drinks can play havoc with your lighting equipment so if you must take liquid refreshments into the lighting box make sure that you keep them well away from the board.

Once all the lanterns are up and working, it's possible to start the *focusing*. Ideally, focusing needs a minimum of three people, one to operate the lighting board and one to alter the settings of the lanterns and the designer on the stage to ensure that the lantern is pointing in the right direction and that the beam is the right size, to check that it will light the actor and to see where the beam hits the scenery. It is the designer who must give instructions to alter the settings of the lanterns.

Now comes the acid test for the lighting designer. With the focusing of individual lanterns completed, the *lighting rehearsal* will give him the opportunity to see whether the actual lighting produces the picture that up to now has existed only in his imagination. The designer will usually be sitting in the theatre with the director and the scenic designer and will call for the lanterns that he wants to build up each cue state. There should be an assistant stage manager or a member of the cast to walk around the stage as requested so that the director can check not only that the light levels on different parts of the stage are correct, but also that the actors are correctly lit at all times. Having got an accurate cue state, the operator on the board is asked to plot it and will write down the intensity setting of every lighting channel that is being used. Once the first cue state is done they can go on to the second, and repeat the process until eventually all the lighting cues are plotted.

Now that modern lighting controls make it possible to have the control board in the auditorium, there are no longer communication problems between the operator and the lighting designer. And with memory systems, the tedium of plotting every lighting setting of a large control system disappears as all that has to be done is to press the record switch and the plot is instantly recorded in the memory, ready to be recalled at will.

It may be that at this stage the operator will want to draw up a *lighting plot*, that is, a list of changes that he has to make for each cue, and the actions that he has to take between cues (Figure 10).

The technical and dress rehearsals give the designer the opportunity to see whether his design has worked, and also an opportunity to make changes if necessary. The dress rehearsal is often the first time that the lights have been on the actors in costume, and this can make a difference to the intensity levels that are needed, or sometimes necessitate changes in colour. It it unwise, however, for the designer to stop a dress rehearsal. These should be organised like performances, with the stage manager in charge, and it is better to make notes during the rehearsal and effect the changes afterwards.

When the curtain rises on the performance, the lighting designer's job

## LIGHTING PLOT

| Q | Time | 1 | 2 | 3 | 4 | 5 | 6 | 7 | 8 | 9 | 10 | 11 | 12 | A | Preset Master |
|---|------|---|---|---|---|---|---|---|---|---|----|----|----|---|---------------|
| | Preset | | | | | | | | | | 6 | | | | Red |
| H/L | & preset out | | | | | | | | | | | | | | |
| 1 | 20 secs | | | | | | | | 7 | 6 | 10 | 6 | | | Build green |
| 2 | Snap | | | | | | | | • | • | • | • | | 10 | |
| 3 | 3 secs | | | 7 | | | | | • | • | • | • | | • | |
| 4 | Snap | 10 | | | | | | | • | • | • | • | | 0 | |
| 5 | Snap | 0 | | 0 | | | | | 0 | 0 | 0 | 0 | | | Fade green |
| 6 | 5 secs | 10 | | 6 | | | | | | | | | | | Build red |
| 7 | 2 secs | • | | 0 | | | | | | | | 7 | | | |
| 8 | 3 secs | 0 | | | | | | | | | 7 | 7 | 4 | 10 | X-fade to green |
| 9 | Snap | | | | | | | | | | • | • | • | 0 | |
| 10 | Snap | 10 | | | | | | | | | • | • | • | | |
| 11 | 10 secs | 0 | 7 | | | | | | | | 4 | 3 | 4 | | X-fade to red |
| 12 | 3 secs | | 0 | | | | | | | | 8 | 6 | 8 | | X-fade to green |
| 13 | Snap | 10 | | | 8 | | | | | 4 | 4 | 4 | 0 | | X-fade to red |
| 14 | 10 secs | 0 | | | 0 | | | | | 0 | 0 | 0 | | | Fade red |
| 15 | 4 secs | | | 7 | | | | | | | | | | | Build red |
| 16 | 10 secs | | | 0 | | 7 | | | 3 | 3 | 3 | | | | X-fade to green |
| 17 | 5 secs | | | | | 0 | | | • | • | 5 | | | | |
| 18 | 5 secs | | | | | | | | 6 | 0 | 0 | | | | |
| 19 | 3 secs | | | | | | | | • | 6 | | | | | |
| 20 | 10 secs | | | | | | | | • | • | 5 | | | | |
| 21 | 15 secs | | | 5 | | | | | 5 | | 0 | 0 | | | X-fade to red |
| 22 | 10 secs | | | • | | | | | 7 | 9 | 9 | 9 | 6 | | X-fade to green |
| 23 | 10 secs | | | 0 | | | | | 0 | 0 | 0 | 0 | 0 | | Fade green |
| | Preset | | | | | | | | | | 6 | | | | Red |
| | H/L | | | | | | | | | | | | | | |

*Figure 10*   Lighting plot

is over – at least from the design aspect. But in many amateur companies the designer will also be the operator for the show, so he will be busy throughout the run. However, if any changes are made during the dress rehearsals or the first night of the show, he must not forget to keep the paperwork up-to-date, for this means that someone else is always able to operate the board should the need arise.

A final word. An excellent way of finding out what lighting can do is to spend time simply playing about with lanterns to see what effects can be created. Go into an empty theatre, switch on a lantern, try altering the focus, try using a gobo, see what colours do, see what colours in combination do. In short, experiment with the tools of your trade so that when you can see in your head the effect you want to create, you know how to create it with the equipment available.

### Exercise 1 – Lighting design
Work out a lighting design for any one act of John Mortimer's *Voyage Round My Father.*

# 7

# Design

'In the acquisition of a script, and the excitement of reading it alone where the author's words conjure up an image to be interpreted in a three-dimensional living picture, is where the art of the designer's work begins. His first job is to make himself very familiar with the play, musical, opera, or whatever it is that he has been commissioned to work on. Then he must formulate in his own mind ideas of how it could look visually. This preliminary work is essential to form his original concept.

After this period his meetings and discussions with the director, his interpretation of the director's ideas, and the personal relationship and rapport set up with the director are, in many ways, the most stimulating, creative, and enjoyable part of the early planning of any production.

Many directors, having once formed this close-knit personal linking of two minds, keep their relationship going for perhaps all of their productions as it develops into a shared language and mutual trust. However, it can be equally stimulating to both director and designer to start off freshly on a new relationship for each job, and therefore to have the added stimulus of different ideas. It's very exciting, at the first meeting between director and designer, to find that the visual stage picture is the same for both, without adjustment.

Nowadays, particularly, with the cost of raw materials, and the fact that the basic function of the designer is invariably to create a broad picture visible from some distance, he must very quickly be realistic and consider what budget and resources are available to carry out his dream-like images. But this is not such a bad thing as it is often more stimulating for the audience to have to work with their visual imagination to conjure up the surroundings of place or time of the play they are watching, and if the designer can help in this, without underlining every detail, so much the better. If it is a period piece the costumes and props can tell us a great deal about the status, style, and time of the characters, so it is not essential to have too much scenery. And lighting must play a very important part in creating the atmosphere of what is seen.

All these means are available to the designer to make up the picture he is trying to create, and must be used to their maximum effect, but as he talks and plans with all the various people concerned he must hold on firmly to the original thoughts he had at the beginning of the venture.'

**Michael Eve**
*Senior designer, ATV*

When evolving the design of the play to be performed consideration must be given, first of all, to two major factors:
1   The nature of the acting area, and
2   The set that is to be built, or placed, upon it.
After that it will be necessary to design and make, or to acquire by borrowing, hire or purchase, suitable props with which to furnish the set. Finally, costumes, lighting and make-up must all be slotted in to the style of the overall design plan.

The director will usually decide, in general terms, what he wants the production to look like, but it is up to the designer to turn his ideas into three-dimensional reality by working with him in an imaginative and creative partnership.

Many amateur companies tend to be conservative about their acting area. Since most of them perform in village halls which have a raised, curtained stage at one end they find it an obvious option to use the picture frame proscenium arch with a box- or curtain-set behind it. But this is very limiting. Some plays – especially pantomime, music hall and realistic domestic drama – lend themselves to proscenium arch presentation, but many can look fresh and exciting if the acting area is kept more open and flexible.

Even in a hall with a raised stage this is perfectly possible. Figure 11 shows a few alternative methods of using the space. Steps are necessary, and rostra desirable, to make the possibilities more wide-ranging.

If the play is to be produced in a hall without a stage, the possibilities are greater, but it is then absolutely essential, not merely desirable, for the society to invest in a collection of rostra which will:
1   Make it possible to create various arrangements of raised levels on which the actors can work; and

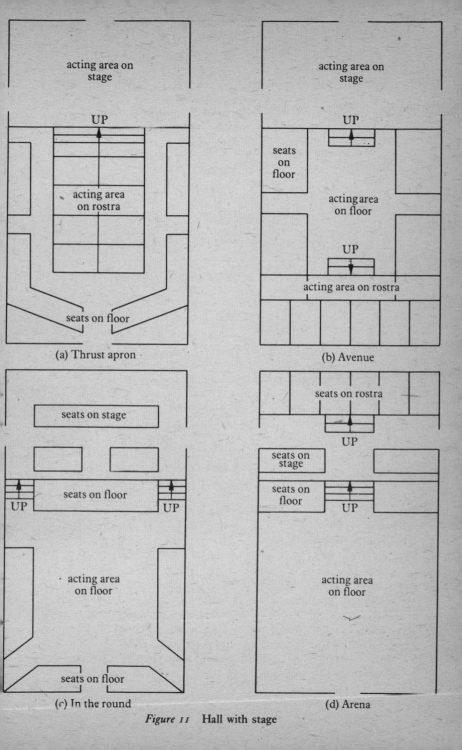

(a) Thrust apron

acting area on stage

UP

acting area on rostra

seats on floor

(b) Avenue

acting area on stage

UP

seats on floor

acting area on floor

UP

acting area on rostra

(c) In the round

seats on stage

UP UP

seats on floor

acting area on floor

seats on floor

(d) Arena

seats on rostra

UP

seats on stage

seats on floor

UP

acting area on floor

*Figure 11* Hall with stage

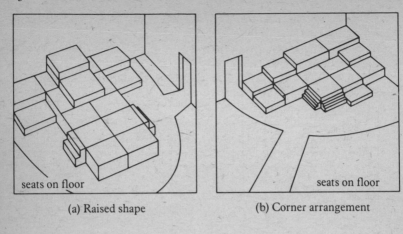

(a) Raised shape        (b) Corner arrangement

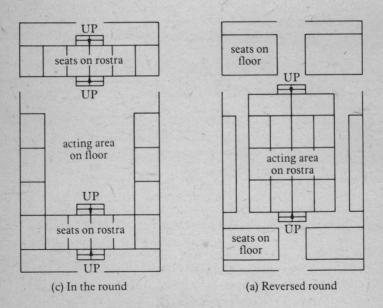

(c) In the round        (a) Reversed round

*Figure 12*  Hall without stage

2 Combine to make flexible seating arrangements, all of which will give satisfactory vision.

Figure 12 shows several alternatives.

A combination of twelve large rostra, in proportions 6:4:3, plus four smaller, 6:4:1½, will give vast permutations of possibilities. Alternatively, use four-foot modules, starting with eight at 4:4:1, and adding four at 4:4:6 and four at 4:4:2 when funds will allow. Remember that they will need to be linked by small blocks or step units.

It's also important to bear in mind that there must be space available to store them when not in use, and that since they will need to be moved quite often, they must be light though sturdy, and preferably fitted with hand-holes.

When the decision is being made as to how to arrange the rostra for the most attractive acting area there are several questions that must be asked.

1 Will the play benefit from being acted on several levels?
2 Is visibility satisfactory?
3 Is there sufficient concealed space for the placing of scenery and props when they are not needed on stage?
4 Is there sufficient concealed space for the actors waiting to make their entrances.
5 Are the exits strategically placed?

If the play is to be performed in a less conventional 'theatre' – in a church, perhaps, or out of doors – rostra will again be useful, both for raising the actors or the audience so that the action can be easily seen, and for delineating various spaces to clarify the action by signifying place.

In any of these types of acting area book-flats and screen-flats add to the practicability and visual richness of the production, especially if they are reversible and decorated on both sides.

*Book-flats* are two rectangular flats of the same size hinged together (Figure 13b). Two book-flats joined form a *screen* (Figure 13c). Alternatively, one large flat and two small ones can be linked with battens to make a *screen background* to facilitate the exits and entrances of the actors.

*The proscenium arch* was originally evolved as a frame for the stage which would divide the actors from the audience (Figure 14a). In some halls and theatres today the archway is a permanent structure. In others it can be a temporary arrangement of flats. Alternatively, curtaining can be used to create a frame when necessary.

*A box set* is a standard interior set showing three walls of a room with the fourth wall removed so that the audience can see in. It is usually realistic and representational. It is very demanding as far as work and

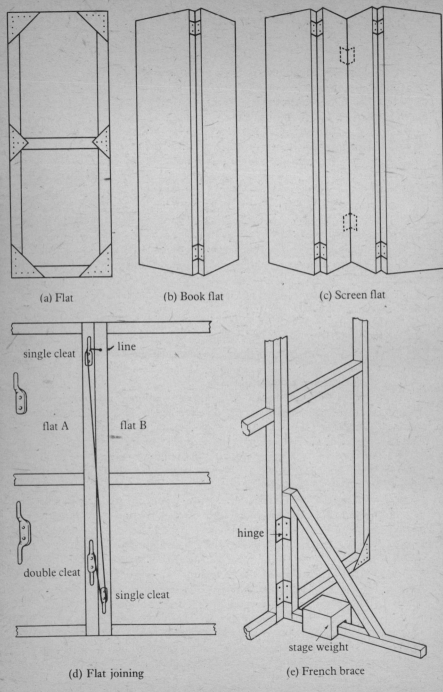

(a) Flat　　　　(b) Book flat　　　　(c) Screen flat

single cleat　line

flat A　flat B

double cleat

single cleat

(d) Flat joining

hinge

stage weight

(e) French brace

*Figure 13*　Flat construction

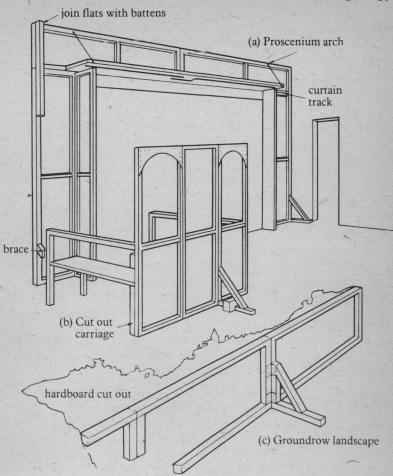

join flats with battens

(a) Proscenium arch

curtain track

brace

(b) Cut out carriage

hardboard cut out

(c) Groundrow landscape

*Figure 14* Using flats as scenery

materials are concerned, requiring the construction of upwards of about twenty flats of various shapes and sizes. Basic flats are wooden frames covered with either canvas or hardboard. Canvas is more expensive and more tricky for amateur craftsmen to handle, but the final result tends to look better and last longer. Interior flats are usually rectangular, with variations for door, window and fireplace.

## Flat construction (Figure 13a)

Cut two uprights to the required height. Cut three cross-pieces – or four if the flat is over 3.5 m high – to the required width.

Butt the joints together and fasten with corrugated wood joiners.

Fasten triangular strengthening pieces into position at the corners making sure that the frame is kept absolutely square.

Cover with hardboard fastened with panel pins, or stretch canvas tightly over the frame and fasten with glue and staples.

## Bracing flats

In order to keep flats firmly upright you can either buy stage braces from a theatrical supplier, or make *French braces*, using 50 × 25 mm timber and strengthening pieces of plywood (Figure 13e). A useful way of fastening French braces is to use hinges to enable them to fold against the back of the flat. If you want to remove the brace from the flat the pin of the hinge can be taken out and replaced with a piece of wire which makes it possible to separate a piece of wire which makes it possible to separate flat and brace at will. Keep the brace in place with a stage weight, hired, bought, or home-made.

## Joining flats (Figure 13d)

The best way is by roping and cleating. Every flat should have rope fastened to the top of one upright – always the same upright on each flat – and this should be matched by a cleat on the next upright. The rope is led from one flat over the top cleat on the next, taken round a bottom cleat on the first flat, and then tied off on the bottom cleat of the second flat. The ropes and cleats should be fastened to the uprights at the same height so that a flat can be joined to any other flat with ease.

When the flats have been erected and joined together to create the required shape, and doors, windows and fireplaces have been added, all that remains to be done is the decoration of the set. However, it is vital to check that all the fixed parts are absolutely sturdy, and that all the moveable parts move easily. There is nothing worse than watching actors struggling with doors that won't open, or closing a window gently only to start the set shaking uncontrollably.

'Rose Ransome' —
Victorian melodrama
Act II sc. i and ii.
Judge's box on truck
witness boxes raised
dark oak — rich red
velvet
Gaol — painted stone
— flats
heavy door with bars.
Court lit sc. i Gaol lit
sc. ii

(a) Preliminary sketch and notes

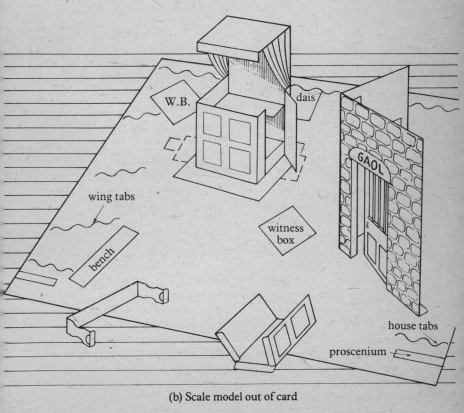

(b) Scale model out of card

*Figure 15* Designer's dossier (Designed by Jane Whittle)

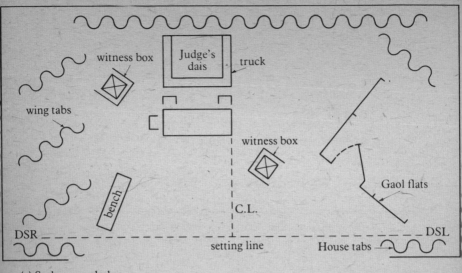

(c) Scale ground plan

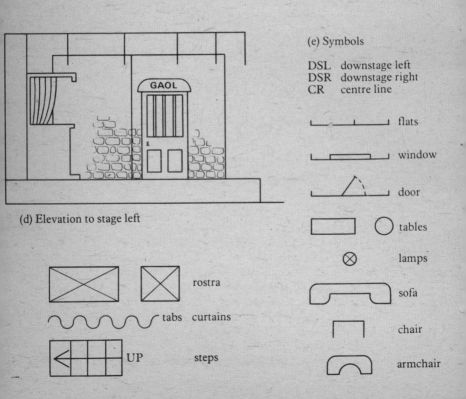

(d) Elevation to stage left

(e) Symbols

DSL downstage left
DSR downstage right
CR centre line

flats

window

door

tables

lamps

sofa

chair

armchair

rostra

tabs curtains

UP steps

A simpler way of staging a play within a box-type acting area is to use a 'curtain set', consisting of wings, back-curtain and borders, combined with either a painted backcloth or a cyclorama, and a combination of cut-outs and groundrows.

*A cyclorama* is a large area at the back of the stage which can be lit to simulate the sky. It can be a fabric drape, suspended from curved battens, or a plaster wall. Its effectiveness depends largely upon imaginative lighting.

*Cut-Outs* are free-standing flats shaped either like natural objects – trees and bushes, for instance – or like architectural features – small buildings, perhaps – or like internal features – for example, a witness box, or a pew (Figure 14b).

*Groundrows* are flats which are placed sideways on the stage, and are cut to represent features of the skyline or horizon – a line of hills, or roof-tops (Figure 14c).

This sort of setting is most effective for productions which do not aim at realism, but benefit from a colourful and dramatic setting. Pantomime is the prime example, but it is also eminently suitable for operetta, revue and musical comedy.

Another sort of stylised setting can be made from scaffolding.

## The designer's precedure

The nature of the acting area and the overall style of the production having been decided in a first consultation with the director, the steps the designer will take in creating his design will be as follows. He will:

1 Re-read the play;
2 Research the period, if necessary, with specific reference to the script;
3 Consider the equipment of the society, its budget, and the nature and extent of the help available to him;
4 Make preliminary sketches and notes (Figure 15a);
5 Have a second consultation with the director;
6 Make (*a*) a scale model of the set from card (Figure 15b)
       (*b*) scale ground plans for the stage staff (Figure 15c), and
       (*c*) elevation drawings in time for the first rehearsal (Figure 15d and e)
7 Consult with (*a*) the lighting designer
              (*b*) the costume designer
8 Cooperate with the stage management team in making up lists of

equipment required – furniture, scenery, props, costumes, and so on;
9    Assist in the building and decorating of the set;
10   Supervise the dressing of the set, through the agency of the stage manager;
11   Attend dress rehearsals and be prepared to make any necessary last-minute adjustments.

## Exercise 1 – Designing the set

Choose any one of the longer dramatic excerpts reprinted in this book and, bearing in mind the facilities of your own society, create a design for it to be staged;
(a) within a box- or curtain-set, and
(b) in an open acting area, using rostra.
Illustrate your design with a dossier.

# Props

There are three kinds of props:
1    Scene (or set) props – including furniture, carpeting, trees, etc;
2    Dressing props, used to decorate the set rather than to further the action – including curtains, pictures, flowers, etc; and
3    Hand props, which are small items used by the actors to reveal character, further the action, or facilitate stage business – including food, cigarettes, weapons, books, etc.

Scene props are particularly important since, in an open production without a box set or scenery, they can be used to denote *place*, *period*, and *life-style*, especially when combined with good lighting. For instance, a lavish chandelier can conjure up an elaborate ballroom, a kitchen range can indicate a humble working-class living room, a wind-bent shrub a lonely heath, and so on.

In the operetta *Don't Blame The Bard*, written for the Salisbury Festival of the Arts, the action spanned four centuries, but had to take place in a curtain set. One central prop managed to set the scene during the time progression. Starting as an Elizabethan players' cart, transforming to a seventeenth century boudoir bed and then a nineteenth century boat, it always indicated, quite clearly, period, place and style. Costumes, wigs and make-up were kept strictly in period, and no other scenery was necessary to clarify the action (Figure 16).

Amateur companies should be flexible and imaginative enough to consider the possibility of using scene props, instead of built scenery, to

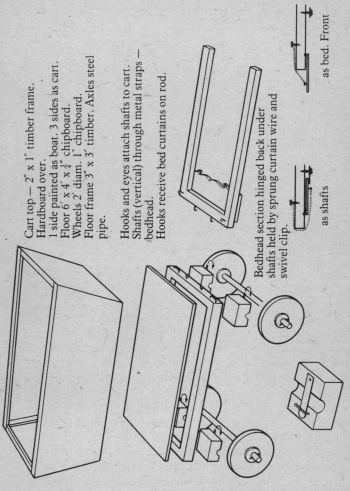

Cart top — 2″ x 1″ timber frame.
Hardboard over.
1 side painted as boat. 3 sides as cart.
Floor 6′ x 4′ x ¾″ chipboard.
Wheels 2′ diam. 1″ chipboard.
Floor frame 3″ x 3″ timber. Axles steel pipe.

Hooks and eyes attach shafts to cart.
Shafts (vertical) through metal straps — bedhead.
Hooks receive bed curtains on rod.

Bedhead section hinged back under shafts held by sprung curtain wire and swivel clip.

as shafts

as bed. Front

Four swivel clips retain axles.
Wheels turn on axles.

CONSTRUCTION DIAGRAM. Cart/Boat/Boudoir bed.
(carries 6 adults)

*Figure 16* One central, versatile prop

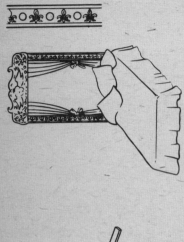

BOUDOIR BED — gilt-painted bedhead is the under side of shafts, with flap up, slotted into base section of cart.
Pale blue silk curtains on rod behind.
Pale blue silk cover — gold silk cushions.

Bedhead can serve as window exit.
All changes performed by cast.
All props kept in cart.

Designs by Jane Whittle for 'Don't Blame the Bard' copyright 1974 by Richard Shephard & Jennifer Curry.

CART — painted to look like wood — back section may be hinged to open.

BOAT painted red, black, white. Top section one side. Mast — sail attached — held by sailor.

*Figure 16*   One central, versatile prop

set the scene. This is not only in step with current practice in the professional theatre, it also pleases the audience in two ways, first by allowing them to make an imaginative response to the design, and secondly by keeping scene changes swift and simple so that they don't slow down or otherwise interfere with the movement of the plot.

Props can be bought, hired, borrowed or made. It is absolutely essential, however, that they should be accurate as far as period and character are concerned, that they should fit in with the style of the production, and that they should function smoothly.

The designer, or one of his team, must research the exact time in which the play is set to make sure that none of the props is an anachronism. This can be an irksome and time-consuming job but it must be done thoroughly. It does not, of course, apply only to period plays. The design of everyday objects changes with remarkable speed. For instance, Alan Bennett's play, *Getting On*, is set in the early seventies. In one scene George reads, and cuts up, a copy of *The Daily Express*. A current copy of this paper cannot be used since its shape and size have changed completely in recent years so somehow an old one has to be tracked down, or a very clever facsimile made. It is detail of this nature which is the hallmark of a meticulous play production, and the stage staff must not balk at the work involved.

Similarly the designer must research the characters carefully to make sure that their dressing props and hand props are true to type. The set must reflect the taste, temperament and interests of the people who are supposed to inhabit it, as must their personal possessions. A delicate, middle-class Victorian heroine would, for instance, dab her eyes with a lace-edged scrap of a handkerchief, not a large square of checked cotton. A poor labourer, about to have his television set reclaimed, would be unlikely to have his table laid with snowy linen, silver and crystal. The problem is to avoid stereotyping – no one wants the Victorian lady or the manual worker to become character clichés – but they must retain credibility.

All props must, of course, fit in with the overall design of the play. The designer and the director may have chosen a coherent 'look' based on a painting, film, or current fashion – or just an exciting visual idea. They may want a very realistic style – or one that works by suggestion and symbol. They may decide that the play should have a light, delicate look – or be rich and sombre. They may want it to look cool and subdued – or dazzle with vibrant colour like a field of poppies. Whatever their decision, all the props should be selected to match up to this picture as effectively as possible.

Note that while stage management is responsible for acquiring and organising props, the choosing or visualising of the props is the task of the design team. In fact, this is yet another shared job where total cooperation is necessary.

## Exercise 2 – Choosing props

Study carefully the scene from *An Ideal Husband* beginning on p. 107. Imagining that it is to be staged on a box set, make lists of:

1  all the set props, and
2  all the dressing props you consider necessary or desirable, as well as
3  all the hand props required by each character.

Add verbal descriptions and coloured sketches so that the stage management team will know exactly what you envisage.

# 8

# Costume

'I would hardly call myself primarily a Costume Designer, as I acted for many years before I got the chance to design any costumes – and that was only because I was directing the production at Chichester! Perhaps for that very reason my experience is more immediate and less complicated than that of someone who has done a great deal of the work. I did, though, train in art and I suppose I approached the designing of clothes very much as I would think about painting part of a picture. Costumes are, after all, only part of the entire concept of production; it's the face of the actor and not the costume that we generally want people to look at – unless of course a costume needs to make a particular effect. Also the actors themselves need to be comfortable in the clothes to do their work properly.

The Designer of course needs to study each character carefully from the text of the play before committing anything to paper. The next thing I did was rush out and buy a number of good illustrated books on the subject. The silhouette and shape is more important than the detail in giving a sense of period.

The better the person making the clothes is at cutting, the better the costumes will look. But in some cases it is advisable to hire the clothes – they will then have a more "lived in" look. Some wardrobes can even be purchased cheaply from market stalls, but you need to make sure they're clean before anyone puts them on!

There is a story of the old American actor who was in a production of *Death of a Salesman* in London. He came down to the footlights during dress rehearsal and said: "Look, these pyjamas I have been given to wear are really smart but I do have a nice old pair at home which might be more in character."'

**Keith Michell**
*Director, actor and artist*

Costume must fulfil several functions, quite apart from the obvious one of simply clothing the character.

First of all, it must convey a great deal of information to the audience about the person wearing it. This will include information about

(a) the period in which the character is living;

(b) his status;

(c) his age;

(d) his temperament;

(e) his tastes.

Since, in most cases, the audience will see the actor before they hear him speak, their first impression of him will be a visual one. For this reason the signals given by his appearance must be absolutely accurate. If the actor's appearance gives false information because his clothes and personal props are wrong he will have an uphill struggle during the course of the play to correct that original misapprehension.

Secondly, costume must fit in with the visual style or 'look' of the play as conceived by the director and designer, and be of an appropriate colour, line and movement.

Thirdly, costume must be practicable:

(a) It must be comfortable and easy to wear, enabling the actor to move freely and carry out any actions required of him by the script or director. Plastics and PVC, as well as crêpe soles, should be avoided as they tend to squeak on stage.

(b) It must be easy to get on and off quickly in rapid scene changes, and must be manageable by the actor unaided if backstage help is limited.

(c) It must be cleanable – at least those parts near neck and wrists which are liable to become soiled by make-up.

(d) It must be sturdy enough to stand up to the wear and tear of an over-crowded dressing room.

There are several ways of acquiring costumes:

1  They can be hired from theatrical costumiers. Many of these advertise in *Amateur Stage*, but local ones can be tracked down through the Yellow Pages of your telephone directory. Alternatively, you may find that your local professional theatre operates a hiring service, or will come to a private agreement with you.

2  They can be bought cheaply from jumble sales, stalls, and second-hand or antique shops.

3  They can be borrowed from members of the society and their friends.

4  They can be made.

There are advantages and disadvantages in all of these.

Hiring costumes is expensive, and often they arrive late and in a tatty condition. Sometimes they don't fit properly, despite carefully taken measurements, and need a great deal of fiddly alteration. What's more, since they cannot be tailor-made for a specific production they may not look right for the set design. However, if the play is a period piece with a large cast, hiring may well be the only option open to the society.

Buying second-hand clothes can be a good idea, and economical too, if the wardrobe team is imaginative and industrious, knows exactly what it is looking for, and is able to transform purchases by clever cutting and adapting. But many hours have to be spent both on the search for suitable clothes, and the work required to create stage costumes from them.

Borrowing clothes works well if the play in production has a con- temporary or comparatively recent setting, and has the distinct advantage of costing nothing. But the clothes must be very well looked after, and returned to their owners in pristine condition.

Undoubtedly, the best way of acquiring clothes is to make them, provided that the wardrobe team possesses skilled dressmakers with a flair for cutting, a knowledge of style, and the time necessary for the work involved. Though it is expensive to buy material in the first place, money spent in this way, as opposed to that spent on hiring, is a useful outlay, since the society can gradually build up an extensive wardrobe which can be used again and again with a little alteration and modification, and can even earn money if it is hired out when not in use. Two things to remember are:

1  If a company creates a new and extensive wardrobe it must have good storage facilities;
2  Few scripts require the characters to wear brand new clothes – do let them be worn before the production so that they can get that 'lived-in' look.

Each company must make its own decisions about how to acquire costumes, and these will depend upon budget, manpower, the period of the play, the size of the cast, and so on. Most will probably find that the best solution is to use a combination of hiring, making and borrow- ing, as is common practice in many professional theatres.

It is important to consider, when choosing the play, that historical costume is expensive, partly because of the intricacy of many of the styles, partly because of the enormous amount of material required for full long skirts, cloaks, puffed sleeves, ruffles and houppelandes. However, it is possible to make quite ordinary material look rich and sumptuous by using a few simple tricks with sprays of paint and glitter, and encrust- ing with pasta shapes, lentils, seeds, beads, cereals, and wine gums, to simulate an exciting and bejewelled texture. And it's no longer necessary to spend hours sewing. The modern wardrobe mistress is as knowledgeable about the various types of adhesive as the different sorts of silks, and as happy with a staple gun as she is with a sewing machine.

It must always be remembered that the theatre, as opposed to television and films, entertains across a distance. Therefore it's more important for the costume designer to concentrate on shape and silhouette, rather than on detail. The shape of a costume is of supreme importance. It is shape that indicates period, so it must be absolutely clean-cut and distinctive (Figure 17).

To capture the distinctive line it is necessary to research carefully. Fortunately, there are many valuable sources of information. The most obvious and easily accessible of these are books. Your library is almost certain to have a good collection. Art galleries are also helpful. For instance, the paintings of Nicholas Hilliard, William Hogarth, Joshua Reynolds, Thomas Gainsborough and John Singer Sargent – to name only a tiny sample – are all valuable guides to the clothes of their period.

But museums, especially museums of costume, like those at Bath, Manchester and the costume department at the Victoria and Albert Museum, London, are the most helpful, since there you can see an original article in its three-dimensional reality, and can often get advice and special facilities for study.

Once you have recognised and defined the period line you will realise that it depends to a large extent on the weight and texture of the material, and the undergarments concealed by the costume.

Fortunately, it is possible to find among the plethora of modern, man-made fabrics several which will match up with those of earlier periods, though it may well be that they will be tracked down among furnishing fabrics and curtaining materials rather than in the dressmaking department. Remember that before the advent of central heating and heated cars, buses and trains, our predecessors had to wear much heavier clothes to keep warm, and that they did not have synthetic fibres.

It is important, though, to be wary about the colours of modern fabrics. Since dyeing techniques have changed drastically over the years some of the shades now available look quite wrong when made up into period costume. In fact, colour is a very important consideration in costume design. As well as being right for the period it must:

(*a*) fit in with the designer's general colour scheme;
(*b*) be reasonably becoming to the actor wearing it;
(*c*) be appropriate to the role, matching up both with the character that

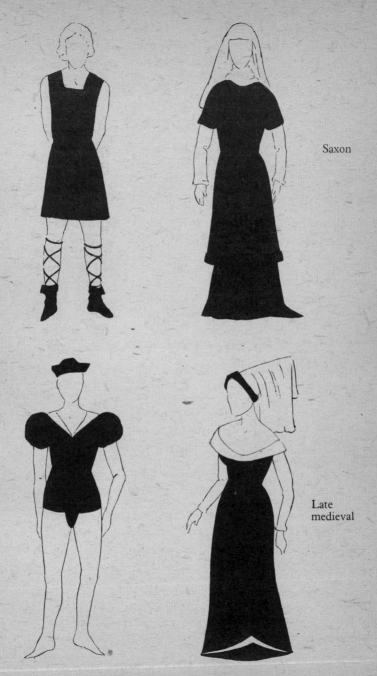

Saxon

Late
medieval

*Figure 17* Costume silhouette

Elizabethan

Restoration

*Figure 17*   Costume silhouette

Victorian

*Figure 17* Costume silhouette

is being played and his significance in the play as a whole. (For instance, a minor character should not be allowed to become the pivot of the audience's attention simply on account of the vibrant colour of his outfit.)

(*d*) take light well – most shades of blue, for example, are notoriously difficult to light.

It is impossible to create the correct outline for period costume unless the appropriate corsetry and underwear of the time is worn, and this must never be neglected. Since it will also affect the way the actors move, stand and sit, it should be used whenever possible during the rehearsal period.

Similarly, both shoes and hats affect movement, stance and carriage, so they must be chosen carefully and worn frequently during the preparation of the production. Footwear poses particular problems to the wardrobe department because a comfortable fit, though so vital, is rarely achieved if boots or shoes are hired. Fortunately it is often possible, in many cases, to adapt the actor's own shoes (Figure 18). For instance, for Greek or Roman plays, low-heeled sandals can be used, or made from soles with lengths of thonging attached. For the medieval period felt shapes can be stuck or stitched to plimsolls. Women wearing concealing long skirts can wear simple flat ballet pumps, or plain court shoes decorated with buttons, buckles or bows. For men, either Wellington boots or leather boots can easily be adapted to fit in with many periods, and ordinary round-toe, elastic-sided casual shoes can be given the addition of a high tongue of stiffened felt, plus a buckle, for an eighteenth century effect. It is simply a matter of studying the footwear of our own period, and studying pictures of the footwear of the period of the play, and working out what can be done, with a few basic materials and objects, plus a certain amount of skill, to transform the one into the other.

In most amateur dramatic societies the costume designer will also fill the role of wardrobe mistress, and will probably have a team of several 'sewing ladies' to help with making the costumes. She will need to have:

(*a*) a certain amount of artistic flair;

(*b*) a basic knowledge of, and interest in, stage costume;

(*c*) a reasonable competency at cutting, sewing, and modern construction and decorative techniques; and

(*d*) organisational ability.

After the first production meeting, the procedure of the costume designer/wardrobe mistress will be as follows. She must:

1 re-read the play;

2 research the period, with specific reference to the script;

3 consider the society's existing wardrobe, its budget, and the help available, then decide what will have to be made and what can be hired, borrowed or bought;

4 make preliminary sketches and notes;

5 have a second consultation with the director and designer, take – and keep for future reference – measurements of all the members of the cast, and order any costumes to be hired;

The required measurements are

(*a*) length from the nape of the neck to the waist,

(*b*) length from the waist to the hem of the garment,

(*c*) length of the shoulder seam,

(*d*) length from the shoulder to the elbow,

(*e*) length from the elbow to the wrist,

(*f*) length from the centre of the back to the top of the armhole seam,

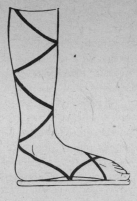

Sandal, made
from sole with
thonging

Boot, with
decorative felt
cuff added

Shoe with added
tongue and buckle

Medieval 'crakowe'
made from felt
stuck on to plimsoll

*Figure 18*   **Footwear**

    (*g*)  circumference of chest, waist, hips and base of the neck,

    (*h*)  for trousers, the length of the inside and outside leg seam;

6   provide, or supervise the provision of, necessary items of rehearsal costume;

7   make detailed coloured drawings of every costume to be worn by each actor, complete with illustrated lists of all the required accessories – hats, shoes, gloves, bags, underwear, etc. – and attach patterns of the materials to be used wherever possible (Figure 19). If any fabric is to be given special decorative treatment enlarged sketches should be made, with notes of the method of ornamentation to be used, for the benefit of the wardrobe team;

8   share out the work of making, altering and acquiring the costumes among the wardrobe team, arrange interim fittings for the actors, and make sure that all the clothes and accessories are ready by the date stipulated by the director;

9   attend dress rehearsals to see that the actors are happy and comfortable in their clothes, and that the designer and director are satisfied with the finished look of the costumes;

10  check over each actor's costume in good time before each show to make sure that it is complete and in good order;

11  do any running repairs or sprucing-up required between shows. There should always be an iron, ironing board, dry cleaning kit and mending kit in the dressing room, complete with pins, stapler, adhesives and iron-on mending tape, for instant repairs;

12  keep the costumes in well-organised order backstage when they are not being used;

13  make sure that adequate help is available at the right time and in the right place for any actors who need help with a quick change during the course of the play;

14  as soon as possible after the play's run has ended, return to their owners items which have been borrowed or hired, in impeccable condition, and store away the others, cleaned and repaired if necessary, in a dry, clean, moth-free place.

## Exercise 1 – Costume design

Design a full wardrobe, complete with accessories and underwear, for Elizabeth Proctor in *The Crucible* by Arthur Miller. Illustrate in colour, and annotate your designs. Add notes indicating which parts of her wardrobe you consider would need to be bought, hired or borrowed, and give directions as to how the others are to be made.

    A final note. A well-organised society will keep an up-to-date,

blonde wig-ringlets

dark red glass beads

straight black
hair or wig

sleeves rolled up

Joyce as Ruby in Acts I and II

dress — cerise satin
petticoat — white lace edge
black lace cap
black high heeled laced boots
wig and beads

as a gypsy in Act III

same
black fringed shawl over
red skirt over
black slippers
basket of apples

*Figure 19*    Costume drawings (Designed by Jane Whittle)

comprehensive and detailed list of the items in its wardrobe, preferably with illustrations and measurements of each costume. This will assist enormously in the smooth planning of each new production.

It is a fact worth considering that amateur dramatic societies can cut their costs and help each other extensively by swopping or hiring out items of costume, lighting, rostra and so on, and detailed lists of all the equipment they possess make this a much more practicable operation.

# 9

# Stage Make-up

'In simplistic terms, the essence of stage make-up must surely be to achieve, by technical and artistic means, the illusion that the actor is not wearing any make-up at all. So the question is posed: why wear any? Indeed, some actors today claim that they do not employ any of the paints and powders and pancakes that are on the market, and see no need for their application.

Yet there is a need. Many actors, by the very nature of their profession, do not choose to risk appearing before the public at a disadvantage, and to this end even a line drawn under the lower eye-lashes or the darkening of an eye-brow or a slight brush of colour on the cheeks constitutes make-up if this application accentuates or highlights the actor's face, in animation, under the bleaching effect of modern stage lighting which is so arranged and directed that practically all shadows, colours and details are eliminated, thus putting the artist at a considerable disadvantage. The application of make-up is therefore to help the actor help himself in presenting the best possible face to his audience by restoring shades, high-lights and mouldings to his features that have been washed out by the deadening effect of an intense battery of artificial stage light. The analogy of the blank canvas is often used. Unassisted by paints and artifices, the actor's face becomes, in consequence of the lighting, like a primed, white canvas waiting for the character to be "painted in".

The range of make-ups available for this "restoration process" is extensive and varied, but by and large there are two methods avail-able: the "dry" pancakes and panchromatic creams as advocated by Max Factor or the beautifully blended grease-paints from the Leichner and Kryolan range. But all these processes are ultimately identical in aim: they are there as an artificial help to the natural foundations of mouldings and lines and bone structure and facial anatomy and the natural creases and muscles of the face to enhance good looks, create beauty, and add to the realism of the character in terms of the particular play in rehearsal.

The performer's face must look right to the audience in the context of the production, its design, and the auditorium in which it is to be presented. If it looks right from the front then how the effect is achieved is really of little account. If it looks wrong then the craft of stage make-up should be studied and practised patiently and with discretion until the results are satisfactory and a sound understanding of the principles involved is achieved.'

**Michael Stroud**
*National Theatre Player*

It is vitally important, when considering stage make-up, to bear in mind that make-up is no substitute for good acting. The healthy young girl playing the part of an ailing old woman will only achieve the transformation if she thinks, feels and moves like an old woman. It is not enough for her to paint herself an appropriate face. Make-up is an aid to acting technique, not an alternative.

Two factors are absolutely crucial to good make-up. The first is a keen-eyed understanding of the bone structure and features of the face to be made up. The second is a knowledge of the way these are affected by light.

The keen actor should, whenever possible, learn how to apply his own make-up, and not leave the job to a make-up artist. To perfect the art he should study his own face very carefully in a well-lit mirror and practise making it up in many different ways. When he has a part in a play he should be thinking about his make-up during the rehearsal period and experimenting at home. Of course, the lights chosen by the lighting designer will affect the make-up but if changes have to be made at the dress rehearsal they will probably be minor changes of tone and emphasis rather than the creation of a whole new look. Remember that during the production meetings the director will have discussed with his designers the visual style of the play, and this too will have a bearing on make-up, so before you start work on your face you should find out what decisions have been taken, whether the look is to be stylised or naturalistic, highly-coloured or delicate, robust or fragile. You should also know all about the part you are to play and make sure that the make-up is appropriate. For instance, the skin colour and texture of a farm labourer will look very different from that of a coal-miner or lawyer. The face of an eighteenth century lady of fashion will look very different from that of a girl student of today, mainly because their life-styles are so different. It is also true that character and experience often etch lines on the face – an anxious, nervous woman, or an embittered one, may look quite different than she would have done if her life had been serene and secure.

Basically, there are two types of make-up styles – 'straight' and 'character'. *Straight make-up* serves only to make the face look on stage much as it does off stage, simply preventing it from being bleached by the lights or losing delineation through distance. *Character make-up* changes the face, making it look older or younger perhaps, or giving it different racial characteristics, or specific features, like a spreading nose or receding chin.

Every actor should build up his own basic make-up kit, though the society should also possess a communal make-up box for general use. There are now various types of make-up available. *Greasepaint* can be obtained either 'hard' in sticks, or 'soft' in tubes. It is applied by hand and has to be 'set' with powder. *Pancake* comes in hard cakes, is applied with a damp sponge, does not need to be powdered, and, being water-soluble, can be washed off instead of being removed with cream. There are also pan-sticks and panchromatic creams but these are less popular, as yet, among amateur groups. Primarily, the important thing is not the type of make-up you use, but the way you apply it.

## Basic make-up kit

A strong box of cardboard, wood or metal, preferably with several compartments:

Several make-up sticks/tubes/cakes
    in standard colours for foundation

| | |
|---|---|
| Liners | Spirit gum |
| Liquid body make-up | Nose putty |
| Powder | Cleansing cream |
| Crêpe hair | Cotton wool |
| Hair-whitener | Tissues |
| False eye-lashes | Hair brush and comb |
| Eyebrow pencils | Scissors |
| | Hand mirror |

## Make-up procedure

Before you start, make sure that you can sit comfortably in front of a large mirror well lit from above and either side preferably with a combination of a strip light and two adjustable table lamps. You will also need a table or bench wide enough to accommodate the clutter that inevitably collects.

1  Cleanse your skin thoroughly.

2  Apply the foundation colours, blending together thoroughly, and covering the whole face, right up to the hair line and including the areas beneath the nose and chin.

3  Colour the cheeks and lips, and re-shape the mouth, if necessary, with foundation and liner.

4  Apply any lines that may be required. For instance, by emphasising those that run from the nostrils to the corners of the mouth, or curve beneath the pouches under the eyes, it is possible to age the face. Do take care, though, not to overdo the lining process – shadowing the natural hollows with a darker colour is usually much more effective in the re-shaping of a face.

5  Make up the eyes, and eye-brows, with eye-shadow, mascara and liners. The eyes are particularly important because they are so expressive and therefore need great care.

6  Add highlights of a paler shade above the cheekbone, on the brow, and on the bridge of the nose.

7  Set the make-up, if you have used greasepaint, with an application of powder.

8  Put the final touches to the eyes.

9  Dress the hair and/or add false hair if required.

10  Make up the neck and any exposed limbs with toning body make-up – this will not need powdering.

11  Make up the hands to match the character's age and role in life.

### Exercise 1 – Straight make-up

Study your face very carefully, using both a mirror and photographs. Then give yourself a straight make-up so that to anyone sitting at the back of an auditorium and watching you on a well-lit stage you would look much as you do in your own home. Don't forget that in a small hall little make-up is necessary because the audience is so near. Most professional actresses only use their day make-up.

Obviously it is always desirable, if at all possible, to match the age of the actors with the age of the characters they are to play, but in a small company this cannot always be done. Besides, some plays cover a long time span and require the characters to age as much as fifty years between the first and final act.

Consequently it is important to know how to age your face convincingly. This is not a simple matter of drawing on a few wrinkles and powdering the hair. The important thing is to examine your face carefully, and to see how age will affect it. Wrinkle your brow, smile and frown, and see where the creases and hollows form. Look at the old people around you and see how age has affected the texture of their skins, and the shape of their eyes and lips, and particularly, their necks. Notice also the various ways that age can affect the hair.

## Creating an impression of age

1　Accentuate the hollows beneath the cheeks, under the eyebrows, along the sides of the nose, under the chin, and at the temples by applying there a darker shade of the foundation colour and adding highlights above.
2　Use a sallow pink (number 6) for an aged skin colour, and stipple with lake (number 25) to give an illusion of broken veins. Alternatively, a combination of ivory and chrome yellow (number 5 and number 59), carefully blended, will give a pale, parchment-like appearance to the skin.
3　Apply shading material in all the natural furrows and wrinkles, with highlights above.
4　Colour the lips with a light application of carmine (number 3) and add fine vertical lines with lake to give a puckered effect. But note that this would only work in a large auditorium. In a small one it would look too obvious, so do be cautious.
5　Line the eyes to give a tired look.
6　Brush the hair very flat – this is easier when it is wet – to make it look sparse, and use hair powder or liquid whitener to change its colour.
7　Make sure that the hands and neck are made up in character. But always remember that, to portray age convincingly, the actor must feel, think, and especially move like an old person.

## Creating an impression of youth

It's rather more difficult to make an old or middle-aged actor look young.

Basically it's a question of freshening the skin tones, filling out the hollows and removing the wrinkles by the application of light shaders, re-shaping the lips to a youthful fullness, and making the eyes look larger and brighter by the use of colour and liners.

### Exercise 2 – Using make-up to look older and younger
Study your face very carefully, then
(a) try to make it look about twenty years older,
(b) try to make it look *at least* ten years younger.

## Hair

Hair is a vitally important part of make-up for several reasons. First of all, the style is often a useful indication of period. Secondly, it can tell a lot about the character's age, status and attitudes. Thirdly, it can enormously enhance, or detract from, physical beauty.

Whenever possible, actors should use their own hair, growing it longer if there is time, or having it cut, if necessary, and having it specially coloured if the part requires it. Wigs are expensive to hire and, despite careful measurement taking, they don't always fit snugly enough to give the actors the necessary confidence. Nevertheless for some period plays they are essential. In this case make sure you go to a reputable firm, even though their charges may be higher – the results will be worth it. It's vitally important, but by no means easy, to disguise the joining line between wig and forehead effectively. The best way is to hide the edge of the wig with a covering of sallow pink foundation (number 6), apply powder lightly, then cover with basic foundation (numbers 5 and 9 mixed together).

It's sometimes better to compromise by adding a hair-piece, which can be dressed in many different styles, to the actor's own hair. All actors should experiment, discover which styles make them look younger or older, plainer or more attractive, and how even a simple change of parting can change their appearance. As a general rule, straightened, sleeked-down hair looks old and unflattering, while hair dressed in a softer way, with more bounce, is more youthful and becoming, though, of course, a lot depends upon the features of the face. Hair brushed hard back can also help to age a man by giving the impression of a receding hair-line. Hair brushed forward will disguise one.

It's also better for men to grow their own beards and moustaches if there is time, and to shape them into the required style. If they are unwilling or unable to do this they should use crêpe hair, stuck to the skin with spirit gum, and removed afterwards with methylated spirit. (But note that false hair will only stick to skin which is completely free from make-up.) First of all the hair, which is bought in the form of a plait, has to be straightened out by being steamed and then ironed flat between dampened cloths. *Moustaches* are built up gradually in small tufts, beginning at the edges and working towards the middle in the direction of natural growth, and then being given a final trim into shape. *Beards* take more time, so the gum should be applied to small areas one by one, otherwise it will dry before it can be of use. Start by applying the hair beneath the chin and working along the jawline, then apply another layer under the lower lip. Continue building up layers of hair, carrying them up the sides of the face to form sideboards, and across the upper lip for a moustache, if desired. Finally, trim into shape with scissors. A slight stubble can be indicated around the edge of the beard with tiny dots of the relevant colour. Alternatively, you can buy a ready-made beard of gauze. Small tufts of false hair can also be used to build up the illusion of bushy eyebrows which add a great deal of character to the face.

Beware of applying too much powder to the hair to make it grey or white – it can be exceedingly embarrassing if an embrace or blow creates a sudden cloud. Powder also dulls the hair which then needs to be brightened up with brilliantine. Liquid hair whitener tends to give better results once you have practised using it.

## Exercise 3 – Management of hair

*Women only*
Using your own hair, plus a switch, if necessary, work out styles to make you look like:
(*a*) a middle-aged lady from one of Jane Austen's novels;
(*b*) the young heroine of a late Victorian melodrama;
(*c*) a flapper from the Twenties.

*Men only*
Using your own, or crêpe, hair, create a beard and moustache to make you look like:
(*a*) a young Elizabethan courtier;
(*b*) an elderly, mid-Victorian gentleman;
(*c*) a 'flower-child' of the Sixties.
Do any research necessary in your local library and/or museum or art gallery.

It is beyond the scope of a general book of this nature to go into character make-up in detail, but good explanatory charts can be obtained from the Leichner studios in London. You can learn most, however, simply by examining faces – either in the flesh, or in portraits and photographs of all types – and by following up your examination with experimentation.

It may be helpful though for all actors to know how to use (*a*) nose putty and (*b*) stage blood.

(*a*) To change the profile view of the nose, as opposed to the full face view, it is essential to use cosmetic putty. First of all, work a small amount of the putty between moistened fingers until it is soft and pliable. Then add a layer of it to the ridge or sides of the nose, attaching it with spirit gum. Shape it carefully with your fingers till you get the outline you require, examining it in the mirror from all angles. Allow it to harden, and when quite dry cover with foundation make-up.

Putty can also be used in the same way to create warts, boils, pimples, or any other lumps on the skin.

(*b*) Bottles of stage blood can be obtained from any make-up supplier – fortunately the lurid reign of tomato ketchup is now over. If a character is to bleed from a wound, he should have a small, sealed, plastic bag of blood securely fastened to the relevant part of his body, ready to be pricked with a pin when the moment comes.

Gelatine capsules are available to simulate bleeding from the mouth. And, for bloody grazes, it's quite easy to smear on a sticky-looking red patch by combining carmine (number 3) in cold cream.

But, as with all stage make-up, be careful not to overdo it. It's often easier to give a vital impression of suffering without having to worry about special effects which, even in the hands of the professionals, don't always work. I vividly remember seeing a performance of Edward Albee's *Zoo Story* in which the blood bag fell from beheath the clothes of the actor playing Jerry, and was deftly kicked beneath the conveniently-situated park bench. Slowly, inexorably, Jerry bled to death. And, though never a drop of blood was spilt, we felt his agony with horrific intensity.

In conclusion, a few important 'do's' and 'don'ts' to bear in mind when applying stage make-up:

1 Don't over-do it.
2 Don't wait until the last moment before learning how to apply the make-up for a specific part – begin experimenting early in the rehearsal period.

3 Do give yourself plenty of time before curtain-up so that you can apply your make-up carefully.

4 Don't do anything just to create an effect. You should have some reason for whatever you do, firmly based upon the characterisation as it emerges from the text.

5 Don't fight your face. Understand it, use it, modify it, develop it, but never try to change it totally.

# 10

# Sound

'I first became involved with sound effects as an assistant stage manager in 1954 (we used disc in those days) and although I am now mainly concerned with specifying sound installations for new theatres, or designing sound reinforcement systems for West End musicals, I still find this the most intriguing aspect of the sound man's art.

First, the creative process of working through the script and deciding with the director what, in addition to the specified spot effects, would add to the atmosphere, aid the audience's sense of time and/or locale, or heighten the drama.

Then the sometimes arduous but always interesting process of compiling the sound track: hunting for commercial recordings, investigating sound effects libraries, and, best of all, making one's own recordings. These may be real or simulated, out in the field or in a makeshift studio. And it should not be forgotten that some of the most convincing effects are achieved by mechanical means during the performance.

But the greatest satisfaction is experienced when, after the experimentation, pruning and re-recording that always takes place during rehearsals, your contribution finally becomes a vital and integral part of the performance.

To me a sound operator is a performer, only instead of uttering words he produces sounds which are equally discernible by an audience. A badly timed or performed sound cue can throw an actor and destroy the illusion just as much as bad acting or forgotten lines. The sound operator must therefore have an excellent sense of timing, a complete involvement, and a 100% valid sound track where every cue has a purpose, no matter how subtle or dramatic.'

**David Collison**
*Sound consultant and director of Theatre Projects*

In most amateur dramatic companies the duties of the sound technician are as follows. He will:

1 attend the production meetings to decide what sound effects are needed throughout the course of the play, in consultation with the director and the stage manager;

2 familiarise himself very thoroughly with the script;

3 decide which sound effects should be made mechanically during the performance, and which should be tape-recorded;

4 decide whether the master tape should be made from commercially-produced sound effects records, and where and how these should be acquired, or whether it should be made up from original sounds (most master tapes will be composed of a combination of the two);

5 make the master tape;

6 ensure that he and the stage manager liaise completely about the manual effects which will be the responsibility of the stage management team;

7 check that permissions for the copyright and performing rights of the recording have been obtained;

8 attend as many rehearsals as possible;

9 operate the master tape, or supervise its operation, during the later rehearsals as well as the performances;

10 be responsible for any auditorium sound reinforcement that may be considered necessary;

11 choose appropriate introductory and interval music for the play, in consultation with the director, and supervise the playing of it.

At one time sound effects were used, usually offstage, to build up an effect of something happening, and this, added to what was occurring on stage, made an overall picture for the audience. These effects were created by backstage staff using all sorts of mechanical equipment to provide an approximation to the type of noise that was required.

However, as with lighting, the advent of modern technology has changed the whole approach to the problem of sound in the theatre. Initially, panatropes, which had a series of record turn-tables, enabled recorded sound effects to be used. This meant that sounds such as cars leaving or arriving could be employed. But one of the difficulties with turntables is accurately locating the place at which to start – to counteract this panatropes had a cueing and lowering device for the pick-up arm.

The introduction of the tape-recorder changed the provision of sound completely. For the first time a device was available which could be accurately cued, and on which tapes could be built up of the various sounds required for a production. The major responsibility for the provision of sound now moved from the stage management to a new specialist, the sound technician. This enabled the director to think of sound in the same way as he thought of his lighting, considering how it could be used most effectively to add to the overall effect that he was trying to create in his production.

Today sound can be used in several ways:

(*a*) to establish the time of the year e.g. carol singing; or of the day e.g. the dawn chorus; or of the type of weather that is prevailing e.g. a howling gale; or the place at which the play is occurring e.g. monks chanting;

(*b*) to provide specially required effects, e.g. cars moving, aeroplanes landing;

(*c*) to create atmosphere, e.g. a tolling bell;

(*d*) to create a link between scenes.

This means that the task of the sound technician is very similar to that of the lighting designer when he is planning the sound for a production. He must work closely with the director so that he understands what the director wants, and he must then use his imagination to create it.

Despite the advent of modern equipment, some effects can still be

MACBETH, ACT I

| Cue | Time | Sound | Page No. | Action |
|-----|------|-------|----------|--------|
| 1 | 15′ 0″ | Background music | 29 | |
| 2 | 15″ | Opening music | 29 | Pre-tabs |
| 3 | 10″ | Thunder | 29 | Witches' entry |
| 4 | 25″ | Electronic music | 29 | Background to witches |
| 5 | 5″ | Thunder | 29 | Witches' exit |
| 6 | 15″ | Fanfare | 29 | Duncan's entry |
| 7 | 20″ | Thunder | 32 | Witches' entry |
| 8 | 1′ 05″ | Electronic music | 32 | Background to witches |
| 9 | 10″ | Drum | 33 | Macbeth's entry |
| 10 | 5″ | Thunder | 34 | Witches' exit |
| 11 | 15″ | Fanfare | 37 | Duncan's entry |
| 12 | 10″ | Oboes | 42 | Duncan's entry |
| 13 | 30″ | Oboes | 43 | Macbeth's entry |

*Figure 20*   Cue sheet

made more realistically by mechanical means, and these will usually be the responsibility of the stage management people, so it is important to establish, right at the beginning, which sounds will be recorded and which live.

The sound technician will then draw up a cue sheet – similar to the one given in Figure 20 – of sounds that will be used during the play, with cue numbers, script page numbers, and a description of what is happening on stage.

Some of these cues may be straightforward, as in the case of introductory music which need only be recorded on to the tape from a record. Others may be complex and will have to be built up from a series of sources. For instance, a scene may begin with:

1 the sound of pouring rain beating against the window panes, through which is heard
2 the arrival of a car,
3 car doors opening and
4 shutting,
5 feet crunching on gravel,
6 a dog barking,
7 a child crying inside the house, then
8 a loud knocking on the front door, followed by
9 the door being opened, and
10 slammed shut.

### Exercise 1 – Cue sheet

Make a cue sheet – and, if possible, a master tape – for these opening moments of *Duet For Two Hands* by Mary Hayley Bell, beginning with appropriate introductory music.

ACT I  SCENE 1

SCENE – *Forsinard. An eighteenth-century castle in the Orkneys. Midsummer, 1904. Sunset.*

*The room, which looks across the Bay of Skail to the Atlantic Ocean, has large high windows which lead through a conservatory on to an emerald and beautifully rolled lawn. The room is high and light, the furniture exquisite, with soft carpets and brocades. A wide stone stairway leads up to the floor above, with a stained-glass window at the turn which pours a lilac light down into the room; below the stairs is an archway leading off to the rest of the house. On the other side of the room is a large Adam fireplace, in*

*front of which are settees and chairs. A large shining grand piano*
*stands alone, down* L., *the shaft of light from the stairs falling*
*across an enormous bowl of tea roses on it. The roses are the*
*most startling thing about Forsinard; they are everywhere, the*
*room is full of them, each seems more perfect a bloom than the last,*
*and their heady intoxicating scent fills the room. Here is a bowl*
*of pink, and there another of lemon and again on the mantelshelf,*
*a single scarlet bloom standing alone in a long, thin Chelsea vase*
*under the portrait of a black-browed man in a crimson cloak.*
   (*See the Ground Plan and Photograph.*)
   *On a small table before the settee, a silver tray with tea and*
*bread and butter stands untouched. There is no sound in the*
*room save for the ticking of the little Spanish clock on the mantel,*
*and the cries of the wheeling kittiwakes as they sail past the*
*windows. A dog barks.*

(*Copyright 1947 Samuel French Ltd*)

Sound effects can be made by:
1  recording the real thing e.g. if you want bird cries, go and find your
   birds and record them;
2  recording a noise effect which sounds like the real thing e.g. dried
   peas swishing around in a tin sound like rain; or
3  taping a sound from a record of the effect.
But do remember that when recording from gramophone records there
are copyright restrictions. Permission must be obtained not only for the
performing rights but also in respect of the mechanical copyright. If in
doubt contact:
(*a*)  The Mechanical Copyright Protection Society Ltd., 380 Streatham
   High Road, London, SW16 6HR.
(*b*)  The Performing Right Society Ltd., 29–33 Berners Street, London,
   W1P 4AA.
   Records can often be borrowed from your local library.
   When deciding what effect you want, listen carefully to the real thing
if you have the chance before making the recording. Often the same noise
can sound quite different according to its locale, for instance church bells
make a different noise in the open country than they do in a town.
Accuracy is extremely important. It is all too easy to create the wrong
mood, or to introduce an anachronism, by being careless over specific
detail.
   The overall sound tape will often be a product of the sound technician's
imagination. Although some of the sounds that are used will be relatively

simple to obtain and to record, others have to be recorded on to the tape from more than one source, with careful cueing to get the various sounds at the right time. Make sure when making recordings that you only record on one track of the tape so that subsequent editing is possible. When all the recording has been done the tape should be edited to provide a master tape. The length of each sound effect cue will have been decided beforehand, so the beginning of each can be found on the tape and then stopped. The tape will then be marked and cut about 1 cm away from the mark. The end of the tape is placed on a splicing block, and a piece of light-coloured leader tape spliced on to it. The same process is carried out for the end of the cue, so that when the master tape is complete it consists of a series of recordings, each with leader tape in between them. In this way it is easy to locate the beginning and end of cues. It is often a good idea to edit in a leader tape of a different colour at the end of a series of cues, or at the end of an act, so that when the tape is being spooled quickly it can be easily seen.

It may be that in some cases the sound cues are so complex that it is necessary to use more than one master tape to create the required effects for the production. In that case the sound design will have to be carefully worked out to ensure that the various master tapes on their respective tape recorders can be brought in on cue.

It is wise at this stage to plan an operating sheet that shows which effects are on which tape recorder so that whoever is operating the sound equipment during the show will know which tape(s) to use for each cue (Figure 21).

The operating sheet will also show the sound level for each tape, and the speed at which it should be faded in and out. These levels will have to be determined at a time when the theatre is quiet prior to the technical rehearsal. It is no good trying to test for sound levels with carpenters erecting sets or electricians rigging lights.

Although this operating sheet will show the levels, it is essential that the sound operator be in a position from which he can hear what is going on on the stage in the same way as the audience can because often the sound can vary if the size of the audience varies, and the operator needs to adjust his levels accordingly.

When the sound technician is satisfied that all sound cues are correctly set and working, he will have to liaise with the deputy stage manager to ensure that the sound effects cues (FXQ's) are recorded in the prompt copy so that the sound operator can be given a warning when a sound cue is about to occur.

Although tape recording can be used for providing many sound effects

MACBETH, ACT I

| Cue | Time | Tape 1 | Tape 2 | Sound |
|---|---|---|---|---|
| | | Tape 1 on channel 1 | | |
| | | Tape 2 on channel 2 | | |
| 1 | 15' 00" | ↑ 8 | | Background music |
| 2 | 15" | ↓ 0 | ↑ 4 | Opening music |
| 3 | 10" | | ↑ 10 | Thunder |
| 4 | 25" | | ↓ 2 | Electronic music |
| 5 | 5" | | ↑ 10 | Thunder |
| 6 | 15" | ↑ 8 | ↓ 0 | Fanfare |
| 7 | 20" | | ↑ 10 | Thunder |
| 8 | 1' 05" | | ↓ 2 | Electronic music |
| 9 | 10" | ↑ 10 | | Drum |
| 10 | 5" | | ↑ 10 | Thunder |
| 11 | 15" | ↑ 8 | | Fanfare |
| 12 | 10" | ↑ 6 | | Oboes |
| 13 | 30" | ↑ 6 | | Oboes |

*Note:* Arrows indicate turning volume control up or down as appropriate.

*Figure 21*  Sound operating sheet

nowadays, there are still some which are better produced by live or mechanical means. These will usually be executed by the stage management team.

For instance, gun shots sound better live than recorded, and are produced by firing blank cartridges offstage. But don't forget that you require a firearms certificate for this. It is always a wise precaution to have two sources or methods of producing the shot. If you cannot get hold of a second revolver, use two planks on the floor, weighted at one end. Simulate the shot by lifting the free ends of the planks and allowing them to drop on the floor.

Rain can be simulated convincingly by perforating a pipe and letting water drip from it into a trough below. Not only does this produce a convincing sound, it can also give the right visual effect if placed outside a window or a door. Remember, if you are creating a wet weather scene, that actors who enter from outside must look as if they have come in from the rain!

A variety of bells, with appropriate switches on a board, can be used to provide the sounds of doorbells, servants' bell, buzzers, telephones ringing, and so on. The operator will have to be in a position from which he can see the action so that he can get the cues right. If this is impossible it might be better to wire up stage-operated bells so that they are worked by the actors on the stage, and to wire telephone bells so that they stop ringing when the hand-set is lifted.

Thunder can be produced by means of the familiar 'thundersheet', which is a large sheet of thin metal hung in the wings at a height from which it can be held. When thunder is required all that is necessary is to shake it.

The sound of wind can be simulated by the use of wind machines. The most common one consists of a slatted wooden cylinder set in a suitable frame and connected to a handle. A piece of canvas is stretched from one side of the frame across the slats to the other side. When the cylinder is rotated the wooden slats rubbing against the canvas produce a convincing wind noise, the pitch of which can be varied by varying the speed of the rotation of the cylinder.

For the sounds of doors opening and closing it is best to construct a 'door-slam'. This is a stout wooden box with one side hinged just like a door, and fitted with various locks and handles so that the appropriate one can be operated when required.

Crashes can be simulated by having a couple of boxes, one full of bits of broken glass and metal, and pouring these, on cue, into the other.

It is usually best actually to break a piece of glass to get the sound of breaking glass. This is most safely done by placing the piece of glass across the top of a padded box and hitting it with a hammer. Extreme care should be taken when doing this, and the stage-hand wielding the hammer should wear gloves and goggles to protect him from any flying glass.

There are many other sound effects which can be created back stage. If a theatre group has an inventive backstage team it can experiment to produce the exact effects required by the director. Don't be afraid to try out what may seem to be the most unlikely noises in an attempt to get the effect you need. As in so many areas of theatre craft, imagination, experimentation, improvisation and practice are of vital importance to the achieving of effective results.

**Exercise 2 – Sound effects**

1   Make a tape recording of:
    (*a*) a large jet aircraft taking off from a nearby airport, and/or
    (*b*) a car parking on a gravel drive.
2   Produce *mechanically* a realistic roll of thunder which tapers off to silence.
3   Produce the sound of pealing bells:
    (*a*) by mechanical means, and
    (*b*) by tape-recording the real thing.

The other main area for which the sound technician is responsible is *sound reinforcement*. This is more commonly used in musical productions, open-air performances, and for creating special effects rather than in straight plays where the correct projection of the voice should be enough to make it perfectly audible to every member of the audience. It's also important to remember that in those exceptional productions requiring sound reinforcement this should enable the audience to hear the performers without, in fact, their noticing that the sound is reinforced.

The primary object in a theatre is to project the sound from the stage so that the whole audience hears it at the same level at the same time. Sound waves tend to reach the audience by a variety of paths, some direct, some by reflection from auditorium surfaces. If it is decided to use sound reinforcement so that the audience can hear more clearly, care must be taken with the installation of the system so that this object is achieved.

Care must also be taken in positioning microphones and loudspeakers to maintain the effect that the sound is coming from the stage – except in a few isolated instances when voices are required to sound as if they are coming from other parts of the auditorium. This means that loudspeakers should be positioned in the front of the auditorium to project the sound at the audience. They should be in front of the microphones to minimise acoustic feedback or 'howl around'. The position of the microphones should be such that the actors for whom reinforcement is necessary can be heard clearly without automatically reinforcing everyone else on the stage.

Often the positioning of microphones and loudspeakers is a matter of trial and error. Consequently, the sound technician must allow himself sufficient time to get the reinforcement systems just right. A rushed job will almost invariably mean an unsatisfactory job.

# I I

# Publicity and Management

'However good a product, it has to be marketed. The public has to be informed of both its existence and its quality. This applies to any field – whether the product being marketed is soap or theatre tickets; and the amateur theatre is in competition with all the effective marketing techniques which are trying to persuade the public to spend its money on their particular product.

In recent years standards of acting, production and presentation in the amateur theatre have improved greatly. Unfortunately this is not always the case with publicity – far too often the important post of publicity manager is filled by some member who does not happen to have been elected to any other job.

A large budget is not necessarily synonymous with good publicity: technical know-how of advertising and printing is important, but the key word is imagination – which surely all those involved in the theatre should possess in abundance.'

**Roy Stacey**
*Managing editor of 'Amateur Stage'*

After the enormous amount of work and preparation that goes into a production it can be very disappointing if the company finds itself playing to empty houses. To avoid this it is necessary to mount an effective publicity campaign, masterminded by an energetic and imaginative team coordinated by an enthusiastic publicity manager.

Publicity involves much more than a few scattered posters and an advertisement in the local paper. It should also include at least some of the following:

Handbills;
Car-stickers;
Centrally-situated displays;
Street banners;
Free give-aways, like badges and balloons, printed with the name or motif of the play;
Competitions;
Personal appearances by the actors, in costume;
Comprehensive coverage by the local mass media, including radio and television.

From the scope and variety of this list it can be seen that the publicity team should be made up of people possessing several different sorts of talents. Some should be good copy writers, others competent artists. At least one member should understand the basics of printing, and another should be a proficient typist. And several need to have the sort of personable self-confidence required to persuade the media, the business fraternity and the relevant public bodies to give the support that is needed.

Posters are important, of course, but they must be well-designed, preferably with an eye-catching and relevant motif which can also be used in advertisements, programmes, car-stickers, hand-bills, balloons, and so on.

The *Fiddler on the Roof* motif printed in Figure 22 was used very effectively in a recent campaign by an amateur operatic society. Since it was so visually explicit it was often used without words and dramatically captured the imagination and curiosity of the public.

The cheapest method of printing a small run of posters is by 'offset litho'. This is a photographic process and has the advantage over conventional letterpress that you can prepare your own designs. The technique also allows of a more ambitious and interesting format. Graphics, for instance, are more easily incorporated since it is not necessary to make a block. Incidentally, printers' quotations for work vary widely so it is worth asking for several estimates. Don't always accept the cheapest though – it's important to see examples of the printer's output before a final decision is made.

Posters should never be too big or you will find that shop-keepers and householders are unwilling to show them because they take up too much of their wall or window. Approximately 30 cm × 45 cm is ideal. When you approach people with a request to display them always take your own adhesive, sticky tape or drawing pins and try to get permission to put them up yourself. If you can see an empty space, it's often quite easy to talk them into letting you use it.

The number of posters you require will depend upon the size and nature of your catchment area, but will not normally be less than fifty or more than one hundred. Always remember though, when you are having any printing done, that the unit cost comes down rapidly as the print run is increased.

*Figure 22*   Advertising motif

A poster should fulfil two functions – it should:
1   attract attention; and
2   give information.
Anyone stopping to read it should be able to discover at a glance:
(*a*)  the name of the play, and of its author;
(*b*)  the date, time and place of performance;
(*c*)  the price of tickets and where they can be obtained; and
(*d*)  the name of the company performing the play.
Nothing more is required.

The same printer will probably make your programmes, tickets, hand-bills and car-stickers too.

It should be possible to cover the cost of the *programmes*, and perhaps even generate some extra money to go towards the printer's bill, by incorporating advertisements in them. Many local businesses will be happy to sponsor a company, and at the same time gain publicity, in this way. Before approaching potential advertisers you must make sure that you know:

1  how many programmes will be circulated;
2  the price of the various sizes of advertisements you are offering – full page, half page or quarter page; and
3  the deadline for copy.

Some of them will want to compose their own advertisement – others may ask you to do it for them. It's a good idea if the theme complements the show in some way, as in this advertisement for *Fiddler on the Roof*'s programme by a local building firm.

> 'We cannot supply a Fiddler for your roof –
> but we *can* supply the roof itself. Come
> and see *our* show at BLOGGS & CO,
> Building Contractors, Main Street, Anytown.'

Some societies like to use a programme 'shell', the outside sheets printed with a basic cover design, advertisements, and information about the company that remains relevant for several productions, with details of the current production rolled off on a duplicator and stapled inside. However, offset litho looks better than duplicating and costs less once you are into a printing run of five hundred sheets or more. Besides, the audience often finds it more interesting to have a freshly designed programme for each play. This is the sort of decision each company must make for itself, depending upon its own circumstances. Do remember that if you want to charge a reasonable price for a programme it must look smart and professional.

*Handbills* should contain at least the same information as the posters and preferably some extra material to attract the interest of casual readers. They can be distributed door to door, either by members of the company or by a local newsagent who will send them out with his papers for a small charge. They can be handed out in the street, or left on the shop counters, and in libraries and information centres. They can be tucked behind the windscreen-wipers of parked cars, or put on the seats in halls and theatres where other entertainments are taking place, provided that the organisers will cooperate with you, possibly on a mutual support basis. If you have developed a good relationship with your local theatre it may even be possible to persuade its management to include your handbill in their mailing list, as well as giving you a mention in their programme and displaying one of your posters on their notice board.

*Car-stickers* don't get read with the same attention as posters and handbills so they don't need to incorporate the same amount of information. It is probably sufficient to put on the visual motif and the place and date of the performance.

Posters will play a large part in any *displays* you mount, but these are most effective if they can also include photographs of the cast, some of the props and costumes, and a collage of cuttings and reports of other performances of the play. Aim for variety and visual appeal.

The local library is a good place for a display. Sometimes it's also possible to persuade estate agents to lend you window space, and to get permission to use empty shop windows in the centre of the town.

*Painted banners* are valuable eye-catching devices, stretched overhead from side to side of a busy street. You could try giving out *badges* printed with the name of the show. Or organise a balloon race with printed *balloons* which will spread the news of your show far and wide, and win a prize for the owner of the balloon which covers the greatest distance. A mobile box office can be set up – perhaps in a busy car park – where the *actors*, *in costume*, can talk to passers-by about the play, hand out information, and sell tickets. *Competitions* can be organised, especially in schools, asking children to design a set or a costume – they are bound to come up with some exciting ideas. And any project of this type has the added advantage that it tends to attract the useful attention of the media. Do remember though that there are laws and bye-laws which must be observed, and always check with the relevant authority – the police, the council, the education authority, and so on – before you begin a publicity exercise.

Finally, make the fullest possible use of the *mass media*. Usually local television and radio stations have 'What's On' programmes in which straight information about your production can be announced, and it's wise to place an advertisement in the paper which serves your area. But if there is a newsworthy story attached to your play – if, for instance, it is by a local writer, or based on local history, or if one of the actors has an interesting background – the media may well give you much more useful coverage in their general interest programmes or pages. Make sure that any good copy is sent in to them well before the first night so that they have time to prepare a piece about it.

Finally, either invite the local paper to send along a reporter and a photographer so that your play can be reviewed, or submit a review written for you by one of the audience whom you know to be competent. Be warned though that either course has its snags. The newspaper reporter may know nothing about theatre and produce a very inept piece of criticism, while the writer of your choice may be considered partial and prejudiced in your favour. Nevertheless I believe that, as a general rule, any publicity is good publicity, so it's probably better to have an indifferent review than none at all.

### Exercise 1 – Publicity campaign
Consider the production your Society is currently preparing. Work out a complete publicity campaign which will include:
1 designing posters, tickets, programmes, car-stickers and give-aways;
2 designing, and writing copy for, handbills;
3 designing displays;
4 arranging publicity events and competitions;
5 preparing an effective advertisement for the local paper;
6 writing copy for human interest stories to be circulated to the local media.
Combine the material into an illustrated dossier.

## Front-of-house and business management

Throughout this book the key-word for success has been organisation, and this applies just as much to front-of-house as it does to back-stage and on-stage activity. It is essential for any society to have a strong front-of-house team, led by a responsible business manager. If he is also in close touch with the publicity group so much the better because there is a great deal of overlap in these two areas.

Usually the business manager will be responsible for:
Box office and ticket sales, and some budgeting;
The seating plan;
The provision and supervision of ushers/programme sellers;
The collection and distribution of programmes;
Refreshments (including a drinks license);
Cloakroom facilities;
The enforcement of no-smoking rules, and the observance of fire regulations;
Complimentary tickets;
General supervision of the audience before, during and after the performance;

Car parking;
The play licence; and
The theatre licence.

## Budgeting

It is a good idea for the business manager to work in close liaison with the director and his production team right from the beginning of the planning meetings to help to evolve a budget. Working preferably from previous records, but otherwise from careful estimates, he should be able to gauge:

(*a*)  the expected income from ticket sales;
(*b*)  the expected income from advertising in the programmes;
(*c*)  the expected income from the selling of the programmes; and
(*d*)  the expected income from selling refreshments.

These estimates must be realistic. It's no good expecting to sell every seat and every programme. It's better to work on the assumption that between one half and one third will be sold, unless the previous experience of the company is of wildly successful shows and 'house full' notices at the door for every night of the run.

The total of these sums adds up to the total expected income from the play – unless there are also sponsors and patrons who donate generously. When working out the complete budget it is necessary to add to the assets the amount of cash already in hand, as provided by the treasurer. This sum will probably be made up of any profit realised by previous productions, the amount raised by members' subscriptions, and any money acquired by fund-raising activities or the hiring-out of equipment.

Against the assets and expected income must be balanced the expected costs of the production. The business manager should be able to provide estimates of the financial outlay required for:

(*a*)  the printing of programmes and tickets;
(*b*)  the provision of advertising of all types;
(*c*)  the fee for hiring the hall for the performances and for some rehearsals and preparation;
(*d*)  the provision of food and drink for refreshments;
(*e*)  royalties.

Other members of the production team must then offer their own estimates of the costs of:

(*f*)  hiring, buying or making costumes and wigs;
(*g*)  buying make-up;
(*h*)  hiring, buying or making sound effects and lighting;
(*i*)  hiring, buying or making scenery and props.

Only when this has been done can a sensible budget be worked out and the money available allocated to the various departments. If the society is prosperous the costume designer, stage manager, lighting technicians, and so on will be given as much money as they need, and should then make an effort to ensure that their expenditure tallies with their original estimate. If, as more often happens, the society is working on a shoe-string, each team will have to make do with only a proportion of what they have asked for, and will have to use all their expertise, ingenuity and energy to achieve the desired effects with what they are given instead of with what they'd like. If this seems totally impossible, four courses of action are open to the society:

1  it can choose a play which is cheaper to produce,
2  it can engage in a few fund-raising activities to provide the required materials and equipment,
3  it can intensify its ticket-selling activities, provided that the extra costs of intensified promotion can be proved to be a good investment,
4  it can raise the annual membership fee. This should be discussed at a general meeting and some consensus of opinion arrived at.

Note that budgets should always be kept for future reference. They are a time-consuming undertaking and, despite changing costs, it is much easier to adjust them to a new production rather than to have to start again from scratch.

It's also worth considering, if a play is very successful and makes a lot of money, that the profits should be banked and/or invested in needed equipment rather than donated to a local charity. It is of the nature of all theatre companies that successes are interspersed with flops, and if the society is to survive it needs a certain measure of financial security as a life-line.

*Ticket sales* are a very important source of income, so it is vital that they should be well organised. To start with, tickets must be designed and printed early in the play production schedule so that they can be in the hands of the sellers as soon as publicity begins. Usually tickets are sold from one main outlet – this might be a central shop or café, or perhaps the local professional theatre or tourist information centre – as well as by members of the society, and at the door on the night of the performance.

Members of the cast should be urged to sell as many tickets as they possibly can to friends, family and the people they work with. Their own enthusiasm and involvement will probably make them effective salesmen. Whatever the selling arrangements, these should be clearly stated on posters and handbills.

If you want a business enterprise to act as a ticket-selling agency it is better not to have a complicated *seating plan* with numbered seats unless you are paying them some commission for the work involved. Busy shop-keepers often can't find the time to help indecisive theatre-goers to choose the most favourable seats when it may be costing them lucrative sales of their own goods. It's much easier to make all the seats the same price, simply having differently-coloured tickets for different evenings. It is important, of course, to collect all unsold tickets, and the money for those sold, before the doors open for the first night.

Usually it isn't difficult to recruit *ushers and programme sellers*. Members and friends of the society are often happy to help in this way, but it's a good idea to have one or two extra standing by in case some don't turn up. If seats aren't numbered ushering responsibilities are minimal – it's simply a matter of pointing out where they are available, and perhaps persuading those already seated to move along slightly to allow groups of friends to sit together. (If possible, seats or empty spaces should be left at the end of some rows for the benefit of the disabled or the accommodation of a wheel-chair. Probably those needing this sort of facility will give details when buying their tickets.) If seats are numbered the ushers need to know beforehand exactly how the numbering works and where seating blocks of specific prices are situated so that the audience can be guided swiftly to their seats without confusions or delays which often get patrons into quite the wrong frame of mind before curtain-up. Ushers will also have to deal with late-comers. Since they can spoil the play for the rest of the audience and unnerve the actors and make them forget their lines, my own solution to the problem they create would be to ask them, very politely, to wait at the back of the hall until there is a break.

The Business Manager should ensure that the *programmes* are in his hands at the latest by the morning of the first day of the performance. He will then distribute them to the programme sellers, in the evening before the doors are opened for the show, with a float of change and a container to keep it in, and station them at strategic places around the hall. It's sensible to price programmes in such a way that change presents no complicated arithmetical problems.

It is a gracious gesture to present a free programme to each member of the cast on the first night. Usually the stage manager does this, but the director may like to take it upon himself. Incidentally, do check – before they go to the printers – that the spelling of all the company's names is correct. Nothing irritates people more than to see their names in print – mis-spelt. You don't want to trigger off sulks and furies just before that first, vital curtain-up.

Most amateur societies provide coffee, squash, biscuits and confectionery during the interval as a service to their patrons and a way of bringing in extra revenue. If possible, coffee should be made and served outside the auditorium to minimise the noise and avoid crowding. The stage manager should be able to tell the *refreshments team* exactly when the interval will begin so that they can be well-prepared and ready for their rush of customers. The whole mood of the play can be destroyed if the audience is kept waiting in long queues and the interval has to be dragged out until everyone is served. The noise of clearing away and washing-up can also be very disturbing. Unless sound-proofing is effective and the work can be done without any overspill of sound into the auditorium the washing-up should be postponed till the end of the play.

Some societies now follow the pleasant and civilised practice of the professional theatre of running a bar before and after the performance as well as during the interval. If the premises are licensed for the sale of intoxicating liquor this presents no problem. If they only have a theatre licence there is normally no need to obtain a justices' licence for the sale of liquor, provided that the licence holder gives notice to the clerk of the local licensing justices of the intention to sell intoxicating liquor, but the local 'drinking hours' must be observed. Alternatively, the society can ask a local publican to run a bar for them, and in this case the business of the licence will be his responsibility. For some sorts of entertainments, especially music hall, revue and participatory shows, a bar can add to the enjoyment of the evening, relaxing the audience and encouraging a warm response which heightens the actors' performance.

Every hall should attempt to provide some basic *cloakroom facilities*. Especially in wet weather the audience will need somewhere to dump coats and umbrellas. If necessary, the business manager should see that there are hanging racks and tables provided for this purpose, and for security reasons, see that someone stays close at hand to keep an eye on them.

Both for the sake of the actors' voices and the audience's comfort and safety there must be a *no smoking rule* in the auditorium and the business manager should make sure that there are large notices explaining this, and that the rule is observed. It is also important to observe the Fire Regulations – details can be obtained from your local council – by indicating the position of exits and keeping these clear, providing fire extinguishers, and so on.

Some people – those who have loaned props, for instance, as well as the Press, and other special guests – will have been offered *complimentary tickets*, and it is up to the business manager to see that good seats are reserved for them, and that they are courteously greeted and presented with a free programme when they arrive. It is natural that those who have made an effort to be generous and helpful enjoy feeling that they are recognised and valued.

If *car-parking* spaces are limited or inconveniently situated it is a wise provision to ask two or three people to supervise the car park so that no minor accidents, incidents or delays occur to mar the evening's enjoyment.

*Supervision of the auditorium:* The business manager should also make sure that the auditorium is comfortable and welcoming, clean and warm, with the chairs properly laid out and the aisles clear, before the audience begins to arrive, and that it is left in good order after they have gone.

And it is his responsibility to cope with any anti-social behaviour during the performance. Fortunately such incidents are rare, but it does occasionally happen that a drunk may wander in unobserved, or a heckler begin to shout or create a disturbance. These people should be quietly asked to leave and, if necessary, firmly led outside. Another sort of disturbance can be caused by someone suddenly taking ill. Again, he should be taken out of the auditorium and any minor upset, like a fainting fit, should be dealt with on the spot. It's always a good idea to keep first aid kits both in the dressing rooms and in the foyer.

Finally, there are two *licences* which may well be considered the responsibility of the business manager. The first of these is the *Play Licence*, which is, in effect, the financial and legal agreement between the author of a copyright play or his agent or publisher, and the company wishing to present his work. Amateur rights for public performance are not always available and this should be checked as soon as the play is chosen. The licence will be specifically agreed for a particular society, it will indicate the number of performances permitted and the place and time of performance as well as the fee payable. Even sketches, jokes, monologues and other short pieces need to be licensed by their copyright owners, who will always be named in the front of a printed script. If the script is unpublished it is still copyright while the author is alive and for fifty years after his death, and in these cases permission must always be sought.

The second obligatory licence is the *Theatre Licence*. The law decrees that premises used for public performances of plays must be licensed. Application for a licence, which lasts a year, must be made to the local council which has the right to inspect the premises to decide whether they are suitable, and to lay down certain conditions, especially as regards

Fire Precautions. This is not merely a matter of officious bureaucracy. It is done for the safety of the audience, and ignoring it is an offence for which there is a heavy fine. However, if the Dramatic Society is merely renting a hall on an occasional basis it may be that it is already licensed by its management committee, in which case no further action will be required.

# Postscript

'I think one of the most important things for an amateur actor to remember is to avoid being ridiculous. Unfortunately, it's only too easy on the stage – and I write as one who has seen an audience at Covent Garden helpless with laughter when Siegfried's sword broke.

We can't all be good, but we can avoid those terrible pieces of bathos which have the onlookers in unintended laughter, such as the corny sword fights between armies of two soldiers each, the guns that don't fire, the crowns that wobble, and the crowds that rhubarb and wave their arms meaninglessly.

In other words, avoid Coarse Acting!'

**Michael Green**
*Writer and amateur actor*

# Recommended Reading

## Papers, magazines and periodicals

| | |
|---|---|
| *Amateur Stage* (monthly) | pub. Stacey Publications 1 Hawthorndene Road, Hayes, Bromley, Kent |
| *Drama* (quarterly) | pub. British Theatre Association 9 Fitzroy Square, London, W1 |
| *Stage and Television Today* (weekly) | pub. Carson and Comerford Ltd. Stage House, 47 Bermondsey Street, London, SE1 3XT |
| *Tabs* (three times a year) | pub. Rank Strand Electric Box 70, Great West Road, Brentford, Middlesex |
| *Theatre Directory* (biennial) | pub. Stacey Publications |

## Books of general interest

Allensworth, Carl: *The Complete Play Production Book* (Robert Hale)
Hartnoll, Phyllis: *The Concise Oxford Companion To The Theatre* (OUP 1972)
Hoggett, Chris: *Stage Crafts* (A & C Black 1975)

# Books of special interest

### Acting
Cotterell, Leslie E: *Performance* (John Offord Publications)
Fishman, Morris: *The Actor in Training* (Herbert Jenkins 1961)
Stanislavsky: *Building a Character* (Methuen 1968)

### Direction
Brook, Peter: *The Empty Space* (Pelican 1972)
Hodge, Francis: *Play Directing* (Prentice Hall)

### Stage management
Stern, Lawrence: *Stage Management* (Allyn & Bacon 1974)

### Lighting
Bentham, Frederick: *The Art of Stage Lighting* (Pitman 1968)
Ost, Geoffrey: *Stage Lighting* (Herbert Jenkins 1954)
Pilbrow, Richard: *Stage Lighting* (Studio Vista 1970)
Reid, Francis: *The Stage Lighting Handbook* (Pitman)

### Costume
Arnold, Janet: *A Handbook of Costume* (Macmillan)
Ewing, Elizabeth: *Dress and Undress* (Batsford 1978)
Jackson, Sheila: *Simple Stage Costumes* (Studio Vista 1968)
Motley: *Designing and Making Stage Costumes* (Studio Vista 1964)
Selbie, Robert: *The Anatomy of Costume* (Mills and Boon 1977)

### Sound
Collison, David: *Stage Sound* (Studio Vista 1976)

### Publicity and management
Cavanaugh, Jim: *Organization and Management of the Nonprofessional Theatre* (Richards Rosen Press, New York 1973)
Frayman, Griffiths and Chippindale: *Into Print* (Teach Yourself Books 1975)

## Play Publishers

(This list does not pretend to include all play publishers, only those which amateur companies will most frequently encounter while searching for general material as opposed to specialised material suitable for children and young people, all-women groups, religious or educational organisations, and so on.)

W. H. Allen, 44 Hill Street, London WIX 8LI3
Allen & Unwin, 40 Museum Street, London, WCI
Calder & Boyars, 18 Brewer Street, London WI
Jonathan Cape, 30 Bedford Square, London, WCI
Davis-Poynter, 20 Garrick Street, London, WC2
Gerald Duckworth, The Old Piano Factory, 43 Gloucester Crescent, London NWI 7DY
English Theatre Guild, 5A South Side, Clapham Common, London, SW4
Evans Bros., Montague House, Russell Square, WCI
Eyre Methuen, 11 New Fetter Lane, London, EC4
Faber & Faber, 3 Queen Square, London, WCI
Samuel French, 26 Southampton Street, London, WC2
Victor Gollancz, 14 Henrietta Street, London, WC2
Hamish Hamilton, 57–59 Long Acre, London WC2E 9J2
George G. Harrap, 182 High Holborn, London, WCI
Wm. Heinemann, 15–16, Queen St, London WIX 8BE
Kenyon-Deane, 129 St John's Hill, London, SWII
Macmillan, 4 Little Essex Street, London, WC2
J. Garnet Miller, 129 St John's Hill, London, SWII
John Murray, 50 Albemarle Street, London, WI
New Playwrights' Network, 35 Sandringham Road, Macclesfield, Cheshire SKIO IQB
Oxford University Press, 37 Dover Street, London, WI
Penguin Books, Bath Road, Harmondsworth, Middlesex
Secker and Warburg, 54 Poland St, London WI

## Plays referred to

* marks those from which excerpts are given, or which are used in exercises, or examples.

| | | |
|---|---|---|
| *All My Sons* | Arthur Miller | Penguin |
| *Alpha Beta** | E. A. Whitehead | Penguin |
| *Anastasia* | Marcelle Maurette | French |
| *An Ideal Husband** | Oscar Wilde | Collins |
| *Arsenic and Old Lace* | Kesselring | English Theatre Guild |

| | | |
|---|---|---|
| *A Ruff for Bess\** | Jennifer Curry and Downton Amateur Dramatic Society | Not in Print |
| *As You Like It\** | Shakespeare | Methuen |
| *A Voyage Round My Father* | John Mortimer | French |
| *Back to Methusaleh* | G. B. Shaw | Penguin |
| *Blithe Spirit* | Noel Coward | Heinemann |
| *Blonde on the Bonnet\** | Jennifer Curry | New Playwrights' Network |
| *Brand* | Ibsen | Methuen |
| *Breath of Spring* | Peter Coke | French |
| *Charley's Aunt* | Brandon Thomas | French |
| *Close the Coalhouse Door\** | Alan Plater | Methuen |
| *Death of a Salesman* | Arthur Miller | Penguin |
| *Design for Living* | Noel Coward | Davis-Poynter |
| *Don't Blame the Bard\** | Curry & Shephard | Not in Print |
| *Duet For Two Hands\** | Mary Hayley Bell | French |
| *Every Man in his Humour\** | Ben Jonson | OUP |
| *Fiddler on the Roof\** | Stein & Bock | Sunbeam Music Corp. |
| *Forget-Me-Not Lane* | Peter Nichols | Faber |
| *Getting On\** | Alan Bennett | Faber |
| *Hamlet* | Shakespeare | Methuen |
| *Hedda Gabler* | Ibsen | Methuen |
| *Heil, Ceasar!\** | John Bowen | French |
| *Home* | David Storey | Penguin |
| *How the Other Half Loves* | Alan Ayckbourn | Evans |
| *In Camera* | Jean Paul Sartre | Hamish Hamilton |
| *Ivanov* | Chekhov | Heinemann |
| *Joseph and his Amazing Technicolor Dreamcoat* | Webber & Rice | Novello |
| *Little Malcolm and his Struggle Against the Eunuchs* | David Halliwell | French |
| *Live Like Pigs\** | John Arden | Penguin |

| | | |
|---|---|---|
| *Long March to Jerusalem* | Don Taylor | French |
| *Look Back in Anger* | John Osborne | Faber |
| *Loot* | Joe Orton | Methuen |
| *Love's Labour's Lost** | Shakespeare | Methuen |
| *Macbeth** | Shakespeare | Methuen |
| *Mahagonny* | Bertold Brecht | Methuen |
| *Maria Marten* | version by Brian J. Burton | Combridge Jackson |
| *Mary Rose* | J. M. Barrie | Hodder & Stoughton |
| *Mixed Doubles* | (anthology) | French |
| *Move Over Mrs Markham** | Ray Cooney & John Chapman | English Theatre Guild |
| *Othello** | Shakespeare | Methuen |
| *Our Town* | Thornton Wilder | French |
| *Plunder* | Ben Travers | French |
| *Pygmalion* | Shaw | Penguin |
| *Richard II** | Shakespeare | Methuen |
| *Roots* | Arnold Wesker | Penguin |
| *Rose Ransome** | Curry & Shephard | Not in Print |
| *Salad Days* | Julian Slade & Dorothy Reynolds | |
| *Salome* | Oscar Wilde | Vision Press |
| *The Apprentices* | Peter Terson | Penguin |
| *The Birthday Party** | Harold Pinter | Methuen |
| *The Caretaker* | Harold Pinter | Methuen |
| *The Cherry Orchard* | Chekhov | Methuen |
| *The Crucible** | Arthur Miller | Penguin |
| *The Dancing Years* | Ivor Novello | Chappell |
| *The Day After the Fair* | Frank Harvey | French |
| *The Glass Menagerie* | Tennessee Williams | French |
| *The Hollow Crown* | John Barton | French |
| *The Importance of Being Earnest** | Oscar Wilde | Methuen |
| *The Incredible Vanishing !!!!* | Denise Coffey | Methuen |
| *The Norman Conquests* | Alan Ayckbourn | French |
| *The Plough and the Stars* | Sean O'Casey | French |

| | | |
|---|---|---|
| *The Royal Hunt of the Sun* | Peter Shaffer | French |
| *The Secretary Bird* | William Douglas Home | French |
| *The Taming of the Shrew** | Shakespeare | Methuen |
| *Waiting for Godot** | Samuel Beckett | Faber |
| *Where There's A Will** | Curry & Shephard | Not in Print |
| *You Never Can Tell** | Shaw | Penguin |
| *Zigger Zagger* | Peter Terson | Penguin |
| *Zoo Story* | Edward Albee | Cape |

# Index

## POETRY

### ROBIN SKELTON

When Boswell said to Dr Johnson, 'Then, sir, what is poetry?', Dr Johnson replied, 'Why, sir, it is much easier to say what it is not. We all *know* what night is, but it is not easy to *Tell* what it is.'

Poetry has always been regarded with awe; in this excellent and penetrating book Robin Skelton brings understanding of it beyond Dr Johnson's honest but evasive answer.

All those who respond to poetry in any form will benefit from reading the book. To the perception of the general reader it gives the added knowledge of the structure, the attitudes and the creative processes in poetry; to the student it offers an invaluable and comprehensive approach to the subject.

**TEACH YOURSELF BOOKS**

# OPERA

## ROBIN MAY

Opera, combining as it does music and drama, is a particularly
exciting experience and can rightly be considered great art.
And yet opera is so often regarded as a rather specialised
interest which can be enjoyed only by a fortunate few.

Robin May's enthusiastic introduction dispels this image and
shows how opera is, in many countries, very much a 'popular'
art form. He traces the history of opera from its beginnings in
Italy, through the development of the Romantic movement and
its full flowering in Wagner and Verdi, to the importance of
opera as a focus of nationalism and to the realism of Puccini
and his followers. Finally, Robin May looks at opera and its
future round the world today.

This is the ideal book for the newcomer to the opera-house
and for all those who want a perspective on what they have
seen and an understanding of what contributes to a great
performance.

**TEACH YOURSELF BOOKS**

# MUSIC

## KING PALMER

This is a book for all those who want an introduction into the world of music and advice on how to pursue their particular interests.

It is designed to be a guide simple enough to be understood by those with little previous knowledge of music, yet comprehensive enough to give a 'bird's eye view' of the entire field. Topics include explanations of musical notation and how music developed, introductions to piano, string, wind, organ and singing techniques, advice on choosing an instrument, how to practise, training your ear and musical appreciation.

**TEACH YOURSELF BOOKS**

**JAZZ**

JOHN CHILTON

'It is I believe the best introduction to the history, practice and meaning of Jazz to date.'
GEORGE MELLY

John Chilton has distilled a life-time of study to provide a wide-ranging, and open-minded book which summarises the development of the music and also provides an outline of the methods which jazz improvisers use. He traces the background of jazz from the music of Africa and its emergence in New Orleans to the jazz of today. It will delight all listeners of jazz and give them a wider appreciation of this unique form of music.

**TEACH YOURSELF BOOKS**

# DANCING

## IMPERIAL SOCIETY OF TEACHERS OF DANCING

Dancing is one of the few occupations that can be enjoyed by everyone, whatever their background and whatever their age.

This book is for the absolute beginner who would like to dance socially and wants to do more than simply 'get round the floor'. It is also a very useful introduction for those who want to take their study of dancing to a more advanced level. The dances cover traditional ballroom dances such as the waltz, Latin American dances, such as the rumba, and social dances particularly suitable for a disco.

**TEACH YOURSELF BOOKS**

# CINEMA: A HISTORY

## KEITH READER

This book is designed for anyone interested in the cinema from the occasional filmgoer to those who wish to see films placed in their broad historical context.

Here you will find a complete survey of the world of the cinema from the very first moving pictures to the latest developments in film criticism. Throughout, the movements discussed are given depth and perspective by relating them to the culture, politics and society in which they evolved. The role of major stars and directors is not neglected, but the book attempts to place their work in a much wider perspective, intended for a proportionately wider readership.

**TEACH YOURSELF BOOKS**

# BALLET

## ·IAN WOODWARD

Here is a book for both the beginner and the keen ballet-goer.
The story of dance is followed from its beginnings with the
Romans and Ancient Greeks, through the Renaissance and the
Romantic Ballet, to the modern dance of the twentieth century.
In addition to this account of the historical development of
ballet, there are unique and fascinating sections on the nature
of ballet and its appeal to audiences today, while an important
feature of the book is its complete reference section of
dancers, choreographers, composers, designers, and ballets –
contemporary and classical – in the international repertory.

Throughout emphasis is placed on twentieth-century ballet
and in this respect every major country in the world is
discussed.

Ian Woodward has written many books on ballet and is ballet
critic of the London *Evening News* and London dance critic of
*The Christian Science Monitor*.

## TEACH YOURSELF BOOKS